D1570761

Duquesne Studies

LANGUAGE AND LITERATURE SERIES

[VOLUME NINE]

GENERAL EDITOR:

Albert C. Labriola, *Department of English, Duquesne University*

ADVISORY EDITOR:

Foster Provost, *Department of English, Duquesne University*

The Sinews of Ulysses

The Sinews of Ulysses

FORM AND CONVENTION IN MILTON'S WORKS

Michael Lieb

DUQUESNE UNIVERSITY PRESS
Pittsburgh, PA

Published in the United States of America
by Duquesne University Press
600 Forbes Avenue, Pittsburgh PA 15282

Library of Congress Cataloging-in-Publication Data

Lieb, Michael, 1941–
   The sinews of Ulysses : form and convention in Milton's works / by
Michael Lieb.
      p.   cm. — (Duquesne studies. Language and literature series
; v. 9)
   Bibliography: p.
   Includes index.
   ISBN 0–8207–0205–6
   1. Milton, John, 1608–1674—Criticism and interpretation.
2. Literary form.   3. Convention (Philosophy) in literature.
I. Title.   II. Series.
PR3588.L46   1988
821'.4—dc19   88–25651
                                                      CIP

For my wife Roslyn, "Associate sole"

Contents

Preface

This study proposes to explore in depth the nature of form and convention in Milton's works. To that end, the subject is approached from a number of corresponding perspectives. Beginning in the first chapter with an examination of Milton's emphasis upon exercise in his pedagogical theories, the study concerns itself with Milton's interest in matters of form at the most basic level, that is, the nurturing of the body as a symbol of the relationship between the material and the spiritual. This relationship extends, in turn, to Milton's understanding of metaphysics. The second chapter, accordingly, examines the extent to which material and spiritual distinctions underlie the metaphysical foundations of Milton's thought. As expressions of metaphysical concerns, these distinctions provide further insight into the nature of Milton's rendering of form and convention in both his poetry and his prose. If form and convention assume a metaphysical bearing in Milton's thought, they are no less important to his vocation as a polemicist. In this respect, Milton's emphasis upon bodily form, as reflected in his pedagogical and metaphysical theories, becomes particularly germane to his polemical practices. Exploring the dynamics that underlie those practices, the third chapter analyzes Milton's use of the convention of the body as metaphor to deploy his rhetorical and polemical ammunition in the prose works, especially those written against the prelates. Moving from the pedagogical, metaphysical, and polemical to the theological, the study next undertakes to illuminate Milton's assimilation of form and convention into his Christology. From the Christological perspective, the fourth chapter explores the kenotic basis of Milton's thought. Here the conventions of divestiture and investiture assume signal importance in the Miltonic view of the mystery of the incarnation, a mystery that manifests itself on a number of occasions in Milton's works. The study next proceeds to an investigation of form and convention as generic imperatives. As categories of genre, form and convention become the focus of Milton's refashioning of pastoral, on the one hand, and epic, on the other. In both respects, a renewed sense of genre emerges. Addressing itself to the conventions of formulaic utterance, the fifth chapter, then, analyzes the way in which Milton's handling of pastoral as a repository of prophetic and amatory meanings discloses the ever-present tensions between classical and biblical norms. These disclosures suggest a poetics of the pastoral that is at once radical and revelatory. With these radical and revelatory dimensions of Miltonic poetics at the forefront of its concerns, the study next addresses itself to the nature of epic dialogue. Focusing specifically upon the conventions of celestial dialogue, the sixth chapter examines the dramaturgical underpinnings of Milton's rendering (and consequent radicalizing) of epic form. These generic considerations, finally, devolve into an extended analysis of Milton's closet drama as a supreme embodiment of the inclination to refashion form and convention into a genre responsive to its own unique demands. Returning to the earlier concern with theology, the seventh chapter explores in depth Milton's delineation of strength as a category of value not only in his closet drama but in his other works as well. This delineation draws upon and amplifies the concept of bodily form as a matter of paramount importance to Milton's outlook. In its reappraisal of bodily form and the conventions that underscore it, the final chapter attempts to provide a renewed sensitivity to the way in which the closet drama functions in the Miltonic canon. From the larger perspective of the study as a whole, the foregoing chapters suggest a variety of approaches to Milton's incorporation of form and convention in his works. Conceived variously (and correspondingly) as pedagogical, metaphysical, polemical, theological, and generic categories, form and convention offer a crucial means of coming to terms with the undercurrents of Milton's thought, as well as with his practices as a writer.

I am indebted to the editors of the following journals and books for permission to incorporate (with revisions) material that has appeared earlier in their pages: chapter 1 in *JGE: The Journal of General Education* 36 (1985) 245–56; chapter 2 in *Studies in Philology* 71 (1974) 206–24; chapter 3 in *Milton Studies*, vol. 4, ed. James Simmonds (Pittsburgh: University of Pittsburgh Press, 1972); chapter 4 in *ELH, A Journal of Literary History* 37 (1970) 342–60. Chapter 5 combines a number of studies published earlier in *Milton Quarterly* 12 (1978) 23–28; in *Milton and Scriptural Tradition: The Bible into Poetry*, ed. James Sims and Leland Ryken (Columbia: University of Missouri Press, 1984); and in *Renaissance Papers 1982*, ed. A. Leigh DeNeef and M. Thomas Hester (Southeastern Renaissance Conference, 1982). Chapter 6 combines two studies published in *Renaissance*

Papers 1974, ed. Dennis G. Donovan and A. Leigh DeNeef (Southeastern Renaissance Conference, 1974); and in *Milton Studies*, vol. 23, ed. James Simmonds (Pittsburgh: University of Pittsburgh Press, 1987).
Research for aspects of this study was undertaken at a number of libraries, including the Folger Shakespeare Library, the Newberry Library, the Regenstein Library of the University of Chicago, the Lutheran School of Theology Library, and the University of Illinois at Chicago Library. I wish to thank the staffs of these libraries for their assistance and support. A fellowship from the Folger Shakespeare Library in 1970 helped me to carry forth the inital research for the material that appears in chapter 3. Portions of the study were delivered as papers at conferences and symposia. The first chapter was originally presented as a paper before the Second International Milton Symposium, Cambridge, England, in 1983. A portion of the fifth chapter was delivered before the Southeastern Renaissance Conference in 1982. Portions of the sixth chapter, in turn, were presented to the Southeastern Renaissance Conference in 1974; before a symposium at the University of Kentucky in 1984; and then again before an NEH-funded Milton Institute at Arizona State University in 1985. I would like to acknowledge with thanks the comments of those who participated in the foregoing conferences and symposia. It is with deep gratitude and abiding respect, moreover, that I extend my appreciation to Professor Albert C. Labriola for his continued faith in my work. The final gesture of thanks and, of course, love is reserved for that "Associate sole, to me beyond/ Compare above all living Creatures dear," my wife Roslyn.

MICHAEL LIEB
University of Illinois
Chicago, Illinois

CHAPTER ONE

The Pedagogical Imperative

A t the conclusion of his tractate *Of Education*, Milton epitomizes his pedagogical outlook by maintaining that the course of study he has recommended "is not a Bow for every man to shoot in that counts himself a Teacher; but will require sinews almost equal to those which *Homer* gave *Ulysses*."[1] The allusion, of course, is to *The Odyssey* (XXI.399–405), in which the supreme strength of Ulysses is made evident in his ability to bend the bow that Penelope's suitors were unable to bend. With that very bow, Ulysses then slays the unfortunate suitors. As an index to Milton's philosophy of education, the allusion has genuine significance. Although the Renaissance characteristically looked upon Ulysses as a paragon of wisdom,[2] Milton made a point of emphasizing his physical prowess as an adjunct to his imposing intellect. In *The Second Defence*, for example, Ulysses is invoked as one who strove with Ajax for the arms of Achilles (8: 83).[3] Assuming various forms, the strength of Ulysses, then, appealed greatly to Milton's sensibility. As the culminating image of his tractate, Ulysses as strong man is, in fact, very much in keeping with Milton's emphasis upon physical exercise in *Of Education*.

Having discoursed at some length upon the program of studies to which the students of his proposed Academy would be subjected, Milton then moves to a discussion of what he calls *"Their Exercise,"* a topic that is given its own heading in his tractate. Upon this enterprise Milton lavishes much attention.[4] Before having lunch each day, his students would devote at least an hour and a half to exercise, and possibly even more time than that, "according as their rising in the morning shall be early" (4: 287–88). The kinds of exercise Milton has in mind for his students are both martial and competitive. "The Exercise which I commend first," he says, "is the exact use of their Weapon, to guard and to strike safely with edge, or point; this will keep them healthy, nimble, strong, and well in breath, is also the likeliest means to make them grow large and tall, and to inspire them with a gallant and fearless courage, which being temper'd with seasonable Lectures and Precepts to them of true Fortitude and Patience, will turn into a native and heroic valour, and make them hate the cowardice of doing wrong" (4: 288). In keeping with these recommendations, Milton himself is described by the Anonymous Biographer as being skilled in using a sword when he had his sight,[5] a fact to which Milton also attests in his *Second Defence*. Armed with his sword, Milton says, "I thought myself a match for any man, though far superior in strength, and secure from any insult which one man could offer to another" (8: 61). In addition to the use of a sword, in *Of Education* Milton advocates training in "all the Locks and Gripes of Wrastling, wherein English men were wont to excell, as need may often be in fight to tugg or grapple, and to close." Such activity, Milton maintains, will certainly "prove and heat their single strength." During the period of "unsweating themselves" after his students perform these exercises, Milton suggests that their "travail'd spirits" be composed with "solemn and divine harmonies of Musick." Whether religious, martial, or civic in nature, such music will smooth the transition between the physical activity of exercise and the mental activity of study.

Milton's program of exercise does not end here, however. For about two hours before supper, the students of his Academy would "be call'd out to their military motions," "first on foot, then as their age permits, on Horseback to all the Art of Cavalry." Such martial exercises would include "Embattelling, Marching, Encamping, Fortifying, Besieging and Battering, with all the helps of ancient and modern strategems," to aid the students in the conduct of a war for "the service of their Country." These "constant exercises at home," in turn, would be complemented by honest recreations away from the Academy, such as "rid[ing] out in Companies . . . to all the quarters of the Land" and gaining "practical knowledge of sailing and of Sea-fight" (4: 289–90). In this respect, Milton's Academy has all the elements of a training ground for soldiers preparing to go to war, as well it might, considering that *Of Education* was published during the Civil War. As Dennis Brailsford so aptly puts it, "the battles of the Civil War were to be won on the exercise grounds of Milton's Academy." Milton describes, in effect, a "New Model Academy" that might well be looked upon as an officer-cadet school for Cromwell's New Model Army.[6] As a counterpart to the rigorous program of intellectual activity that Milton recommends earlier in his tractate, the exercises that constitute his program of physical activity would, in their own way, go far to realize his definition of "a compleat and generous Education" as "that which fits a man to perform justly, skilfully and magnanimously all the offices both private and publick of Peace and War" (4: 208).

In order to appreciate the full significance of this definition, one must recognize the extent to which Milton correlates exercise as physical enterprise with exercise as spiritual enterprise. For Milton, the transition between the two enterprises has an inevitability born of the conviction that body and soul are inextricably united. It is hardly necessary to invoke Milton's materialism here, although it might be seen as an extension of the outlook implicit in his discussion of exercise. An examination of Milton's conception of the end or purpose of education should help to clarify that outlook. As one might expect, for Milton the purpose of an education has a decidedly theological bearing. In addressing what he calls "the end of Learning," Milton speaks not only as educator, but as theologian addressing postlapsarian man. At the outset of his tractate, Milton declares that the purpose of education is "to repair the ruines of our first Parents by regaining to know God aright, and out of that knowledge to love him, to imitate him, to be like him, as we may the neerest by possessing our souls of true virtue, which being united to the heavenly grace of faith makes up the highest perfection" (4: 277). Implicit in this postlapsarian view is a process of transformation by which ruins are repaired and knowledge regained as the soul, possessed of true virtue and heavenly grace, achieves a fully spiritualized form. In *Of Education*, Milton expresses this idea as the movement from physical to spiritual, visible to invisible: "But because our understanding cannot in this body found itself but on sensible things, nor arrive so clearly to the knowledge of God and things invisible, as by orderly conning over the visible and inferior creature, the same is to be found in all discreet teaching" (4: 277). From the perspective of Milton's pedagogy, the movement from physical to spiritual, visible to invisible is not undertaken without difficulty. Indeed, the working of body up to spirit in the process of refinement is both difficult and laborious. The "right path of a vertuous and noble Education," Milton observes, is "laborious indeed at the first ascent." To prove his point, Milton conducts us to "a hill side" to show us the path. Like those "that labour up the hill of heav'nly Truth" in Milton's ninth sonnet (4), the strivers after spiritual perfection must condition themselves for the rigors of the task. As Donne suggest in *Satire III* (79–87), he that will reach Truth, who stands on "a huge hill" cragged and steep, "about must, and about must goe; / And what th'hills suddennes resists, winne so." As the goal of "the mindes indeavours," "hard knowledge" implies "hard deeds, the bodies paines."[7] Yet once the ascent is accomplished, observes Milton, the purified soul will be presented with a "goodly prospect, and melodious sounds on every side, that the Harp of *Orpheus* was not more charming" (4: 280).

We can now better understand the sense of physicality that underlies Milton's definition of "a compleat and generous Education." Expressing the idea of mental exertion through the metaphor of physical exertion, Milton's view of such an education implies the idea of bodily conditioning as a concomitant of mental conditioning. It is for this reason that Milton calls "a compleat and generous Education that which *fits* a man to perform justly, skilfully and magnanimously all the offices both private and publick of Peace and War" (*italics mine*). The "fitness" that Milton has in mind is as much bodily as mental; in fact, the one presupposes the other. Implicit in his use of "fitness," then, is that all-pervasive athleticism by which body works up to spirit in a process of transformation at once laborious and strenuous. Undergoing this process, one attains a fitness worthy of "a compleat and generous Education." If the attainment of that fitness requires the sinews of Ulysses, those so equipped will have been superlatively trained both in body and in mind. Such an outlook, then, accounts for the great emphasis Milton places upon exercise as physical activity in *Of Education*.

Although this emphasis is fundamental to Milton as educator, the prominence that exercise receives in *Of Education* was not apparent either in the reformist movement with which Milton's tractate is customarily associated, or in the educational practices of Milton's own day. From the perspective of the reformist movement, Milton's concern with exercise as crucial activity is not a significant aspect of the programs espoused by Comenius and his followers. "If Milton belongs chronologically and by association to the Comenian movement, he was *in* the movement and not *of* it."[8] Nor was exercise of the sort that Milton advocates an integral part of the school curriculum when his tractate was published. Neither at St. Paul's nor at Cambridge was Milton exposed to exercise—martial or otherwise—as a designated curricular activity; in his time exercise as such was simply not a part of the school statutes. It was either disregarded or discouraged by the schools, both at the lower level and at the university.[9] Departing from established practice, Milton restores exercise to the prominence it once enjoyed in the "ancient and famous Schools of *Pythagoras, Plato, Isocrates, [and] Aristotle*" (4: 287).

We may take Plato and Aristotle as prime examples of the attitude Milton has in mind. In the *Laws*, for example, Plato invokes the commonplace notion that gymnastics is one of the two branches of education. (The other is music.) Plato includes under the heading of gymnastics not only wrestling but "all military exercises, such as archery, and all hurling of weapons, and the use of the light shield, and all fighting with heavy arms, and military evolutions, and movements of armies, and encampings, and all that relates to horsemanship."[10] The purpose of such exercises, Plato says in the *Republic*, is to breed a race of "warrior athletes."[11] In the *Politics*, Aristotle follows suit. "It is an admitted principle," Aristotle says, "that gymnastic exercises should be employed in education." As one of "the customary branches of education," "gymnastic exercises are thought to infuse courage." Aristotle would have boys "handed over to the trainer, who creates in them the proper habit of body, and to the wrestling-master, who teaches them their exercises."[12] As E. Norman Gardiner has demonstrated, the educational theories enunciated by Plato and Aristotle, among others, were in fact put into practice in the daily curriculum of the Greek schools. "From the day that the Greek boy went to school about the age of seven he spent a considerable portion of each day in the palaestra [or wrestling school] and gymnasium [or sports arena] exercising himself under trained supervision, and he continued to do so till he reached manhood and often indeed much longer."[13]

The classical world's emphasis upon gymnastics was reflected in the educational theories of Renaissance humanism. In works ranging from Juan Luis Vives' *De Tradendis Disciplinis* (1531) to John Brinsley's *Ludus Literarius* (1627), the virtue of exercise was extolled. Entire treatises were written on the subject,[14] and gymnastics was looked upon as essential to the educational background of the Renaissance courtier. According to Baldassare Castiglione's *Libro del Cortegiano* (1528), the courtier must "have understanding in all exercises of the bodie that belong to a man of warr." For this purpose, Castiglione singles out wrestling and the handling of weapons, as well as other forms of exercise, such as hunting and swimming.[15] As part of the same tradition, Sir Thomas Elyot reflects a similar point of view in *The Boke Named the Gouernour* (1531). Devoting a sizable section of his work to gymnastics, Elyot advocates exercise not only to preserve health and increase strength, but also to encourage valor.[16] In *The Scholmaster* (1570), Roger Ascham follows suit. Among the exercises that Ascham recommends are riding, wrestling, swimming, playing at weapons, and, of course, archery.[17] If such a view produced Ascham's *Toxophilus* (1545), it also inspired such works as Gervase Markham's *The Art of Archerie* (1624).

For our purposes, one of the most important treatments of gymnastics in all its forms may be found in the *Positions* (1581) of Richard Mulcaster, first headmaster of the Merchant Taylors school and high-master of St. Paul's school before that position was assumed by Alexander Gil, high-master during Milton's own tenure at St. Paul's. Devoting large sections of his treatise to exercise, Mulcaster insists "that the exercise of the body still accompanie and assist the exercise of the minde, to make a dry, strong, hard, and therefore a long lasting body: and by the fauor therof to haue an actiue, sharp, wise and therwith all a well learned soul." As part of his treatise, Mulcaster provides a history of exercising (especially of the martial sort) and distinguishes various kinds of exercises, including swimming, wrestling, fencing, walking, running, riding, and hunting, among others.[18] What makes Mulcaster so pertinent here is his insistence upon the inextricable relationship between exercise as bodily phenomenon and exercise as spiritual phenomenon. A well-rounded education involves, for Mulcaster, the complete conditioning of the body as the means by which the soul itself might realize its full "athletic" potential.[19] If the idea was to reappear much later in John Locke's concept of "a sound Mind in a sound Body,"[20] it was of crucial importance to Milton.

As early as the sixth Prolusion on "sportive exercises," Milton maintained "that just as those who accustom themselves to wrestling and to field sports are rendered much more vigorous than others and better trained for every kind of work; so likewise it comes about by use that the sinews of the mind [*nervus animi*] are much strengthened by this exercise of wit [*ingenii palaestram*], and a better blood and spirit, as it were, is obtained; so that the native ability itself becomes finer and keener, both pliable and versatile for all things." (12: 216–19). The attitude was pervasive during Milton's Cambridge years. Milton looked upon the prolusions themselves—albeit somewhat ironically—as a form of mental gymnastics (*ingenii palaestram*). The prolusions were, after all, academic exercises (*exercitationes*) formed by a rhetorical tradition that had its roots in the concept of physical combat. Accordingly, the gymnasium as an athletic arena and the palaestra as a wrestling school were known in the later classical period as centers for the study of academic subjects. In these schools of rhetoric, "exercises" were of the oratorical sort, the prototypes of Milton's own *exercitationes*.[21] It is in this sense that Cicero in his *De Oratore* speaks of the orator as one who engages in the exercises of the palaestra.[22] Like Renaissance school children, Roman school children were well trained in their *progymnasmata*, elementary exercises taught in that school of games the *ludus literarius*.[23] There budding rhetoricians became well equipped to engage in *controversia*, a concept associated by Cicero with gymnastic contests and even warfare.[24] Polemic (from *polemos*, war), as Milton well knew, involves a warfare all its own.[25] The training ground for Milton's career as polemist, the prolusions represented the perfect means by which the future controversialist might engage his *ingenii palaestram*.

In keeping with the pedagogical outlook espoused in *Of Education*, Milton's seventh Prolusion is a case in point. There he speaks of contending for the glory of the orator through long and strenuous study (*"longo & acri studio ad illam laudem veram contendere"*). Invoking the power of eloquence (*"vim Eloquentiae"*), he looks upon himself as one who is armed for combat. As warrior-athlete, Milton will argue that "knowledge renders man happier than ignorance" (12: 247). To gain knowledge, Milton contends, one must not be slothful (12: 273). Exercising oneself fully through appropriate study, one must gain sufficient strength to overcome the debilitating effects of ignorance. To be ignorant is the most grievous of weaknesses (12: 275). Accordingly, Milton counsels, let us preserve at all costs "the heavenly vigor of the mind" (*"coelestem animi vigorem"*) (12: 274–75). In doing so, we shall be like Alexander the Great, who conquered all the world. With that victory, ignorance will have breathed its last (12: 278–79).

The athleticism implicit in Milton's seventh Prolusion is fundamental to his stance as a controversialist. If the seventh Prolusion emphasizes the spirit that was to assume curricular form in *Of Education*, *Areopagitica* is Milton's most eloquent defense of his pedagogy. Equating the process of tyrannical licensing with what he terms the "disexercising" of Truth (4: 297), Milton advocates the kind of laws that will allow true exercise to prevail. In keeping with Richard Mulcaster's insistence upon exercise as both bodily and spiritual phenomenon, Milton accordingly maintains in *Areopagitica* that "our faith and knowledge thrives by exercising, as well as our limbs and complexion" (4: 333). For this reason, Milton refuses to condone "a fugitive and cloister'd vertue, unexercis'd & unbeath'd, that never sallies out and sees her adversary" (4: 311). Instead, he extols the "warfaring Christian," one who is "strong in the Lord, and in the power of his might" (Eph. 6:10).[26] It is this warrior-athlete who wages what Milton refers to as the "wars of Truth" (3: 348). His speech for the liberty of unlicensed printing, in turn, provides an arena for the waging of those wars. "So Truth be in the field," Milton says, "we do injuriously by licensing and prohibiting to misdoubt her strength. Let her and Falsehood grapple; who ever knew Truth put to the wors, in a free and open encounter" (4: 347). Taking its cue from Milton's emphasis upon exercise in *Of Education*, Truth, no doubt, has been trained in "all the Locks and Gripes of Wrastling" and knows well how "to tugg or grapple, and to close." Like the outcome of the contest between knowledge and Ignorance in the seventh Prolusion, the result of the battle between Truth and Falsehood in *Areopagitica* is never in doubt.

Nor is it in doubt in all those poems Milton wrote to portray such combats.[27] Whether one thinks of the Lady and Comus in *A Mask*, the Son and the rebel angels in *Paradise Lost*, Jesus and Satan in *Paradise Regain'd*, or Samson and his adversaries in *Samson Agonistes*, in Milton's poetry the wars of Truth are constantly being waged by the warrior-athlete or *agonistes*. In his *Nativity* ode, Milton appropriately exults in the prowess of the divine Infant: "Our Babe to shew his Godhead true, / Can in his swadling bands controul the damned crew" (221–27). The allusion, of course, glances at the infant Hercules, who, according to Pindar, strangled serpents in his cradle.[28] In accord with the athletic nature of Pindar's odes, the event culminates Milton's own celebration of the Herculean *Christus victor*, that athlete of athletes. If this "Most perfect *Heroe*, try'd in heaviest plight / Of Labours huge and hard, too hard for human wight" (11–12) was to appear again in *The Passion*, he makes his most dramatic appearance in *Paradise Regain'd* as Hercules grappling with an Antaeus-like Satan. In his ability to withstand Satan's final temptation, Christ demonstrates an athleticism that transcends physicality and culminates in the triumph of the Son of Heaven over all the powers of earth. Just as the Herculean "Babe" of the *Nativity* ode strangles serpents in his cradle, the *Christus victor* of *Paradise Regain'd* fulfills his promise as athlete in a wrestling match to end all wrestling matches. Here as elsewhere, Milton's warrior-athlete is trained in all strategems of combat to defeat his adversary. The prime example of this training is Milton's own Samson, the agonist par excellence. As the final chapter of this study will attempt to demonstrate, Samson represents a profound expression of the way in which the emphasis upon athleticism in Milton's thought assumes dramatic form. For the moment, however, it is sufficient to observe that the attitude expressed in the poetry is fully in keeping with the educational principles espoused in *Of Education*. "Regaining to know God aright, and out of that knowledge to love him, to imitate him, to be like him," we "possess . . . our souls of true virtue, which being united to the heavenly grace of faith makes up the highest perfection" (4: 277). This perfection can be achieved only by under-going the rigors—athletic as well as intellectual and moral—of Mil-ton's proposed Academy. Sustaining those rigors, the warrior-athlete as Milton conceives him will have every opportunity to develop the sinews of Ulysses necessary for his task.

CHAPTER TWO

The Metaphysics of Form

JUDGING by Milton's early attacks upon scholastic philosophy in his prolusions,[1] we might well hesitate to consider with any seriousness the metaphysical application of form in his works. As indicated in Prolusion VII, his unflinching castigation is epitomized in his reference to the subject of metaphysics as simply "a kind of Lernian swamp of sophisms, contrived for shipwreck and destruction" (12: 277). Despite his impatience with the subject, however, his prolusions do give evidence of how thoroughly he has absorbed the principles of metaphysics and how ably he applied them in metaphysical disputes.[2] Having attacked scholastic philosophy in Prolusion III, Milton goes on in the next two prolusions to argue as an accomplished metaphysician that the destruction of any substance does not result in the resolution into first matter (Prolusion IV) and that no partial forms reside in an animal in addition to the whole (Prolusion V). Setting aside the abstruseness of such considerations (and Milton's dismay at having to engage in them),[3] we may observe that both prolusions demonstrate his concern to support his views on the proper relationship between form and matter. Essentially, his arguments are based upon the following premise: If matter and form are to preserve their integrity in any metaphysical disputation, the characteristics of each must be fully understood.[4] For our purposes, the clearest exposition of those characteristics may be found in Milton's *Art of Logic*, a work setting forth with care and precision the fundamental attitudes upon which so much of his prose and poetry are founded.[5]

Defining matter in the *Logic* as "the cause from which a thing is [*causa ex qua res est*]," Milton proceeds to define form as "the cause through which a thing is what it is [*causa per quam res est id quod est*]" (11: 58, 59).[6] The distinction is important, for through it Milton gives apt expression to his ontology, to his view that "matter and form . . . constitute the thing itself [*materia autem et forma . . . rem ipsam constituunt*]" (15: 21). It is on the basis of such an assumption that Milton conducts his argument in *Animadversions* against the Anglican liturgy. In support of the Anglican liturgy, the *Remonstrant* argues

that although the "forms" might be "spurious," the substance is
"holy" (3: 128). The Answerer's response is perfectly in accord with
Milton's metaphysics: "Let it be suppos'd the substance of them [the
forms] may savour of something holy . . . this is but the matter; the
forme, and the end of the thing may yet render it either superstitious,
fruitlesse, or impious, and so, worthy to be rejected. The Garments of
a Strumpet are often the same materially, that cloath a chast Matron,
and yet ignominious for her to weare. . . ." (3: 128). Therefore, the
Answerer concludes, "'tis not the goodnesse of matter . . . which is
not, nor can be ow'd to the *Liturgie*, that will beare it out, if the form,
which is the essence of it, be fantastick, and superstitious, the end
sinister, and the imposition violent" (3: 129–30).

Implied is the idea that the "nature" of a thing depends upon the
relationship between its material and its formal causes (15: 268). The
significance of that relationship is particularly discernible in the emphasis Milton's *Logic* places upon form as a *principium* (11: 31).[7]
Without the presence of the formal cause, the material cause is
deprived of its efficacy (11: 59).[8] Providing "the peculiar essence of the
thing [*rei essentia*]," form distinguishes that thing "from all other
things" (11: 59–61).[9] It is thereby "the source of every difference":
"When the form is given," states Milton, "the thing itself is given;
when the form is taken away, the thing is taken away [*posita forma, res
ipsa ponitur; sublata tollitur*]" (11: 61). Referring to such an idea as
one that was commonly held, Milton reveals his awareness of the long
tradition, stemming from Aristotelian metaphysics,[10] that viewed form
precisely as he had.[11] For purposes of expediency, we may glance at
Francis Bacon's *Novum Organum*, which reflects Milton's view in the
statement that "the form of a thing is the very thing itself": "Given the
form the nature infallibly follows. Therefore it is always present when
the nature is present, and universally implies it, and is constantly
inherent in it. Again, the form is such, that if it be taken away the
nature infallibly vanishes."[12]

The importance of this idea for Milton's metaphysics may be seen in
his attempt to reconcile the apparent discrepancies between the Platonic and the Aristotelian views of form. As he states in his *Logic*:
"This definition joins those of Plato and Aristotle. For Plato defines
form as the cause through which [*per quam*], Aristotle as that which is
[*quod quid est esse*]" (11: 59). Such an approach is discernible in
writers ranging from St. Thomas to George Downame.[13] The point
apparently to be reconciled is that while Plato conceives of form as
transcendent entity imposed upon matter, Aristotle views form as that
which is already immanent in matter.[14] For Plato, the *idea* or *eidos* is

the separate self-sufficient pattern that constitutes the essence (*ousia*) of a thing.[15] For Aristotle, form is the inherent "active force that activates the proper shape of the thing and actuates the process by which it becomes that thing."[16]

Thus we find Plato referring in the *Timaeus* to "self-existent ideas unperceived by sense, and apprehended only by the mind" (2: 32). All things with form have participation (*koinonia*) in these self-existent entities, which in turn are the source of generation (*Phaedo* 1: 484). In fact, to describe the process of generation, Plato distinguishes three principles: "first, that which is in the process of generation; secondly, that in which the generation takes place; and thirdly, that of which the thing generated is a resemblance" (*Timaeus* 2: 31). The first is the formed substance to be created; the second, the matter out of which the formed substance is to be created; the third, the absolute, self-existent form in which the formed substance is to "participate" in its creation. The matter itself, Plato makes clear, is "formless" (*amorphon*), "free from the impress of any of those shapes which it is hereafter to receive from without": "that which is to receive all forms should have no form" (*Timaeus* 2: 31).[17]

It is precisely this approach that was to come under fire from Aristotle, who states quite categorically in the *Metaphysics* that "it is manifestly impossible for that which is the substance of a thing to exist apart from it. How, then, can the Ideas, which are supposed to be the substances of things, exist apart from them?" (78). Indeed, the Platonic "Forms (if there are such things) do nothing to explain generation or substances, and therefore cannot be considered self-subsistent substances" (185). "Hence of course it is unnecessary to posit a Form as pattern" (185). Instead, we should concern ourselves with the true process of generation in which the creation of a formed substance is definable not in terms of any self-existent pattern but entirely in its own terms. Thus, Aristotle states, "Now just as a craftsman does not make the substratum of his product (e.g., the bronze), neither does he produce the sphere—except accidentally inasmuch as the bronze sphere is a sphere, and he produces the former. For to make an individual thing is to make it out of a substratum in the full sense of the word"—that is, as an entity including both matter and form. "To make the bronze round," then, "is not to make 'the round' or 'the sphere,'" since form *qua* form is not generated, "nor does production apply to it" (184). With this emphasis upon the inseparability of a thing from its essence, Aristotle concerned himself with what "exists" rather than with any ideal, self-existent pattern in which existence participates; he concerned himself with "what a thing is" (*ti estin*), with the substance of a thing as "the immanent cause of being," both "defining" individual things and "marking them out as individuals" (173).

In his attempt to reconcile these two approaches, Milton envisions a cosmogony in which both Platonic and Aristotelian conceptions are at work. On the one hand, God in *Paradise Lost* creates the universe out of a "formless Mass" (III.708), thereby fulfilling in true Platonic fashion "his great Idea" (VII.557). As Milton states in the *Logic*: "For the efficient [*efficiens*] produces the form [*formam*] not yet existing and induces it into the matter [*inducit in materiam*]" (11: 58, 59; 50, 51). On the other hand, once the form is induced into the matter, something like an Aristotelian process occurs: in *Paradise Lost* the Earth is both "form'd" (VII.276) and, "satiate with genial moisture" (VII.282), produces new forms. In accord with Milton's *Logic*, "the form is also the cause of the effect" (11: 59). Or, as Milton states in *Christian Doctrine*, God "blended" the "breath of life" "so intimately with matter" that the production of form became "the proper effect of that power which had been communicated to matter by the Deity" (15: 53). Referred to by Milton as "the power of matter" that generates every form (including human), this concept is thoroughly Aristotelian in nature. According to William B. Hunter, Jr., Milton follows the Aristotelian system in which "formed substances educe new forms from the *dynamis*,"[18] from a matter which in Milton's *Logic* also acts as that "cause" or "force" that produces an "effect" (11: 50, 51).[19]

This attempt to reconcile the two views gives rise to an important tendency in Milton's thought. We see his predisposition to envision form on the one hand as that which transcends the visible world (*per quam*), and on the other, as that which constitutes it (*quod quid est esse*). That is, we see a metaphysics that maintains the integrity of the phenomenal world from the vantage point of a supraphenomenal perspective. The repercussions of this attitude have an immense bearing upon Milton's conduct in both the prose and the poetry, a conduct that can be understood only through further recourse to the distinctions implicit in Platonic and Aristotelian views of form.

According to Richard Kroner, these distinctions represent a movement "from the invisible to the visible sphere, from the Idea to the thing, from the self-existing essence to that entity in which the essence exists."[20] The movement that Kroner speaks of is, of course, not unfounded. We obviously have in Plato an emphasis upon the invisible: the "simple self-existent and unchanging forms," Plato says in the *Phaedo*, are perceived not with the "senses" but with the "mind," since the Ideas are "invisible" (*oux orata*) (1: 463). They are, in fact, comparable to the soul, as distinct from the body (1: 464):

> And he attains to the purest knowledge of them who goes to each with the mind alone, not introducing or intruding in the act of thought sight or any other sense together with reason, but with the very light of the mind in her own clearness searches into the very truth of each; he who has got rid . . . of eyes and ears and . . . of the whole body . . . is likely to attain to the knowledge of true being. . . . (1: 449)

In Aristotle however, we find an emphasis upon the visible. Take some "perishable things," quips Aristotle, "and simply add the word 'Ideal' to the names of these things—Ideal Man, Ideal Horse"—and one is faced with the Platonic conception of form (203–04). Plato might have returned the quip: conceive of form in any of its manifestations, place the word "sensible" before it, and one is faced with the Aristotelian conception. These are oversimplifications, of course, but they have their truth. Thus Aristotle admonishes Socrates for "ignor-[ing] the material world" and for seeking "universals" in the transcendent sphere. "Plato," states Aristotle, accepted Socrates' method and argued that the true understanding of form "is properly concerned with something other than sensibles." Since, as Aristotle insists, "forms must be substances," that is, "the shape of a sensible thing" (*aistheto morphen*), to speak in the Platonic sense of form is "to talk in empty metaphor" (67, 76–77, 167).

It is these contrary points of view that lead Milton, in part, to distinguish between "external" and "internal" form in the *Logic*. While the external form, "more easily observed," is "exposed to the senses [*sensibusque exposita*]," the internal form, difficult to be observed, is "very remote from the senses [*a sensibus . . . remotissimam*]" (11: 62, 63). External form is characteristic of "artificial" entities, internal of "natural" entities (11: 63).[21] Appropriately, Milton is careful to distinguish in his works between external entities, such as the form of "walls" or the form of a "port" (11: 62, 63), and internal entities, such as the form of "marriage," which has "no corporal subsistence, but only a respective being" (4: 100).[22] Elaborating upon the second example, Milton says in *Tetrachordon*: "First therefore the material cause of matrimony is man and woman; the Author and efficient, God; and their consent, the internal *Form* and soul of this relation, is conjugal love arising from a mutual fitnes to the final causes of wedlock, help and society in Religious, Civil and Domestic conversation, which includes as an inferior end the fulfilling of natural desire, and specifical increase; these are the final causes both moving the efficient, and perfecting the *form*" (4: 100).

The distinction is one that can be found as early as Plato's *Cratylus*, which emphasizes the difference between "natural" and "artificial" form. Whereas the "natural" form accords with the ideal and the invisible, the "artificial" form accords with the material and the visible (1: 179). Using as examples the ideal shuttle, as opposed to the material one, Plato states: "When a man has discovered the instrument which is naturally adapted to each work, he must express this natural [*pephukos*] form and not others which he fancies, in the material . . . which he employs" (1: 179). When the distinction appears in Aristotle, the terms are defined to accord with his philosophical outlook. Although Aristotle concedes that things may be "produced artificially whose form is contained in the soul of the artist" (181), there is no sense that "natural" form is internal or that "artificial" form is external. "Natural genesis is that which takes place according to the laws of nature," while artificial genesis is that which takes place (or is "produced") according to the laws of "art, faculty, or thought." If, in the process of generation, Plato is careful to distinguish between the immaterial or "natural" and the material or "artificial," Aristotle insists characteristically that the "material element" (*ulen*) is "present throughout the process." Matter becomes an essential element in the "definition" (181).

These differences lead us to conclude with John Elof Boodin that internal form is uniquely Platonic in its bearing. If, as Boodin states, "Plato's form has to do with internal structure,"[23] Aristotle's has to do with the essential continuity between form and its visible manifestation in the world of matter. The importance of both points of view for Milton will become still clearer if we examine in more detail the Platonic and Aristotelian influences on his works. A study of those influences will indicate why Milton was able to assert with such confidence in the *Logic* that his definition of form reconciled the Platonic and Aristotelian views.

We may begin by examining the Platonic influence through the perspective of St. Augustine, whose observations about form are of the first importance to Milton's outlook. In *The City of God*, St. Augustine states that "the word 'form' has two meanings. Every material body has an outer [*extrinsicus*] form shaped by . . . [an] artisan who can paint or fashion even forms that look like the shapes of animals. But there is also an inner [*intrinsicus*] form which is not a shape but a shaper, with an efficient causality deriving from the secret and hidden determination of some living and intelligent nature which can shape not merely the outer forms of physical bodies but the inner souls of living things. The first kind of form we may attribute to any artificer but the second, only to the one Artificer, Creator and Maker, who is God."[24] It is this second kind of form to which St. Augustine addresses himself in his *De Diversis Quaestionibus* ("*De ideis*," XLVI). There he refers to Platonic form as an "interior" entity, the perception of which is accorded to eyes that are "*sancta et pura*": "*id est, quae illum ipsum oculum quo videntur ista, sanum, et sincerum, et similem his rebus quas videre intendit, habuerit.*"[25]

In line with this observation, we find Milton early in pursuit of the "idea of the beautiful [*tou kalou idean*]," "through all the forms and faces of things (for many are the shapes of things divine)" (12: 26, 27), a pursuit he later applies to the vindication of his own blindness in the *Second Defence*: "Blindness," he says, "deprives things merely of their colour and surface; but takes not from the mind's contemplation whatever is real and permanent in them," as a result of which God illumines his darkness with "an inward and far surpassing light [*interiore ac longe praestabiliore lumine*]" (8: 71, 73). One recalls Milton's impassioned plea in *Paradise Lost*: cut off from the sight of those forms that inhabit the external world, he calls upon the "Celestial light" to "Shine inward, and the mind through all her powers" to "Irradiate, there plant eyes, all mist from thence / Purge and disperse that [he] may see and tell / Of things invisible to mortal sight" (III.51–55). We must not conclude from this statement that Milton in his blindness loses touch with the visible world: although deprived of immediate visible contact with its superficies, he is able to accommodate his knowledge of its external forms to a higher knowledge of its internal makeup. Like Raphael, he is able to "delineate" "what surmounts the reach / Of human sense . . . / By lik'ning spiritual to corporal forms, / As may express them best" (V.571–74). Underlying such a statement is what we have seen as the Platonic movement from visible to invisible, external to internal, a movement that is fundamental to Milton's outlook as a writer.

The various ways in which that outlook expresses itself may be seen, for example, in Milton's theories concerning the acquiring of knowledge. Arguing in *Of Education* that "the end . . . of learning is to repair the ruins of our first Parents by regaining to know God aright," Milton envisions the learning process in a way that we have seen as distinctly Platonic: "But because our understanding cannot in this body found itself but on sensible things, nor arrive so clearly to the knowledge of God and things invisible, as by the conning over the visible and inferior creature, the same method is necessarily to be follow'd in all discreet teaching" (4: 277). Metaphysically, the import of this statement may be found in the discussion of form in the *Logic*, where Milton states unequivocally that of all other causes, form is "the fount of all knowledge [*fontem . . . omnis scientiae*]. For the cause which especially constitutes the essence . . . above all brings knowledge" (11: 60–63). Even if the knowledge of "the internal form of anything . . . is especially difficult," we are assured that "there is nothing that does not have its form, though unknown to us [*res enim nulla est quae suam non habeat formam, nobis licet incognitam*]" (11: 58–63).

In Milton, that idea is visualized repeatedly. One thinks, for instance, of his vision of "discipline" in *The Reason of Church-Government*:

> And certainly discipline is not only the removall of disorder, but if any visible shape can be given to things divine, the very visible shape and image of vertue, whereby she is not only seene in the regular gestures and motions of her heavenly paces as she walks, but also makes the harmony of her voice audible to mortal ears. Yea the Angels themselves, in whom no disorder is fear'd as the Apostle that saw them in his rapture describes, are distinguished and quaterniond into their celestiall Princedomes, and Satrapies, according as God himself hath writ his imperiall decrees through the great provinces of heav'n. The state also of the blessed in Paradise, though never so perfect, is not therefore left without discipline, whose golden survaying reed marks out and measures every quarter and circuit of new Jerusalem. (3: 185)

In its form, discipline is depicted visually through its distinguishing attributes: its gestures, motions, paces, and harmonious voice as a female; its "quaterniond" formation as an emblem of angelic order; its "measured" regularity as a vision of the blessed state in paradise.[26] From the point of view of his *Logic*, Milton is here putting into practice those theories regarding the proper depiction of form. If "definition" constitutes "the essence of a thing," we may more readily arrive at an understanding of that essence as the result of a proper "description" (11: 261–69). Especially in the representation of forms that "cannot be had," description can provide an insight into their definition by drawing upon "qualities that can be experienced," as a result of which there is not merely a "mutual affect . . . between the description and the thing described, but also a reciprocation [*reciprocatio*]" (11: 267–71).

In the case of comprehending the divine nature of God, we may know him, as Milton states in *Christian Doctrine*, by "that form which he attributes to himself in the sacred writings": "For granting that both in the literal and figurative descriptions of God, he is exhibited not as he really is, but in such a manner as may be within the scope of our comprehensions, yet we ought to entertain such a conception of him, as he, in condescending to accommodate himself to our capacities, has shown that he desires we should conceive. For it is on this very account that he has lowered himself to our level" (14: 32, 33, 37). Commonly known as the concept of accommodation, this approach is further reinforced by Milton's distinction between "definition" and "description" in the *Logic*. It is a distinction that he similarly applies in his theological tract. Although, he states, "it is impossible to comprehend accurately under any form of *definition* the divine nature" or "divine image," "some *description* of it . . . may be collected from his [God's] names and attributes," which "*show* his nature" (14: 38, 39; my italics). Providing an analysis of those names and attributes, Milton reveals his method of coming to terms with the divine form. In so doing, he gives expression to the Platonism in his methodology, a Platonism whose significance is discernible not only in the realm of learning and perception but in the realm of behavior as well.[27] For if we consider that, as Plato states in the *Meno* (1: 366–68), the end of knowledge is virtue, a striving for the Good,[28] we shall not be surprised to find Milton imposing a moral framework upon his metaphysics.

Such a framework is discernible at the very outset in *Of Education*, which, we recall, addresses itself to the "end" of "learning" as a process of repairing "the ruines of our first Parents" through a proper knowledge of God. That knowledge, in turn, will allow us, "to be like him," to possess a form worthy of His (4: 277). To achieve such a state, we must undergo a process of refinement not unlike what the Lady is said to experience in *A Mask*. There the Lady's knowledge of the divine is accompanied by a movement from visible to invisible, external to internal: "Till oft convers with heav'nly habitants / Begin to cast a beam on th'outward shape, / The unpolluted temple of the mind, / And turns it by degrees to the souls essence, / Till all be made immortal" (459–63). The Platonic nature of that process becomes particularly discernible when the process is reversed, when the "spiritualizing" of form, owing to chaste behavior, gives way to the "materializing" of form, owing to unchaste behavior: "but when lust / By unchaste looks, loose gesture, and foul talk, / But most by lewd and lavish act of sin, / Lets in defilement to the inward parts, / The soul grows clotted by contagion, / Imbodies, and inbrutes, till she quite loose / The divine property of her first being" (463–69). We are reminded here significantly of Plato's discourse on the soul-body relationship in the *Phaedo*:

> But the soul which has been polluted . . . and is the companion and servant of the body always, and is in love with and fascinated by the body and by the desires and pleasures of the body, until she is led to believe that the truth only exists in a bodily form, which a man may touch and see and taste, and use for the purposes of his lusts . . . is held fast by the corporeal, which the continual association and constant care of the body have wrought into her nature. . . . And this corporeal element . . . is heavy and weighty and earthy, and is the element of sight by which a soul is depressed and dragged down again into the visible world below. . . . [Such souls] are cloyed with sight and therefore visible. (1: 466)

The Platonic implications of the entire process, as Milton envisions it, are unmistakable. Through the renunciation of the senses, we experience a transcendent flight from body to soul, visible to invisible, external to internal. Through the cultivation of the senses, we experience an immersion in the bodily, a movement from invisible to visible, internal to external. The dichotomies could not be more distinct. From the metaphysical point of view we are returned to the Platonic *perquam*, the dynamic and transcendent source of all movement as it is embodied in form. Christianized by St. Augustine, that principle, we recall, is associated with "the one Artificer, Creator, and Maker, who is God." A movement toward this Absolute First Mover is a movement away from the material (*extrinsicus* to *intrinsicus*); a movement away from the Absolute First Mover is a movement toward the material (*intrinsicus* to *extrinsicus*).

Were it not for Milton's stance as a metaphysician, we might well be content to look upon such a process as an example of his unqualified indebtedness to the concept of form implicit in Platonic and Neoplatonic metaphysics. We are reminded, however, that Milton's metaphysics "join" Platonic and Aristotelian conceptions, that he maintains the integrity of the phenomenal world from a supraphenomenal perspective. As a result, we should be prepared to come to terms with the Aristotelian bearing of what appears to be a distinctly Platonic point of view, as may be seen in Milton's own statements in the *Logic* about what is involved in the process of transformation. Significantly, Milton explains that process not in Platonic but in Aristotelian terms. In the "change" (*mutatio*) from one state of being to another, the material element is *always* present. Matter merely assumes a different form: "that is the thing," Milton states in the *Logic*, "which the matter makes evident, to wit, the effect produced by the matter, since we know that matter is common to all entities and nonentities, not peculiar to sensible and corporeal things. But of whatever sort these things are, such the matter of them ought to be; the sensible should be composed of sensible things, the eternal of eternal things, and so in the rest" (11:50–3).

Thus, in *Paradise Lost*, we are made aware of "one first matter all,/ Indu'd with various forms, various degrees of substance" (V.472–4), "proceed[ing]" from God and "return[ing]" to Him "if not deprav'd from good" (V.469–70). The nearer these forms are placed to God the "more refin'd, more spiritous, and pure" they become, "Till body up to spirit work" (V.475–6) as man is "rais'd" to heavenly stature "by degrees of merit" (VII.157). (The reverse of such a process is discernible, of course, in the "foul descent" of Satan's enforced "incarnat[ing] and imbrut[ing]" within serpentine form [IX.163–71].) Referring to this process in *Paradise Lost* as one in which matter is "sublim'd" by a "gradual scale" (V.484), Milton similarly speaks in *Christian Doctrine* of that impulse in all things to a higher order which provides for "degrees" (*gradus*) of perfection (15:20, 21). At the same time, he emphasizes in *Paradise Lost* the fact that distinctions of "degree" are not distinctions of "kind" (V.490), that material refinement from "body" to "spirit" constitutes not a dichotomy but a progression. As Milton states in *Christian Doctrine*, all forms are material: there is simply no dichotomy between "body" and "spirit" (15:23). In this way, he insists upon the material continuity that underlies all changes in form, even changes that suggest some sort of purifying or spiritualizing process (or the reverse). For Milton, then, the movement from "body" to "spirit" must be seen in terms that take into account the undeniable presence of the material world, the *quod quid est esse* of Aristotelian metaphysics.[29]

We may now see the particular significance of Walter Clyde Curry's observation that from the Miltonic point of view, "a material continuity is established between the invisible and visible worlds."[30] As we have noted, that continuity causes Milton's Platonism—his concern with form conceived externally and internally, with the ability of the mind to perceive the unperceivable, with the influence of behavior upon form—to be grounded firmly in the Aristotelian world of the "sensible," the "actual." His ontology never loses sight of the material continuity uniting all phenomena,[31] even while it is insisting upon such dichotomies as body-spirit, external-internal, visible-invisible, corporeal-incorporeal. The result is to give credence to those dichotomies by maintaining that in fact they do not exist. It is to assert the reality of the transcendent by emphasizing the inescapable presence of its opposite. Even as body becomes spirit, external internal, visible invisible, corporeal incorporeal, a continuity underlies that movement so categorically that the transcendent, the *per quam*, takes on a meaning it would otherwise never have, a reality that language could never bestow upon it. It becomes what it is, a *quod quid est esse*. In that way, Platonic and Aristotelian conceptions of form become integrated into Milton's metaphysics with a force that permeates his work, and that suggests at once the harmony and the complexity of his vision.

CHAPTER THREE

The Organicist Polemic

WE are already familiar with the Renaissance predisposition to view the world in bodily terms. Referred to by the sociologists as *organicism*, that tendency in thought is one which "constructs its picture of the world on an organic model."[1] If the universality of the organicist tendency is attested by the fact that it may be found in "ancient Hindu, Chinese, Greek, and Roman writers,"[2] its presence in the Renaissance is no less pervasive. Basing his entire treatise upon the idea, Edward Forsett, in *A Comparative Discourse of the Bodies Natural and Politique* (1606), devotes a full introductory section to the matter. First he traces organicism to "that thrice renowned philosopher *Trismegistus*," who "imagined an huge and mightie Gyant, Whose head was aboue the firmament, his necke, shoulders, and upper parts in the heauens, his armes and hands reaching to East and West, his belly in the whole spaciousnesse under the Moone, his legges and feet within the earth."[3] Then he justifies his use of the organicist analogy by invoking the commonplace Renaissance association of the body of the world (macrocosm) and the body of man (microcosm). For Forsett, this was no arbitrary correspondence; he insisted, as Michael Walzer states, "that the whole system of analogies was the creation of God" and that "they had a real existence prior to their recognition by men."[4] Thus, Forsett concludes, "Wherefore seeing that the uttermost extent of mans understanding, can shape no better forme of ordering the affayres of a State, than by marking and matching of the workes of the finger of God, eyther in the larger volume of the uniuersall (that is, the body of the world), or in the abridgement thereof, the body of man: I account these two to be the two great lights for enquiry and meditation concerning this business" (2).

That Renaissance writers would have concurred with Forsett's views may be seen by the proliferation of works (predominantly allegorical) based solely upon the organicist analogy. One thinks of works as diverse as Phineas Fletcher's *The Purple Island, or The Isle of Man* (1633); Richard Bernard's *The Isle of Man: or, The Legal Proceeding in Man-shire against SINNE* (1626); and *Lingua: or The Combat of the*

'Tongue,' and the fiue Senses for 'Superiority,' A pleasant Comoedie (1607), attributed to Thomas Tomkis. But perhaps the most apt illustration of the tendency in the Renaissance to look upon the world in bodily terms is discernible in Francis Gray's *The Judge's Scripture or, God's Charge to Charge-givers* (1637). In that work, Gray envisions at least five bodily categories: "body celestial," "body astronomical," "body natural," "body economical," and "body politic."[5]

With so great a stress upon the organicist analogy in the Renaissance, then, it is little wonder that organicism should be brought to bear upon polemic. Indeed, so pervasive was the tendency in Renaissance polemic to formulate one's position through a bodily correspondence that controversies in general tended to resolve themselves into arguments about bodies. Hooker's *Of the Laws of Ecclesiastical Polity* provides a case in point. In Book 8, chapter 4, he quotes Thomas Cartwright as saying: "If the Church be the body of Christ, and of the civil magistrate, it shall have two heads, which being monstrous, is to the great dishonour of Christ and his Church." Hooker reponds: "It is neither monstrous nor as much as uncomely for a Church to have different heads," since God has made Christ "the supreme head of the whole Church; the head not only of that mystical body which the eye of man is not able to discern, but even of every politic society, of every visible Church in the world."[6] Implicit in Cartwright's statement and Hooker's response are those elements that formed the cornerstone of the organicist polemic in the Renaissance. Their importance to Milton's use of the body as polemical device will become apparent only after we have explored, within the context of his times, his view of the church, both invisible and visible, and the relationship of the church to the state. An understanding of these matters will provide the necessary background for an appreciation not only of Milton's polemical practices but of the organicist polemic in general.

As invisible entity, the church for Milton had its source in the concept of the mystical body of Christ (*corpus mysticum*). Thus, Milton states in *Christian Doctrine*: "from [the] union and fellowship of the regenerate with the Father and Christ, and of the members of Christ's body among themselves, results the mystical body called *The Invisible Church*, whereof Christ is the head" (16: 61). Milton's statement derives, of course, from 1 Corinthians 21: 12–31: "For as the body is one, and hath many members, and all the members of that one body, being many, are one body: so also is Christ. . . . Now ye are the body of Christ, and members in particular."[7] Despite the New Testament source, however, the concept of the invisible church as *corpus mysticum* is of medieval origin. As Ernst H. Kantorowicz makes clear, although the idea of the church as *corpus Christi* goes back to Saint Paul, it was the medieval world that ascribed to the church those sacramental and sociological characteristics underlying the concept of the *corpus mysticum*.[8] This is precisely the view that emerges in John of Salisbury's *Policraticus*, which compares "the commonweal with the organism of the human body, a simile popular among the jurists." "Similar comparisons of the Church with a human body, stimulated by St. Paul . . . are found sporadically throughout the Middle Ages, and it was only an adaptation to the new terminology that Isaac of Stella, a contemporary of John of Salisbury, applied the metaphor of the human body with great precision to the *corpus mysticum* the head of which was Christ and whose limbs were the archbishops, bishops, and other functionaries of the Church. That is to say, the anthropomorphic imagery was transferred as a matter of course to both the Church as the 'mystical body of Christ' in a spiritual sense and the Church as an administrative organism styled likewise *corpus mysticum*."[9] For the Renaissance understanding of the idea, we might invoke Richard Hooker's eloquent exposition in his *Laws*: "That Church of Christ, which we properly term his body mystical, can be but one; neither can that one be sensibly discerned by any man, inasmuch as the parts thereof are some in heaven already with Christ, and the rest that are on earth (albeit their natural persons be visible) we do not discern this property, whereby they are truly and infallibly of that body. Only our minds by intellectual conceit are able to apprehend, that such a real body there is, a body collective, because it containeth an huge multitude; a body mystical, because the mystery of their conjunction is removed altogether from sense" (1: 220).

In contradistinction to the mystical body of the invisible church, Hooker refers in the same place to the corporeal body (those who are "incorporated into . . . *one body*") of the visible church. Comprised, as Milton says, of "those indiscriminately who have received the call, whether actually regenerate or otherwise," the visible church functions temporally in various congregations throughout the world (*Christian Doctrine* 16: 219). As such, its importance is decidedly inferior to that of the invisible church. This may be seen particularly in the fact that Milton associated the visible church with the Old Dispensation, the invisible church with the New. For Milton, the Old Dispensation emphasized the ceremonial law (the "materiall Temple," as he calls it), which prefigured but was superseded by "the new alliance of God to man" (*Reason of Church-Government* 3: 190–91). According to that new alliance, "the spiritual eye may discerne more goodly and gracefully erected then all the magnificance of Temple or Tabernacle, such a heavenly structure of evangelick discipline . . . that it cannot be wonder'd if that elegant and artfull symmetry of the promised new temple in *Ezechiel,* and all those sumptuous things under the Law were made to signifie the inward beauty and splendor of the Christian church thus govern'd" (3: 191). The ceremonial law, therefore, becomes important in its prefigurative capacity but "must not be subscribed to literally . . . unlesse," Milton says, "we mean to annihilat the Gospel" (3: 191), for the gospel expresses the word of the Holy Spirit, which, enlightening us "inwardly," impresses itself upon our hearts, "according to the promise of God" (*Christian Doctrine* 16: 273). Such an idea bears directly upon the place of the visible church in Milton's beliefs: "For with regard to the visible church, which is also proposed as a criterion of faith, it is evident that, since the ascension of Christ, the *pillar and ground* of *the truth* has not uniformly been the church, but the hearts of believers, which are properly 'the house and church of the living God'" (16: 279). This movement in Milton from the corporeal to the mystical, the external to the internal, the visible to the invisible, has prompted Malcolm Ross to observe that for Milton the church became "*utterly* invisible, as is the fellowship it is said to contain."[10]

If this is so, then we can more nearly appreciate the thrust of Milton's criticism of the prelates in his antiprelatical tracts, where he exploits the bodily associations of the invisible and visible churches for polemical purposes. *Of Reformation* is a case in point. At the outset we encounter "the mysticall body" (*corpus mysticum*) of the invisible church, whose "every joynt, and sinew" is inspired by "the Spirit of unity and meeknesse" (3: 18). In that form, Milton reveals to us "our Saviour *Christ,* suffering to the lowest bent of weaknesse, in the *Flesh,* and presently triumphing to the highest pitch of *glory,* in the *Spirit,* which drew up his body also, till we in both be united him in the Revelation of his Kingdome" (3: 1–2). The pure body, then, is represented through a spiritualizing movement, whereby "that Doctrine of the *Gospel*" is "winnow'd, and sifted, from the chaffe of overdated Ceremonies, and refin'd to such a Spiritual height, and temper of purity" that the body is "purifi'd by the affections of the regenerat Soule, and nothing left impure, but sinne" (3: 1). In connection with that idea, one might once again recall the Elder Brother's statement in *A Mask* that the effect of chastity is "to cast a beam on th' outward shape, / The unpolluted temple of the mind" and to turn it "by degrees to the souls essence / Till all be made immortal," while the effect of lust ("By unchast looks, loose gestures, and foul talk, / But most by lewd and lavish act of sin") is to let in "defilement to the inward parts" so that "the soul grows clotted by contagion, / Imbodies and imbrutes, till she quite loose / The divine property of her first being" (459–69).

The uniquely ecclesiastical bearing this idea assumes in *Of Reformation* may be seen in the organicist vision of that "Corporation of Impostors," "misshapen and enormous *Prelatisme*" (3: 12), a fitting contrast with the elect members of the mystical body of Christ. Through the prelates, "the inward acts of *worship* issuing from the native strength of the SOULE, run out lavishly to the upper skin, and there harden into a crust of Formallitie" (3: 3). Having caused the purity of doctrine "to backslide one way into the jewish beggery, of old cast rudiments, and stumble forward another way into the new-vomited paganisme of sensuall Idolatry," the prelates have brought "the inward acts of the *Spirit* to the outward, and customary ey-Service of the body, as if they could make God earthly, and fleshly, because they could not make themselves *heavenly*, and *Spirituall*":

> they began to draw downe all the Divine intercours, betwixt God, and the Soule, yea, the very shape of God himselfe, into an exterior, and bodily forme, urgently pretending a necessity, and obligement of joyning the body in a formall reverence, and *Worship* circumscrib'd, they hallow'd it, they fum'd it, they sprincl'd it, they be deck't it, not in robes of pure innocency, but of pure Linnen, with other deformed, and fantastick dresses in Palls, and Miters, gold, and guegaw's fetcht from *Arons* old wardrope, or the *Flamins vestry*: then was the *Priest* set to *con his motions*, and his *Postures* his *Liturgies*, and his *Lurries*, till the Soule by this meanes of over-bodying her selfe, given up justly to fleshly delights, bated her wing apace downeward: and finding the ease she had from her visible, and sensuous collegue the body in performance of *Religious* duties, her pineons now broken, and flagging, shifted off from her selfe, the labour of high soaring any more, forgot her heavenly flight, and left the dull, and droyling carcas to plod on in the old rode, and drudging Trade of outward conformity. (3: 2–3)

Characteristically inveighing against what he considers to be the results of prelatical corruption, Milton causes the many aspects of that corruption to express themselves in a vision of a deformed body. The fraud of traditions, idolatry, formal worship, vestments, set liturgy—all these are resolved into an image of God's being reembodied, reincarnated in human form. Once "triumphing to the highest pitch of *glory*, in the *Spirit*," the *corpus mysticum* now becomes a "dull, and

droyling carcas," a debased version of what the corporeal body of the
visible church is supposed to signify. Ideally, as Milton states in
Christian Doctrine, the visible church should serve, especially in
matters of worship, as an outward manifestation of the invisible (16:
221). After all, as Hooker says, the members of the corporeal body of
the visible church are "one in outward profession of those things,
which supernaturally appertain to the very essence of Christianity" (1:
220). This view is certainly in agreement with Milton's attitude, as
indicated in *Christian Doctrine*, that the visible church should express
itself in "the proper external worship of God" (16: 221). When it does
not, however, an embodying occurs. In matters of worship, Milton
articulates this idea in a number of ways.

For example, implicit in the *corpus mysticum* image we are discuss-
ing is a liturgical dimension. The debased "joyning" of the body "in a
formall reverence and *Worship*" (characterized by the hallowing, the
fuming, the sprinkling, and the bedecking) suggests a perversion of the
rite of communion. That suggestion is perfectly in accord with the
corpus mysticum concept, since "traditionally, there was a close
connexion . . . between the Eucharist as the body of Christ and the
Church as His mystical body."[11] Indeed, *corpus verum* and *corpus
mysticum* bore an integral relationship: "Holy bread," states *The
Rationale of Ceremonial* (circa 1540), reminds us "that all Christian
men be one mystical body of Christ as the bread is made of many
grains and yet but one loaf."[12] What results from the implicit association of the Eucharist and the mystical body in Milton's tract is a
criticism of the prelatical overemphasis upon the ritual trappings of the
communion. To Milton, such ostentation, with its stress upon externals rather than what they symbolized, represented a return to popery,
whose implications he treated graphically in *Christian Doctrine*. There
he criticizes the doctrine of the Real Presence by contrasting Christ's
true presence in the incarnate flesh with his symbolic presence in the
Lord's Supper. Attributing to "the outward sign the power of bestowing salvation or grace by virtue of the mere *opus operatum*," the
papists in their Mass have "converted the Supper of the Lord into a
banquet of cannibals" (16: 197). Similarly, with their acceptance of
outward signs to the exclusion of all else, the prelates have caused the
corpus mysticum, in its association with the rite of communion, to
become perverted.

From an organicist point of view, that idea represents only one
aspect of Milton's antiprelatical criticism. Also important is his castigation of the prelates through the imagery of investiture. Thus we
recall that the prelates are accused not only of "joyning" the body in

"a formall reverence and *Worship*" but of investing it as well: "they be deck't it, not in robes of pure innocency, but of pure Linnen, with other deformed, and fantastick dresses in Palls, and Miters, gold, and guegaw's fetcht from *Arons* old wardrope, or the *Flamins vestry*" (3: 2). The use of the imagery of investing as a characteristic of the embodying process is not arbitrary: ecclesiastically, it has its roots in existing controversies over ministerial vesture. First becoming an issue in 1549, the idea of proper ministerial attire made itself felt when by 1552 "albs, copes, and vestments were forbidden throughout England." Such strictures were reflected in the 1552 Edwardine Book of Common Prayer, in which "all references to vestments were deleted" from "the directions for the ordering of deacons, priests, and bishops."[13] That atmosphere was, of course, altered when Mary (and, even after her, Elizabeth) came to the throne. As a result, in 1565, three hundred of the Fellows of Saint John's College, Cambridge, appeared in church without their surplices. "When Sir William Cecil, Chancellor of the University, commanded the students to wear their vestments or be expelled, the heads of the Colleges, along with John Whitgift . . . petitioned for dispensation because of the threatened loss of students."[14] Shortly thereafter disputes were waged like the Vestiarian controversy, comprised of such tracts as *A briefe discourse against the outwarde apparell and Ministring garments of the popishe church* (1566). The issues implicit in tracts like these became part of the Admonition controversy between Whitgift and Cartwright, were treated at length by Richard Hooker in his *Laws*, and were taken up again with renewed virulence in the seventeenth century.

From the Puritan point of view, ministerial vesture recalled popery and was therefore a defilement. John Wyclif had earlier admonished the clergy in "De Papa" (circa 1380) by saying that God's "men shulden not be clothid" in rich garments.[15] His admonition was, in turn, elaborated upon by such later writers as William Prynne, who complained, in *A Looking-Glasse for all Lordly Prelates* (1636), that although Christ's clothing was very poor, "one poore thread-bare Coate without a seame," the prelates "have many silken, sattin, scarlet, Gownes, cassockes, robes, coapes . . . patterned up with many seames and piebalde colours," which "poore Christ never wore" (67–68). This clothing led the Puritans to refer to prelatical attire as "abominable rags, polluted garments, marks and sacraments of idolatry," indeed, downright "filth."[16] That criticism found ample expression in *The Letany of John Bastwick* (1637), where we discover the following castigation: "One would think that hell were broke loose and that the devils, in surplices, in hoods, in copes, in rochets, and in foursquare cowturds upon their heads, were come among us and beshit us all—foo, how they stink!"[17]

In contrast to the extreme Puritan view, the Anglican position on ministerial vesture reflected their via media attitude. Whitgift, Hooker, and Hall should provide a firm foundation for understanding this attitude. Countenancing the use of ministerial vesture, Whitgift says, in his *Defence of the Aunswere* (1574): "Wherefore that which I say is true, that even then ministers of the gospel might be known by their apparel, as Christ and John the Baptist, and therefore not to be so strange a matter that ministers should also differ from other men in their apparel."[18] Hooker restates this position in his *Laws* when he sanctions the minister's attire as "but a matter of mere formality" and when he admonishes: "as we think not ourselves the holier because we use it, so neither should they with whom no such thing is in use think us therefore unholy, because we submit ourselves unto that which . . . the wisdom of authority and law hath thought comely. To solemn actions of royalty and justice their suitable ornaments are a beauty. Are they only in religion a stain?" (1: 347–48). But the most telling defense may be found in Joseph Hall's *Episcopacie by Divine Right. Asserted* (1640). Reflecting a major tendency of the organicist impulse, Hall causes the issue of ministerial vesture to represent his via media stance regarding the problem of ornaments in general. In doing so, he reveals an essential aspect of the Anglican mind in its understanding of the relationship between external things and what they represent: "The accession of honourable titles, or (not incompatible) priviledges, makes no difference in the substance of a lawfull and holy calling: These things, being merely externall, and adventitious, can no more alter the nature of the calling, than change of suits, the body. Neither is it otherwise with the calling, than with the person whose it is; the man is the same whether poore or rich. . . . As a wise man is no whit differently affected with the changes of these his outward conditions, but looks upon them with the same face . . . so the judicious beholder indifferently esteems them in another . . . valuing the calling according to its own true worth, not after the price or meanenesse of the abiliments wherewith it is cloathed; if some garments be coarse, yet they may serve to defend from cold; others, besides warmth, give grace and comelinesse to the body; there may be good use of both; and perhaps one and the same vesture may serve for both purposes" (66–68).

Essentially, what Hall is doing in this statement (through his recourse to the organicist idea of changing clothing, is invoking the concept of adiaphorism or indifferency. Derived from Saint Paul, the concept became important to such reformers as Luther and Calvin and emerged in the sixteenth- and seventeenth-century disputes between the Puritans and the Anglicans.[19] Hall voices the Anglican point of view when he says that externals such as titles and privileges cannot alter the nature of a calling, that outward conditions are of no consequence to inward makeup. Milton, of course, would respond by saying that outward conditions are of absolute importance to inward makeup, that the form a thing assumes is integral to its nature (the matter of which it consists).[20] By extension, to call the form of something indifferent, as the prelates do, is to violate that matter which it manifests. With respect to the liturgy, for example, Milton felt that since the form of it had been tainted by its Romish use, its matter had been likewise tainted, so that we could not assume the form of the liturgy without being subject to its corruptions: " 'Tis not the good-nesse of matter therefore which is not, nor can be ow'd to the *Liturgie*, that will beare it out, if the form, which is the essence of it, be fantastick and superstitious, the end sinister, and the imposition violent" (130).

Such assumptions led the Puritans to remove root and branch all vestiges of Romish use from their church. They sought to purge their church of all those corruptions brought upon by forms that smacked of popery, forms that were imposed, as Laud's *Constitutions and Canons Ecclesiastical* (1640) makes clear, for the sake of "decency."[21] We might recall, for instance, that the Commons, on 1 September 1641, "issued resolutions for the reform of ceremonies" previously attacked, "with fanatical fervor," by the Puritans: "the communion table to be removed from the east end of the church; rails around the communion table to be taken away; crucifixes and images of the Virgin Mary to be removed; candlesticks and tapers not to be used on the communion table; bowing at the name of Jesus to cease."[22] Even more to the point, however, was the "unauthorized destruction of images in many cathedrals" in the summer of 1642 by the Puritan troops. "On 26 August 1642 Colonel Sandys led his men into Canterbury Cathedral where 'were demolished that day . . . many Idolls of stone, thirteen representing Christ and his twelve Apostles standing over the West doore of the Quire, which were all caste doune headlong and some fell on their heads and their Myters brake their necks.' "[23] With all ornaments purged away, the Puritans worshiped in unadorned places. As Donne complains, the Puritans "think they cannot . . . call upon God out of the depth, except it be in a Conventicle in a cellar (or) . . . in a garret, and when they are here [in the Anglican service] wink at the ornaments, and stop their ears at the musique of the Church."[24]

What relationship this iconoclastic, purgative impulse has to the organicist idea will become clear if we examine the rhetoric with which the Puritans justified their activities and with which the Anglicans responded to that justification. In Book 5, chapter 15 of his *Laws*, Hooker records the Puritan view that unadorned places are most "suitable unto the nakedness of Jesus Christ and the simplicity of his Gospel" (1: 312). Undoubtedly Hooker's understanding of the Puritan view is accurate. An integral part of the Puritan impulse is the need to divest the body of its trappings, a need that we already witnessed in those Fellows of Saint John's College, Cambridge, who appeared in church without their surplices. This impulse in polemic is discernible in Milton's desire, expressed through a language of divestiture, to purge the church of its corruption. He first accuses the prelates of investing "*Christs* Gospell," that "thred-bare Matron," with pompous attire, of overlaying "with wanton *tresses*" her "chast and modest vaile surrounded with celestiall beames," and of bespeckling her "in a flaring tire" with "all the gaudy allurements of a Whore" (*Of Reformation* 3: 25). Then he reproaches them: "Tell me ye Priests wherfore this gold, wherfore these roabs and surplices over the Gospel? is our religion guilty of the first trespasse and hath need of cloathing to cover her nakednesse?" (*Reason of Church-Government* 3: 246). Milton's impulse is to divest the prelates themselves, "undresse them of all their guilded vanities" (*Reason of Church-Government* 3: 271), in order to have their "inside nakednesse thrown open to publick view," thereby revealing their "deformed barenesse" (*Animadversions* 3: 112; *Reason of Church-Government* 3: 198).

It is precisely this attitude that the Anglicans saw as a primary Puritan characteristic: the need to divest, to lay bare. Appropriately, to defend their position they responded in language that drew upon the same organicist concept of divestiture and investiture. Thus, Donne justifies the Anglican via media by saying: "we stript not the Church into a nakedness, nor into rags; we divested her not of her possessions, nor of her Ceremonies" (4: 106). Rather, like his Anglican counterparts, Donne saw the necessity of clothing the church lest it be unseemly: "God is said in the Scriptures to apparell himself gloriously; (God *covers* him *with light as with a garment*). And so of his Spouse the Church it is said, (*Her clothing is of wrought gold, and her raiment of needle worke*) and, as though nothing in this world were good enough for her wearing, she is said *to be cloathed with the Sun*. But glorious apparell is not pride in them, whose conditions require it, and whose revenews will beare it" (2: 290).

Organicist in import, such a defense of the Anglican via media represents only one aspect of the way in which the body was incorporated into the Puritan-Anglican disputes. Intimately associated with the Anglican accusation that the Puritan impulse is one of divesting appears the accusation that that impulse, in its zeal, expresses itself in terms of tearing as well. Thus we find the following statement in Donne: "To a *Circumcision* of the *garment*, that is, to a paring, and taking away such *Ceremonies*, as were superstitious, or superfluous, of an ill use, or of no use, our *Church* came in the beginning of the *Reformation*. To a *Circumcision* we came; but those *Churches* that came to a *Concision* of the *garment*, to an absolute taking away of *all ceremonies*, neither provided so safely for the *Church* it self in the substance thereof, nor for the exaltation of *Devotion in the Church*" (10: 116). The pervasiveness of these ideas is indicated by the fact that as late as *A Tale of Tub*, they may be found in Swift's satirical thrust at Jack: "Having thus kindled and enflamed himself as high possible, and by Consequence, in a delicate Temper for beginning a Reformation, he set about the Work immediately, and in three Minutes, made more Dispatch than *Martin* had done in as many Hours. For . . . *Zeal* is never so highly obliged, as when you set it a *Tearing*. . . . Thus it happened, that stripping down a Parcel of Gold *Lace*, a little too hastily, he rent the *main Body* of his *Coat* from Top to Bottom."[25]

That the association of divesting with tearing does indeed reflect the Puritan attitude is discernible in Milton's castigation of the prelates in *The Reason of Church-Government*: "As for the rending of the Church, we have many reasons to thinke it is not that which ye labour to prevent so much as the rending of your pontificall sleeves: that schisme would be the sorest schisme to you" (3: 215). Milton's statement is especially revealing because it relates the rending of clothing to the rending of the body, that is, the church itself. That form of rending is precisely what Donne warns against when the he says: "they pretend *Reformation*, but they intend *Destruction*, a tearing, a renting, a wounding the body, and frame, and peace of the Church." Further, those who pretend Reformation enact a "*Concisionem corporis*, the shredding of the *body* of Christ into Fragments, by unnecessary wrangling in *Doctrinall points*; and then *Concisionem vestis*, the shredding of the *garment* of Christ into rags by unnecessary wrangling in matters of *Discipline*, and *ceremoniall* points; and lastly *Concisionem spiritus* . . . the concision of thine own spirit, and heart, and minde, and *soule*, and *conscience*" (10: 104, 105).

The Anglican ideal is to keep the body intact at all costs, to beware of "*Concisio corporis*," as Donne says, lest we "break Jesus in pieces" by departing from "any fundamentall Article of faith, for that is a skin that covers the whole body, an obligation that lies upon the whole *Church*" (10: 115). For this reason, we find such writers as Edward Forsett advocating a via media approach, an encouraging of what is good before a severing of what is bad: "That as in the bodie it is a greater mischiefe not to nourish and sustaine the sound and seruiceable parts, than not to cut off the diseased and corrupted: so in the Commonweale, not to reward and aduaunce the worthie, is more pernicious and of more dangerous consequence, than to afflict, punish, or pare away the hurtfull and infectious: for where the one is but spared awhile by lenitie and impunitie in some hope of amendment, the other unrespected in his goodnesse, is so pinched by that coldnesse of entertaynment, as hee seldome or neuer can come forward and put forth any shoots of vertue" (*Comparative Discourse* 46–47). Forsett's statement introduces a new point of reference into our discussion, and in order to appreciate the full impact of the Puritan impulse to tear and sever one part of the body from the other, we must take careful note of it.

Obviously the organism to which Forsett refers in his via media approach is that of the state. The reference to the body politic at this point is scarcely arbitrary, first because its use is universally sanctioned. Otto Friedrich von Gierke states quite unreservedly that "there was hardly a single system of political theory which entirely escaped this 'organic' tendency of thought."[26] We are perhaps most familiar with the idea from Book 5 of Plato's *Republic*, in which the state is compared to "an individual man," an "organism" (2: 724–25). But even more important for our immediate purpose is the intimate association of the state as political organism with the church as ecclesiastical organism. The association has a long tradition going back at least as early as the thirteenth century, when Vincent of Beauvais, in his *Speculum doctrinale*, used the term *corpus reipublicae mysticum*.[27] The idea received juristic emphasis when "the venerable image of *sponsus* and *sponsa*, Christ and his Church, was transferred from the spiritual to the secular and adapted to the jurist's need for defining the relations between Prince and State." As a result, "the Church as the supra-individual collective body of Christ, of which he was both the head and the husband, found its exact parallel in the state as the supra-individual collective body of the Prince, of which he was both the head and the husband." Appropriately, as late as 1603, we discover James I drawing upon precisely that association in the speech to his first Parliament: "What God hath conjoined then, let no man separate. I am the husband, and all the whole island is my lawful wife; I am the head, and it is my body; I am the shepherd, and it is my flock."[28] Moreover, in line with this idea was the belief that the king was the single head not only of the civil realm (political organism) but of the religious realm (ecclesiastical organism) as well. That is, he was one head over two bodies. His power over the second realm was explained by the fact that as ruler, he had dominion (at least within a temporal context) over the visible church.[29] Defending precisely that idea, Whitgift voiced the Anglican point of view when he argued that he was able to "perceive no such distinction of the commonwealth and the church that they should be counted, as it were, two several bodies, governed with diverse laws and diverse magistrates."[30]

Countering the Anglican impulse to unite the two bodies under one head, the Puritan impulse sought to separate them. Specifically, the Puritans maintained that the jurisdictions of church and state were different, the church concerning itself with inner things, the state with outer. That is exactly the point of view Milton assumes in *The Reason of Church-Government*, where he argues that man, "consisting of two parts, the inward and the outward," is left by "the eternall providence" "under two sorts of cure, the Church and Magistrat." To prove that "the magistrat hath only to deal with . . . the outward man," Milton sets out "to shape and fashion this outward man into the similitude of a body, and set him visible before us; imagining the inner man only as the soul." But even "the inner man" takes the form of what Milton calls "the ecclesiastical body" (3: 254, 258). When these bodies are unnaturally joined, a monstrosity results. As Milton says in *Considerations touching the likeliest means to remove hirelings out of the Church*, "And for the magistrate in person of a nursing father to make the church his meer ward . . . is neither just nor pious . . . and upon her (the church), whose only head is in heaven, yea upon him, who is her only head, sets another in effect, and, which is most monstrous, a human head on a heavenly, a carnal on a spiritual, a political head on an ecclesiastical bodie; which at length by such heterogeneal, such incestuous conjunction, transformes her oft-times into a beast of many heads and many horns" (6: 82–83). Such is the basis of the organicist impulse as it expresses itself in Puritan polemic.

With that idea in mind, we can more readily understand the Puritan need to tear and sever one part of the body from the other. The Puritans saw themselves in that act not as destroying what was healthy but as curing (by radical means, to be sure) what was unhealthy. That is, they saw themselves as physicians administering treatment and effecting cure. That attitude is apparent in the very titles of their pamphlets, such as Anthony Tuckney's *The Balme of Gilead, For the Wounds of England* (1643).[31] Moreover, in the passage we have just considered from *The Reason of Church-Government*, Milton looks upon both the civil magistrate and the clergyman as physicians who cure the body according to the nature of their office. While the clergyman applies "phisick" to the "inward bed of corruption," the civil magistrate "seres," "cauterizes," and even "cuts off" the corrupt limbs of the outward body if the treatment warrants it (3: 255–56).

Such an attitude is dramatized in *Of Reformation*. There Milton presents us with a little self-contained drama, in which a body summons "all the Members to meet in the Guild for the common good" in order to contest the presence of "a huge and monstrous Wen little lesse than the Head it selfe, growing to it by a narrower excrescency." The wen defends his position by saying "that as in place he was second to the head, so by due of merit; that he was to it an ornament, and strength, and of speciall neere relation, and that if the head should faile, none were fitter than himselfe to step into his place; therefore hee thought it for the honour of the Body, that such dignities and rich indowments should be decreed him, as did adorne, and set out the noblest Members." The body responds by sending for "a wise and learned Philosopher," who examines the wen's "claime and Petition of right" and then says disdainfully: "Wilt thou . . . that art but a bottle of vitious and harden'd excrements, contend with the lawfull and free-borne members? . . . Lourdan . . . thy folly is as great as thy filth. . . . thou containst no good thing in thee, but a heape of hard, and loathsome uncleannes, and art to the head a foul disfigurment and burden, when I have cut thee off, and open'd thee, as by the help of these implements I will doe, all men shall see" (3: 48–49). Freely adapting the popular fable of the belly and the bodily members found in Livy's *Historiarum . . . Libri* (2: 32) and elsewhere, Milton causes his satiric drama to embody succinctly his organicist assumptions regarding church and state and the need for their separation. By doing so, he ironically inverts the fable to suit his own needs. Customarily used to placate those who criticize policy, the fable, as Milton conceives it, serves to bolster that criticism. In order to appreciate how Milton does this, we will discuss briefly the way in which he adapts to his own polemical purposes the fable as it was commonly understood.

A glance at the version appearing in North's *Plutarch* should provide the needed perspective. The belly, charged by the mutinous bodily members of only remaining "in the midst of the body, without doing anything," defends its usefulness in this manner: "It is true, I first receive all meats that nourish man's body; but afterwards I send it again to the nourishment of other parts the same."[32] What the Renaissance gathered from the fable is discernible in Forsett's statement in his *Comparative Discourse*: "This similitude was both fitly and fortunately enforced by *Menenius Agrippa*, who being imployed in the appeasing and persuading of the seditious reuoulting commons of Rome, did . . . so sensibly shew them their errour, that surseasing their malignant enuy wherewith they were inraged against their rulers (whom they accounted as the idle belly that swallowed the labors of their hands) they discerned at the last, that their repining against, and their pining of that belly, whence was distributed unto them their bloud and nourishment, necessarily tended to their owne destruction; and were thereuppon forthwith reclaymed into their bounds of obedience" (p. 3).

The thrust of the fable is ironically the exact opposite in Milton. As Milton interprets the fable, the wen (that is, the belly become episcopal encumbrance) is shown to be not only completely useless, but destructive, despite his protestations that his "Office" is the body's "glory" and that "so oft as the soule would retire out of the head from over the steaming vapours of the lower parts to Divine Contemplation, with him (the wen) shee found the purest, and quietest retreat, as having been most remote from soile, and disturbance." The "wise and learned Philosopher" counters that argument like a true organicist by maintaining that "all the faculties of the Soule are confined of old to their severall vessels, and *ventricles*, from which they cannot part without dissolution of the whole Body" (3: 49). A self-sustaining entity, complete unto itself, the body should not be joined with or encumbered by any other organism at the risk of creating something unnatural, even monstrous. Thus Milton concludes that the wen must be severed from the head in order to restore comeliness and health to the body. As he states later in *Of Reformation*, "if we will now resolve to settle affairs either according to pure Religion, or sound policy, we must first of all begin roundly to cashier, and cut away from the publick body the noysom, and diseased tumor of Prelacie" (3: 62).

That Milton's language reflects prevailing Puritan attitudes may be seen in William Prynne's *Lord Bishops, None of the Lord Bishops* (1640), which distinguishes between "the Body it selfe of the Church" and the prelates. The second are "but *wennes*, or *swellings* grown up, and so incorporated into the Body, as overspreading it like a Leprosie, it assumes the denomination of the Body." As such, continues Prynne, they are "great *Swellings*, like the Kings Evil, which are commonly next the Head, or about the necke, in the most principall parts of the Body" (25). Our only recourse, as Alexander Leighton says, in *An appeal to the Parliament; or Sions Plea against Prelacie* (1628), is surgery: "as a knob, a wen, or any superfluous bonch of flesh, being no member doth not onely overburthen the body, but also disfigureth the feature, yea killeth the body at length except it be cut; so these Bishops be the knobs & wens and bunchie popish flesh which beareth down, deformed & deadeth the bodie of the Church, that ther is no cure . . . but cutting off" (p. 11).

Finally, the decorousness of Milton's adaptation of the fable of the belly and the bodily members to suit his own purposes is even further enhanced if we consider the following observation by E. K. Chambers: "St. Paul probably had [the fable] in mind when he wrote I Cor. 12:12–26."[33] Chambers's observation implies the existence of an intimate correspondence, possibly conceived at the very root of organicist thinking, between the body of the state, as represented by the fable, and the body of the church, as represented by the biblical source. If accurate, such an observation would go far to reinforce Milton's political application of the fable to his antiprelatical argument, an argument, as we have seen, based upon fundamental organicist relationships. Accurate or not, Chambers's observation at least underscores the Renaissance predisposition to think of the fable and the passage from 1 Corinthians in the same terms. For example, immediately after speaking about the moral import of the fable, Edward Forsett states: "The like comparison is most diuinely enlarged by a much better Orator, and in a much more important poynt of the unseparable union of the members of Christ with their head, and of the necessary communion of their distinct gifts and works amongst themselves" (*Comparative Discourse* 4–5).

In the context of Milton's organicist concerns, Forsett's statement throws a good deal of light upon the attitudes embodied in Milton's prose. It allows us to see the underlying unity of Milton's use of the body for polemical purposes: the body of the church, with all its ramifications, finds appropriate correspondence in the body of the state. Unlikely what Forsett would maintain, however, the two bodies in Milton's thought are to be brought into conjunction only to reveal their essential disparities. Complete unto themselves, they must not be joined for fear of creating a monstrosity. An unnatural joining necessitates a forcible disjoining, a disjoining enacted not for the sake of mutilating the body but for the sake of restoring it to health. For that reason, the thrust of Milton's reforming zeal is ultimately, in his terms, constructive rather than destructive. His final vision involves not the tearing down of the body but the re-forming of it. That is the impression one receives from Milton's apocalyptic vision of Truth in *Areopagitica*:

Truth indeed came once into the world with her divine Master, and was a perfect shape most glorious to look on: but when he ascended, and his Apostles after him were laid asleep, then strait arose a wicked race of deceivers, who . . . took the virgin Truth, hewd her lovely form into a thousand peeces, and scatter'd them to the four winds. From that time ever since, the sad friends of truth . . . imitating the carefull search that *Isis* made for the mangl'd body of *Osiris*, went up and down gathering up limb by limb still as they could find them. We have not yet found them all . . . nor ever shall doe, till her Masters second comming; he shall bring together every joynt and member, and shall mould them into an immortall feature of lovelines and perfection. Suffer not these licencing prohibitions to stand at every place of opportunity forbidding and disturbing them that continue seeking, that continue to do our obsequies to the torn body of our martyr'd Saint. (4: 337–38)

The import of this passage for our discussion is significant, especially as it comments upon the way Milton incorporated the organicist idea into his outlook as a reformer. For him, the Reformation itself, as J. Max Patrick suggests, implied a re-forming of the bodily members.[34] Philosophically, in his impassioned plea for the toleration of those who desire "to unite those dissever'd peeces that are yet wanting to the body of Truth" (3: 338), Milton was inclined to see the fulfilling of the Reformation as the attempt to approach bodily wholeness. This idea would seem not only to substantiate still further the argument that as a polemicist, Milton viewed the world in decidedly organicist terms, but also to indicate that when called upon, he could rise above the immediate contentions of the time and envision a body that must be called transcendent.

CHAPTER FOUR

The Kenotic Christology

A FTER William B. Hunter Jr.'s assertion that kenosis has no real place in Milton's Christology,[1] we are liable to suspect any study that presumes to approach Milton's works from a kenotic point of view. We should withhold our reservations, however, until we consider Hunter's assertion within its proper context, which involves a form of kenoticism made evident in the later disputes of the Lutheran Church. Hunter's strictures are therefore not all-inclusive, nor can they be, since one cannot categorically dismiss the concept of kenosis from a full consideration of Christ's nature. Indeed, as Vincent Taylor states, "some form of *kenosis* is essential to any worthy doctrine of the Incarnation": "if we dismiss it [kenoticism] at the door, it comes back through the window."[2]

To gain a fuller perspective of how kenosis operates in Milton's thinking, we must distinguish between the later Christologies, to which Hunter alludes, and the earlier Christologies of the Church Fathers. The validity of such a distinction is attested to by Friedrich Loofs. As his detailed discussion of kenotic doctrine makes clear, the radical views arising out of the controversies between the seventeenth-century theologians of Giessen and Tübingen and culminating in the kenoticism of the nineteenth century find no adequate support in the Church Fathers.[3] At most, patristic commentary reflects "an exegetical predisposition . . . for a theory similar to the modern *kenosis*-theory."[4] The essence of that theory is stated clearly by J. M. Creed: "The Divine Logos by His Incarnation divested Himself of His divine attributes of omniscience and omnipotence, so that in His incarnate life the Divine Person is revealed and solely revealed through a human consciousness."[5] This is quite foreign to Milton's beliefs. Like the Church Fathers, he views kenosis as the Son's preincarnate act of emptying himself of his godhead in order to take upon himself the nature of man, but also like the Church Fathers, he does not feel that kenosis implies Christ's "actual denuding of his power and divine attributes."[6] Rather, in his conception of the hypostatic union, "Milton assumes a fusion of the divine and human natures and persons into the one person of Christ at the Incarnation."[7] Milton says as much in *Christian Doctrine*: "There is then in Christ a mutual hypostatic union of two natures, that is to say, of two essences, of two substances, and, consequently, of two persons" (15: 271).[8]

We are not to assume from Milton's statement, however, that the kenotic experience is unimportant to his Christology. On the contrary, Barbara Lewalski finds kenosis to be "of central importance" to Milton.[9] If, as Hunter says, Milton "remains aloof" from the later Christologies,[10] he is very much aware of the earlier ones. Their influence upon him may at least be seen in their view of kenosis "as a divine act" voluntarily undergone by the preincarnate Son, who imposed "real limitations . . . upon Himself during the incarnate life."[11] Such an attitude undoubtedly bears upon Milton's own view of the kenotic experience. To appreciate fully the extent to which he is influenced by the earlier commentaries, however, we must examine his glosses of Philippians 2:6–11, the source of the kenotic concept. Through his glosses, we shall be able to see how the traditions that constitute kenotic theory underlie his conduct as a writer.

Milton's glosses of Philippians 2:6–11 in *Christian Doctrine* reveal a great deal about his awareness of past traditions. We might examine, for example, the way he interprets Philippians 2:7 ("But made himself of no reputation, and took upon him the form of a servant") in Book 1, chapter 5 of *Christian Doctrine*: "he [Christ] emptied himself of that form of God in which he had previously existed" (14: 343). Using "*exinanivit*" in this context (elsewhere, "*inanivit*") in order to render the Greek *heauton ekenosen*, Milton "seems to prefer a stronger expression than the rather colorless 'he made himself of no reputation' [found] in both the Geneva and the Authorized translations."[12] His language, however, is certainly in accord with the earier commentaries on the Philippians text. Indeed, the tradition in which Milton writes is well established.

Clement of Alexandria, Irenaeus, and Tertullian all make use of the concept of self-emptying denoted by the word *ekenosen*.[13] Origen likewise "understands the official doctrine to assert that the Son of God, "emptying himself (*se ipsum exinaniens*) and becoming man, was incarnate," and recalling the older tradition, Augustine states: "Thus he emptied himself, taking the form of a servant, not losing the form of God; the form of a servant was added, the form of God not subtracted."[14] These examples should suffice to show the common patristic practice of viewing Christ's sacrifice as an exinanition. But this is not the only way of viewing his sacrifice. As a further consideration of Milton's glosses of the Philippians text will indicate, the kenotic experience may be interpreted in other ways as well.

Earlier in Book 1, chapter 5 of *Christian Doctrine*, Milton interprets Philippians 2:7 (here with particular reference to "and took upon him the form of a servant") as Christ's laying aside the form of his divinity (*"posita forma ponatur"*) in order to assume the form of man (14: 274, 275). In kenotic thinking, a laying aside of one's divinity accords with the idea of self-divestiture, a "surrender . . . of the form of God ('the glories, the prerogatives of deity' . . .)," as means of investing oneself with "the likeness of man."[15] To deal fully with kenosis, we have to concern ourselves with both self-divestiture and self-investiture in relation to the idea of self-emptying. Indeed, the term self-divestiture and self-investiture are often used concurrently in theological discussions to describe the kenotic experience.[16] For the purpose of clarity, however, I shall treat each term individually.

We recall that J. M. Creed refers to self-emptying through a language of self-divestiture. He echoes a well-established tradition. Gregory of Nazianzen equates self-emptying with self-divestiture in his *Orations*: "But inasmuch as He strips Himself for us, inasmuch as He comes down (and I speak of an exinanition, as it were, a laying aside and a diminution of His glory), He becomes by this comprehensible."[17] Hilary of Poitiers likewise speaks of "the Form of God divesting Itself of that which It was,"[18] and to show how widely the idea is disseminated throughout history, E. H. Gifford cites the important modern kenoticist M. Godet, who uses the term *dépouillement* in his *Etudes Bibliques* to refer to the act of self-emptying.[19] Finally, in his commentary on Philippians, J. B. Lightfoot uses precisely the language of self-divestiture by saying that the Son "emptied" or "stripped" himself in his kenosis.[20] Milton is no exception to this tradition. In his poem *Upon the Circumcision*, he speaks poetically of Christ's having "emptied his glory, *ev'n to nakednes*" (20; my italics). Such a statement undoubtedly reveals Milton's awareness of the common practice relating self-divestiture to self-emptying. His awareness of the complementary practice relating self-investiture to self-emptying will become apparent if we examine additional theological commentaries.

Hilary of Poitiers, who has much to say about the process of self-emptying, offers a fitting point of departure. In Book 9, chapter 14 of his *De Trinitate*, he states: "When He emptied Himself [*se evacuaverit*] to become Christ the man, . . . the changing of His bodily fashion, and the assumption of another nature [*in corpore demutatio habitus et assumptio naturae*], did not put an end to the nature of His eternal divinity, for He was one and the same Christ when He changed His fashion [*demutans habitum*], and when He assumed our nature.[21] How closely Hilary accords with Milton's view of the incarnation is not my concern here. What is of concern is the fact that in Hilary a "change of fashion" (which implies divestiture as well as investiture) is used concurrently with the process of self-emptying.[22] Variations of the same approach are discernible in Origen, to whom kenosis implies a veiling of the "splendors and brilliancy of deity," and in Cyril of Alexandria, to whom kenosis implies "the acceptance of a human vesture."[23]

Such language, says Donald G. Dawe, forms part of a well-founded tradition "usually referred to as the divine occultation, *occultatio Dei*."[24] Underlying the tradition is a Platonic pattern of thought that appears as early as the Church Fathers of the second century and reaches its height in the mystical theology of the Middle Ages.[25] The medieval fusion of the Christian and Platonic frames of reference is discernible, among other places, in Peter Lombard's assertion that Christ invested himself with humanity as with a veil.[26] According to Charles Gore, "among the authorities for this position, St. Augustine is quoted, commenting on the Latin version of Philippians 2:7 *habitu inventu est ut homo*."[27] That approach does not terminate with the Middle Ages, however; it is likewise discernible in both Renaissance and Reformation theology.

In his *Institutes of the Christian Religion*, for example, John Calvin speaks numerous times of Christ's being "clothed with our flesh" and of Christ's "allow[ing] his divinity to be hidden" by a "veil of flesh."[28] (Compare Hebrews 10:19–20: "Having therefore, brethren, boldness to enter into the holiest by the blood of Jesus, By a new and living way, which he hath consecrated for us, through the veil, that is to say, his flesh.") At another point, Calvin resorts metaphorically to the same idea to discourse upon the meaning of "form" in Philippians 2:6–11: "*The form of God*," he says, "here signifies majesty. For just as a man is known from beholding his form, so the majesty, which shines in God, is the figure of Himself. Or if you would prefer an apter simile, the form of a king is the apparel and splendour which indicates the king, as sceptre, diadem, cloak, apparitors, tribunal, and the other ensigns of royalty; the form of a consul is a toga bordered with purple, an ivory chair, lictors, with rods and axes."[29]

Such a statement reveals Calvin's awareness of an entire tradition expressing the kenotic experience through the concept of attire. Form manifests itself metaphorically as the apparel that invests the body. To change one's form is to disrobe oneself of one's apparel; to assume a new form is to invest oneself with new apparel. The metaphor becomes a very accessible and convenient way of describing an experience that ultimately defies metaphor. Some of us, however, might be inclined to feel that the metaphor is almost too accessible, that it incurs the danger of leading us to underestimate the gravity of the kenotic experience. The profound transformation that Christ undergoes in his kenosis signifies, after all, more than a mere change of clothing. To think otherwise is to slight the immense repercussions of Christ's humiliation. Etymologically, the idea of self-divestiture and self-investiture is foreign to the true meaning of kenosis. As Ralph P. Martin makes clear, the verb *kenoun* means nothing more than "to empty," and "in its literal sense it is used . . . of Rebekah's emptying the water from her pitcher into the trough (Gen. 24:20; Septuagint: the verb is *exekenosen*)."[30]

Calvin is undoubtedly aware of the possible dangers of his metaphor; yet we must also realize that he is using form to imply not that which is superficial and changeable, but that which depends for its expression upon the very existence of a thing. Form does not merely describe: it signifies, it manifests. According to J. B. Lightfoot, this is precisely the philosophical and doctrinal sense in which Paul uses form in Philippians 2:6 and 7 ("form of God" and "form of a servant").[31] As opposed to the "fashion" of Philippians 2:8 ("fashion as a man," implying external semblance), "form" implies "essence" or "nature."[32] E. H. Gifford tells us that this basically Aristotelian interpretation of form is a philosophical commonplace discernible in such writers as Hooker and Bacon.[33]

As we have seen, the idea likewise holds true for Milton, in whose *Art of Logic* we find the association of form with essence and the statement that "form is the cause through which a thing is what it is" (11: 59, 61). That definition has a direct bearing upon Milton's practices as a writer, for it allows him to depict spiritual matters in human terms. This approach, central to Milton's handling of the divine, is commonly referred to as the concept of accommodation. Its relevance to the present discussion is discernible, among other places, in *Christian Doctrine*. There Milton views God's attributing to himself human characteristics in the Bible as an accommodating of the divine to the human. "Let us be convinced," he says in *Christian Doctrine*, "that those have acquired the truest apprehension of the nature of God who submit their understanding to his word; *considering that he has accommodated his word to their understandings, and has shown what he wishes their notion of Deity should be*" (14: 35, 37; my italics). That statement becomes especially significant to a consideration of the incarnation, since the manifestation of the divine form in the Bible is complemented by that manifestation as an actual event in history. By God's own example in the Bible and in the incarnation, man may enact through metaphor what God enacts through miracle. He may "delineate" "what surmounts the reach / Of human sense . . . / By lik'ning spiritual to corporal forms / As may express them best" (*P.L.* V.571–74).

As Milton's metaphorical practices make clear, form is most concretely represented through a language of attire. Thus, in *Il Penseroso*, Milton "hail[s] divinest Melancholy, / Whose Saintly visage is too bright / To hit the sense of human sight; / And therfore to our weaker view, / O'er laid with black staid Wisdoms hue" (12–16). The importance of Milton's apostrophe resides in his implicit attitude concerning the relationship between form and attire. By "overlaying" Melancholy with "black," Milton is not merely "dressing" the divine figure. Rather, he resorts to attire as the means by which we experience the otherwise unbearable aspect of the divine. The nature of divinity is thereby revealed to us through the apparel that invests it. Apparel expresses Milton's recognition of the power and sanctity of the manifested form. By representing the spiritual in human terms, it allows us to transcend the physical and experience the nonphysical. Of such great significance is this concept to Milton's treatment of kenosis, in both the prose and the poetry, that it illuminates an essential feature of his metaphorical conduct. As a preliminary examination of the prose will indicate, the precise nature of that conduct makes itself felt in Milton's polemical attitudes.

Milton's argument against the prelates reveals how kenosis may be brought to bear upon polemic. In the antiprelatical tracts he invokes the kenotic experience in order to point up the irreverence of the prelates toward Christ. The nature of their irreverence is of particular interest to our discussion, for it recalls what has been said about the relationship between form and apparel. Specifically, Milton bases his argument upon the assumption that the prelates violate the form of Christ through their improper concern for apparel. Those very dangers we have seen lurking in a metaphor that views Christ's kenosis as a change of clothing, Milton finds actualized in the prelates.

How the prelates disregard God's purpose in manifesting himself to us in human form is indicated, for instance, in *The Reason of Church-Government*. There Milton admonishes the prelates: ". . . if to doe the work of the Gospel Christ our Lord took upon him the form of a servant, how can his servant in this ministry take upon him the form of a Lord? . . . The form of a servant was a mean, laborious and vulgar life aptest to teach; which form Christ thought fittest . . . choosing the meaner things of this worid. . . . Now whether the pompous garb . . . of Prelaty be those meaner things of the world . . . be it the verdit of common sense" (3: 244). Perverting the proper relationship between form and apparel, the prelates reject "the meaner things of this world" by attiring themselves in "pompous garb." In so doing, they take upon themselves "the form of a Lord" rather than following the example of Christ, who voluntarily took upon himself "the form of a servant." The results are disastrous. Exalting themselves through an apparel that does not befit their office, they not only parody Christ's exaltation (Phil. 2:9–11), but metaphorically effect an enforced incarnation. As we recall from our discussion of the organicist metaphor that initiates *Of Reformation*, this is precisely the thrust of Milton's argument in the first antiprelatical tract (3: 1–3). From the kenotic point of view expressed in that complex metaphor of prelatical bedecking, Milton implies that when the world of externals (of outward fashion, false ceremony, and custom) becomes an end in itself, what results is a perversion of Christ's original self-humiliation. Almost as if in mockery of the first incarnation, "the very shape of *God*" is made manifest again, to be worshipped for its own sake rather than for what it represents.

What is important about such an idea is that Milton invokes the whole tradition of divestiture and investiture in order to effect his metaphor. Reversing the motif of Christ's kenosis (represented by the *in corpore demutatio habitus* that we saw in Hilary, Origen, Cyril of Alexandria, and others), Milton shows how the prelates' concern with investiture (or bedecking) debases rather than exalts. With the prelates' misdirected concern, the entire purpose of the kenotic experience becomes self-defeating. As a result of the prelates' perverted emphasis upon externals, the inward or spiritual moves to the outward or material, there to "harden into a crust of Formalitie" (3: 3). The clothed body becomes a symbol of the inability to go beyond the corporeal in order to attain the spiritual, of the inability to recognize, that is, the proper relationship between form and apparel. The importance of that recognition to Milton's handling of kenosis in the poetry cannot be over-estimated. There the pattern of divestiture and investiture underlying Milton's respect for the manifested form takes on renewed significance.

Because of its obvious concern with the incarnation, the *Nativity* ode offers a fitting point of departure. The traditions that constitute the kenotic idea are certainly apparent in the depiction of the humiliation of Christ, who "la[ys] aside" "that glorious Form, that Light unsufferable, / And that far-beaming blaze of Majesty" (8–12) in order to take upon himself the form of a servant. (Compare Christ's "Lay-[ing] down the rudiments / Of his great warfare" in *Paradise Regain'd* [I.157–58].) We need not look far for the poetic significance of Christ's act. His sacrificial humiliation finds its counterpart, for example, in the posture assumed by the speaker of the *Nativity* ode. In order to anticipate the coming of the "Star-led Wisards," the speaker desires to "lay" his "humble ode" "lowly at [Christ's] blessed feet" (22–25; compare Phil. 2:10). That is, through both the humility of his posture and the humble nature of his gift, he desires metaphorically to take upon himself the form of a servant. His desire, in turn, reveals his gratitude for Christ's corresponding act.

But this is not all that is implied by Christ's humiliation. As we recall from our discussion of *Christian Doctrine*, a laying aside of one's form is comparable to self-divestiture. Indeed, we have seen that Gregory of Nazianzen, Hilary of Poitiers, and others support Milton's own view that Christ's kenosis involves an emptying "ev'n to nakedness" (*Upon the Circumcision*, 20). Furthermore, since we have also seen that in kenotic thinking self-divestiture is followed by self-investiture, we might likewise expect to see such a concept expressed in the *Nativity* ode. Appropriately, in "The Hymn," we find that the "Heav'n-born child" "lies" "all meanly wrapt in the rude manger" (30–31). The meanness in which Christ is "wrapt" refers not only to his clothing (see line 27 and Luke 2:7) but metaphorically to his incarnate state (compare 1 Pet. 5:5; Rev. 19:23). The idea is quite common. In a little poem called *Christ Took Our Nature*, Robert Herrick says that Christ "dressed him with our human trim," / Because our flesh stood most in need of him."[34]

Milton provides parallel examples, as in his address to Anne in the *Fair Infant* elegy: "wert thou of the golden-winged hoast, / Who . . . clad thy self in human weed [?]" (57–58). (Anne, of course, assumes the role of a sacrificial figure "let down in clowdie throne to do the world some good" [56].) Even more compelling, however, is the figure of the Attendant Spirit, who states in *A Mask*: "But first I must put off / These my sky robes spun out of *Iris* woof / And take the weeds and likeness of a swain / That to the service of this house belongs" (82–85). The Attendant Spirit's willingness to "put off" his immortal garments in order to assume the form of a servant as Thyrsis is similar to the Son's willingness in *Paradise Lost* to "put off" his "glorie" (III.239–40) in order to assume the form of a servant as man. (Both acts of humility contrast implicitly with the opposite act that characterizes man's fall in *Paradise Lost*: "putting off / Human to put on Gods" [IX.713–14]; compare Col. 3:9–10: "ye have put off the old man with his deeds; and have put on the new man, which is renewed in knowledge after the image of him that created him.")

That the Attendant Spirit deigns to appear in the "likeness of a swain," furthermore, gives added impetus to Milton's handling of the Christian perspective, for in the *Nativity* ode, Christ likewise appears as the Good Shepherd (see John 10; 1 Pet. 2:25, 5:4) or the "mighty *Pan* / . . . kindly come to live with [us] below" (89–90). The pun on "kindly" is certainly appropriate: it suggests not only Christ's "kindness" to man but his "kinship" (in the sense of being human as well as divine) with man. Milton thereby fuses the pastoral conception with the idea of the incarnation.

Significantly, in contrast to the pastoral habits of Christ, on the one hand, and the Attendant Spirit, on the other, we find Satan in *Paradise Regain'd* attired "in Rural weeds" (I.314) and Comus in *A Mask* attired as a shepherd (271) or "harmless Villager" (166). Their disguises, in turn, parody the tradition that sees Christ's assumption of the human form as a disguising of the godhead. Indeed, C. A. Patrides mentions the very interesting (if grotesque) view of such writers as Gregory of Nyssa, in whose *Oratorio chatechetica* we find the idea that Christ, through, "a kind of deceit and trickery," disguised himself as man, so that he could catch Satan unawares.[35] Although Milton does not expressly agree with that concept, he does reflect what we have seen to be the patristic interpretation of Christ's kenosis as an *occultatio Dei*. Thus, in *The Passion*, he celebrates Christ's assuming man's form in these terms: "O what a Mask was there, what a disguise!" (19). For our purposes, the meaning of such a statement becomes evident within the context of accommodation. Divinity takes human form (metaphorically disguises itself) in order to *reveal* itself to human understanding. Unlike Christ (and, implicitly, the Attendant Spirit), on the other hand, Satan and Comus disguise themselves in order to deceive, but they become "undisguised" through the scrutiny of Christ (*P.R.* I.348, 355, 356; compare Heb. 4:13, Nah. 3:5), and the Attendant Spirit (*A Mask*, 570–71), respectively. (What happens, incidentally, when a deceitful disguise is uncovered is discernible in *Samson Agonistes*. Samson "undisguises" Dalila by metaphorically divesting her of her clothing; thus, although she approaches him "bedeckt, ornate, and gay" [714], she leaves him, as Samson says, "bare in [her] guilt" and "foul" to look upon [902].)

What holds true for Milton's prose, then, likewise holds true for his poetry: the negative or positive overtones of investiture depend upon the essential relationship between form and attire. Obviously that relationship comments significantly upon moral stature. When Milton is describing a virtuous character, for instance, form and attire correspond gloriously. We might consider Milton's description of his "late espoused saint," who "came vested all in white, pure as her mind" (Sonnet 23,9); of the chaste person "clad in compleat steel" (*A Mask*, 421; Compare Ephes. 6:14); or of Michael "invest[ed]" with "Majestie," "Not in his shape Celestial, but as Man / Clad to meet Man" (*P.L.* XI.232–33; 239–40).

When, on the other hand, Milton is describing a sinful character, form and attire comment upon each other ironically. Attire attempts to hide or "disguise" form, with the result that investiture debases rather than glorifies. In the prose, the prelates become the prime examples of such an occurrence. In the poetry, the fallen angels fulfill the description: once "cloth'd with transcendent brightness" (*P.L.* I.86), they are destined to become "disguis'd in brutish forms" (*P.L.* I.481). The idea of investiture implied here gives rise, of course, to the whole matter of the bestial shapes (vulture, wolf, cormorant, lion, tiger, toad, serpent) that characterize Satan's own degradation in *Paradise Lost*. Ironically, his greatest moment of triumph becomes his greatest moment of disgrace: along with his cohorts, he is "punish't in the shape he sin'd" (X.516) by having to reassume what had been his previous disguise as serpent.

The theological bearing of such a disguise has already been conclusively demonstrated by Mother Mary Christopher Pecheux.[36] According to Mother Mary Christopher, Satan's self-imbruting as a means of effecting man's damnation (IX.163–67) contrasts implicitly with the Son's willingness to incarnate himself in human form as a means of effecting man's salvation (III.238–40). Despite Bentley's objections to the idea of associating Satan's activities with the word "incarnate" (IX.166),[37] Milton deliberately uses that term in order to effect one of the many contrasts that unify his poem. We must conclude, therefore, that Milton has no qualms about transforming theological doctrine into poetic fact, even if it means allowing us to view divine acts within a debased context. This particular context John T. Shawcross sees as an example of reverse kenosis.[38]

That Milton would agree with such an observation is clear from statements he makes elsewhere. In Prolusion VII, for example, he resorts to kenotic doctrine to admonish the soul that would deliberately embody itself in a lower form. His statement brings to mind Satan's complaint about the need to "incarnate and imbrute" his "essence" (*P.L.* IX.166). Thus Milton admonishes: "let it lay aside [*exuat*] the human; let it be given the Circean cup; stooping let it migrate to the beasts [*ad bestias prona emigret*]" (12: 280, 281). The language combines a number of associations that have an implicit bearing upon kenoticism. Humiliation is indicated not only in the laying aside of one form and the assumption of another but also in the act of stooping in order to enter a lower form. (The act of stooping, for example, is central to the description of Christ's incarnation in *The Passion*: "stooping his regal head," Christ "entered" the "poor fleshly Tabernacle" of man's body [15–17].)[39]

But of equal importance is the allusion to the "Circean cup," in which Milton fuses the idea of kenotic embodiments with that of Circean transformations. The precise nature of such transformations is discernible from the philosophy expressed in *A Mask*. We are told that, as a result of intemperance and fleshly indulgences, "the soul grows clotted by contagion, / Imbodies, and imbrutes, till she quite loose / The divine property of her first being" (467–69). Man thereby loses his "upright shape" (52) and godlike countenance (69) and is transformed "into som brutish form" (70) without once perceiving his "foul disfigurement" (74).

That is precisely what happens to Adam and Eve in *Paradise Lost* as a result of their fall: "corrupted to forsake / God thir Creator," they are "transform[ed] / . . . to the Image of a Brute" (I.368–71; compare Rom. 1:22–23: "Professing themselves to be wise, they became fools, And changed the glory of the uncorruptible God into an image made like corruptible man, and to birds, and four footed beasts, and creeping things.") The physical transformation of fallen man is made evident in the "Lazar-house," where Adam witnesses those who "disfigure" the image of God in themselves (XI.478–525). Although Adam and Eve are not themselves physically disfigured, they experience a symbolic transformation. That idea is implicit, for example, in Adam's statement that Eve is "defac't" (IX.901; compare XI.522) as a result of her transgression. The same, of course, may be said of Adam when he falls.

The nature of their defacement is made evident in the shame they experience in response to their own nakedness: "innocence, that as a veil / Had shadow'd them from knowing ill was gon," and they are "naked left / To guiltie shame" (IX.1054–58). With the loss of their innocence, they gain a knowledge of evil, a knowledge that is indicated in the repulsion they feel toward their bodies. Previously a sign of their glory, their nakedness now becomes a sign of their debasement. Thus, in response to their "middle parts," they complain that "Shame" sits in opposition to them and reproaches them as "unclean"

(IX.1097–98). Their complaint recalls the earlier one of Sin: in response to the serpentine transformation of her "middle parts," she complains that Death sits in opposition to her as a constant reminder of her bestiality (II.803–04). The shame Adam and Eve experience as a result of their nakedness, then, places them within the context of bestial disfigurements.[40]

A parallel situation is discernible in the figure of Nature in the *Nativity* ode. Nature's "foul deformities" (44) are intimately involved in the shame that she feels toward her nakedness (40). As Adam and Eve are repelled by their nakedness when they fall, Nature is ashamed of her own corruption. This idea has a particularly kenotic bearing in the *Nativity* ode, for Christ's willingness to take upon himself the uncleanness and corruption of man finds its counterpart in Nature's activities. We are told that "Nature in aw to [Christ] / Had doff't her gawdy trim / With her great Master so to sympathize" (32–34). Recalling that aspect of Christ's kenosis seen as a self-divestiture, we are not hard put to understand the significance of Nature's doffing her "gawdy trim." As Albert S. Cook correctly observes, Nature's act parallels Christ's.[41] While Christ disrobes himself of the insignia of his dignity, Nature appropriately disrobes herself of the outward signs of her corruption. Christ undergoes kenosis as a means of sacrificing himself for the world's sins; in sympathy for Christ's act, Nature undergoes a metaphorical kenosis as a means of preparing herself for Christ's sacrifice.

Milton's use of the expression "to sympathize" indicates as much. Nature does not merely "commiserate with"; her sympathy is much stronger: it actually causes her to resemble in disposition or to be in harmony with (see *OED*, "Sympathize," 2.b.). That is, Nature's sympathizing with Christ's humiliation involves a corresponding experience on Nature's part. (Compare the language Milton uses to describe another humiliation, one we have already associated with the kenotic experience. The "horrid sympathy" Satan's cohorts feel for their master's serpentine transformation in *Paradise Lost* compels them ironically to undergo a similar transformation: "for what they saw, / They felt themselves now changing" [X.540–41].)

With the knowledge of her own "foul deformities," however, Nature desires "to hide her guilty front with innocent Snow, / And on her naked shame / Pollute with sinfull blame, / The Saintly Vail of Maiden white to throw" (39–42). Surprisingly enough, William Riley Parker finds this passage "inartistic . . . because of the idea's utter irrelevance."[42] It seems to me, however, that the passage is entirely relevant to Milton's celebration of the incarnation. We have already seen how Nature's self-divestiture acts as a counterpart to Christ's. Appropriately, then, her desire for investiture in this passage completes the pattern of divestiture and investiture implicit in Christ's kenosis. Indeed, with Nature's emphasis upon the need to "hide" her guilt behind a veil of innocence, we should be reminded of the tradition that sees Christ's kenosis as a divine occultation. The effect of that occultation, of course, will be to relieve Nature of the need to hide her guilt in the first place. Purified of corruption, Nature will be fulfilled in her desire to exchange her "gawdy" vestments for "the Saintly Vail of Maiden white." (Compare Zech. 3.3–4: "Now Joshua was clothed with filthy garments, and stood before the angel. And he answered and spake unto those that stood before him, saying, Take away the filthy garments from him. And unto him he said, Behold, I have caused thine iniquity to pass from thee, and I will clothe thee with change of raiment.")

The full implications of such an idea become dramatically apparent in *Paradise Lost.* There the desire to "hide" one's "guilty front" culminates in the plight of Adam and Eve, who attempt to "cover round / Those middle parts" (XI.1096–97). Once in glorious nakedness spared the task of assuming the "troublesom disguises" that plague fallen man (IV.739–40), Adam and Eve now must try desperately "to hide / The Parts of each from other" (IX.1092–93). (Indeed, in his despair, Adam calls upon the very pines and cedars that surround him to "cover" and "hide" him "with innumerable boughs" [IX.1088–90].) But the more the fallen pair cover, the more they uncover (IX.1058–59; 1113–14). Milton makes clear in his account of the Son's coming to clothe their nakedness that only through the Son can their covering be effective.

With his awareness of the tradition that sees Christ's kenosis as a self-investiture, Milton appropriately uses the language of Philippians 2:7 to describe the Son's act. Thus, the Son, "pittying how they stood / Before him naked to the air . . . / . . . disdain'd not to begin / Thenceforth *the form of servant to assume,* / As when he wash'd his servants feet, he clad" their outward nakedness with the "Skins of Beasts" and their "inward nakedness, much more / Opprobrious, with his Robe of righteousness, / Arraying cover'd from his Fathers sight" (X.211–23; my italics). As the passage indicates, the assumption of the servant's form corresponds to the act of investiture, which has not only physical but spiritual repercussions. Thus the Son attends to Adam and Eve's spiritual, as well as to their physical, nakedness. (Compare Rev. 3:18: "I counsel thee to buy of me . . . white raiment, that thou mayest be clothed, and that the shame of thy nakedness do not appear.")

Furthermore, his act is given added significance through the allusion that associates his becoming a servant with his washing of his servant's feet (John 13:4–16).[43] Although Simon Peter is not then aware of it, the bathing of his feet symbolizes the purification that man will experience through Christ (compare Tit. 3:5–6; Rev. 1:5). The allusion is important, then, because it emphasizes washing as that which represents a future spiritual cleansing (compare *P.L.* XII.442–44). "What I do thou knowest not now," Christ says to Simon Peter, "but thou shalt know hereafter" (John 13:7). Similarly, Adam and Eve are not immediately aware of the relationship between the Son's assumption of the servant's form and his clothing of them. But the allusion clarifies the relationship for us: the Son's clothing of man prefigures what will be the effect of his future self-humiliation. He will voluntarily take upon himself the corruption of man so that man may be purified, and given the possibility of regeneration. "Clothed with humility" (1 Pet. 5:5), he will be able to "change [his] vile body, that it may be fashioned like unto [Christ's] glorious body" (Phil. 3:21).

That idea is implicit in the kind of clothing the Son provides for Adam and Eve. The "Skins" in which they are "clad" are both those of "Beasts" that have been "slain" and of "Beasts," like the "Snake," that have had their "youthful Coat[s] repaid" (X.216–18). If the skins of slain beasts say something about the necessity of experiencing death, the skins of beasts whose coats are "repaid" say something about the possibility of experiencing rebirth. (Compare the reference in *Areopagitica* to "cast[ing] off the old and wrincl'd skin of corruption" and "wax[ing] young again" [IV.344].) But man's regeneration is not the only consequence of Christ's kenosis, for if Christ reveals through his role as servant how man is to humble himself, he also reveals through his exaltation how man is to be regenerated.

Made evident in Philippians 2:9–11, the idea of Christ's exaltation is basic to the kenotic concept. Through the exaltation of Christ, we are allowed to witness the glorious culmination of his humiliation. Appropriately, then, the Son's prefigurative assumption of the form of a servant in *Paradise Lost* is followed by his ascent to God in order to "reassum[e]" his "glory as of old" (X.225–26). We are made to think of God's earlier promise that the Son's "Humiliation shall exalt" both him and his "Manhood also to this Throne," where he "shalt . . . sit incarnate" and "shalt Reign / Both God and Man" (III.313–16; compare XII.456–58).[44] What God promises in Book III is thereby prefiguratively fulfilled in Book X through Milton's handling of kenotic doctrine. The Son's dressing of Adam and Eve and subsequent ascent to God, therefore, expresses in small the hymn of praise implicit in Philippians 2:6–11. Beginning with Christ's humiliation and ending with his exaltation, that hymn becomes integral to the overriding sense of celebration discernible in *Paradise Lost*. (I refer, of course, to the poem's essentially positive outlook, based upon God's willingness to save man through the Son as Messiah.)

To develop adequately the kenotic repercussions of that idea is impossible here. The subject invites another full-length study. If the present study may claim to have provided the basis for such an investigation, however, its purpose has been more than fulfilled. If not, it has at least attempted to reveal Milton's sensitivity to the traditions that constitute kenotic theory and his willingness to accommodate those traditions to his own particular needs. That is, it has attempted to demonstrate the importance of seeing how the matter of Christ's kenosis forms an integral part of Milton's conduct as a writer.

CHAPTER FIVE

The Poetics of Pastoral

JAMES Holly Hanford's seminal essay "The Pastoral Elegy and Milton's *Lycidas*" first drew attention to the immense range of the poem's allusiveness and its unprecedented ability to reshape and veritably transform earlier traditions of pastoral into a new and vital construct.[1] In no other work by Milton does this "transformative" aspect function more compellingly and dramatically than it does in *Lycidas*. As a profoundly self-conscious and indeed self-reflexive document, Milton's poem establishes an ongoing dialogue with its forebears, drawing upon their conventions, their *topoi*, in order to refashion them and finally to re-create them in its own image. An encounter with *Lycidas* is an encounter with a "new song," one that is *sui generis*. It is this quality of the *sui generis* that distinguishes Milton's pastoral elegy on Edward King.

The extent to which such is the case is discernible from at least two interrelated perspectives, both of which underscore the nature of form and convention in Milton's poem. The first perspective has to do with the way in which patterns of phrasal formulation and verbal repetition disclose hidden meanings. The second has to do with the way in which complex networks of allusion redefine generic expectations. The first perspective addresses the textural dimensions of the poem, the second the formal dimensions. Both dimensions are already at work in the opening of *Lycidas*:

> Yet once more, O ye Laurels, and once more
> Ye Myrtles brown, with Ivy never sere,
> I com to pluck your berries harsh and crude,
> And with forc't fingers rude
> Shatter your leaves before the mellowing year. (1–5)

As what is in effect an announcement of subject, this opening gives rise to the two dimensions that will represent the focus of the discussion that follows. The first dimension I shall call revelatory, the second amatory. The first is signaled by the phrase "Yet once more," the second by the reference to the plants (in particular the "Myrtles brown") whose foliage the speaker has come yet once more to pluck and finally to shatter. It is to the revelatory and amatory dimensions of *Lycidas*, as embodied in its opening declaration of poetic intent, that the discussion will here attend. Focusing upon these dimensions, the discussion will attempt to suggest the way in which Milton's pastoral elegy is a profoundly self-conscious and self-reflexive document, one that not only establishes an ongoing dialogue with its forebears but refashions and re-creates the *topoi* of earlier traditions into a form that is *sui generis*.

If the ongoing *Variorum Commentary on the Poems of John Milton*[2] is any indication of the status of Milton criticism at the present time, its gloss of the first line of *Lycidas* should be of some help in coming to terms with the phrase "Yet once more." In accord with Todd's early-nineteenth-century variorum,[3] the editors of the new *Variorum*[4] refer to Thomas Warton's singling out of the phrase "Yet once again my muse," which opens the elegy on the Countess of Pembroke in *Tottel's Miscellany*.[5] As the *Variorum* editors note, the reference "drew a protest from Coleridge . . . for citing a phrase any poet might think of."[6] "Why, in Heaven's name!," exclaims Coleridge, "might not 'once more' have as well occurred to Milton as to Sydney?"[7] Leaving aside the accuracy of Coleridge's ascription of the Pembroke elegy to Sidney, we can question the validity of his response to Warton. Warton invokes the opening of the Pembroke elegy not as a source but as a convention in the form of a "phrase," or more accurately a "formulary," used by other poets as well.[8] The *Variorum* editors suggest that Milton's use of the phrase in this manner causes it to become "a formula of identification" like that with which Renaissance poets were wont to allude to their earlier productions after the Vergilian fashion ("Lo I, the man whose muse whilom did mask," etc.).[9] In *Lycidas*, the "formula of identification," as the editors indicate, refers to Milton's "earlier memorial poems," such as the Fair Infant elegy and the *Epitaph on the Marchioness of Winchester*.[10] But as a "formulary," the phrase "Yet once more" certainly has wider application. The *Variorum* editors suggest this fact through a reference to its earlier appearance in Sannazaro's *Eclogue XI*, which employs the refrain "Once more, Muses, begin your lament."[11] Its appearance in Sannazaro, as we shall see, is no surprise considering that in one form or another, its occurrence in the tradition of the pastoral elegy causes it to assume something of the status of a *topos*.

Thus, as early as Theocritus' first *Idyll*, the refrain "Begin, dear Muses, begin the pastoral song" opens *The Song of Thyrsis* and, in modulated form, closes it: "End, Muses, come end the pastoral song."[12] The *Lament for Bion*, attributed to Moschus, employs the refrain "Begin, Sicilian Muses, begin the dirge," throughout. According to Watson Kirkconnell, Moschus's *Lament for Bion* was first printed in 1495 in the Aldine edition of Theocritus, and its impact on Sannazaro led to much imitation in *Eclogue XI*, cited above. "One such feature is the cyclic refrain of lamentation."[13] It can be found thereafter in such pastoral elegies as Alamanni's *Eclogue I* ("Begin, you Muses, the mournful song" and "Conclude now, you Muses, the mournful song") and Marot's *Lamentation for Madame Louise of Savoy* ("Sing, my verses, sing bitter grief," "Sing, my verses, sing grief once more," "Cease, my verses, cease here your lamentation," etc.).[14] In this context, we think of Milton's own modulation of the *topos* in *Lycidas*: "Begin then, Sisters of the sacred well" (15) and "Weep no more, wofull shepherds weep no more" (165). As a variation of the latter formulary ("Weep no more"), we recall the *Epitaphium Damonis*: "neither do tears for you befit, nor shall I shed them more. / Away, away my tears" (202–03). A call either to begin or to cease weeping through the medium of the pastoral elegy as "melodious tear" is little more than a variation of a *topos* that goes back to Bion's *Lament for Adonis* ("I weep for Adonis; lovely Adonis is dead") and reappears in pastoral elegies like Alamanni's *Eclogue II* ("Weep now for evermore, you Tuscan sisters"), Ronsard's *Adonis* ("Alas, poor Adonis, all the Loves weep for thee"), and Spenser's *November Eclogue* ("Let streaming tears be poured out in store: / O carefull verse," which becomes "Cease now, my Muse, now cease thy sorrowes: / O joyfull verse").[15] Finally, everyone remembers Shelley's *Adonais*, which begins "I weep for Adonais—he is dead!" and concludes with such verses as "Nor let us weep" and "Mourn not for Adonais."[16] With their variations, these and the foregoing formularies constitute the structural foundation of the epicedium as it moves from lamentation to consolation.[17] As such, they are the stock in trade of the pastoral elegist. By opening his elegy with "yet once more," Milton is invoking through one formulary the multitude of formularies that had been employed for ages, dating back to Theocritus. Through the formulary "Yet once more" (and its variations "Begin then, Sisters of the sacred well" and "Weep no more, wofull shepherds weep no more"), Milton in effect is invoking the entire pastoral elegiac tradition. This is hardly news, but it does bear reiteration, particularly as it heightens our awareness of the multifaceted nature of the opening of *Lycidas*. With its formulaic quality, however, that opening assumes ever further meaning from the biblical point of view.

That the phrase "Yet once more" alludes to Hebrews 12:26–29 has already been established by a number of scholars, including David S. Berkeley and Joseph A. Wittreich, Jr.[18] In fact, this biblical passage represents a veritable discourse on "Yet once more." Distinguishing between God's voice as it once thundered from earth at the giving of the Laws from Sinai and as it will ultimately thunder from Heaven at the Last Judgment, the author of Hebrews admonishes us that God "hath promised, saying, Yet once mose I shake not the earth only, but also heaven. And this *word*, Yet once more, signifieth the removing of those things that are shaken, as of things that are made, that those things which cannot be shaken may remain. Wherefore we receiving a kingdom which cannot be moved, let us have grace, whereby we may serve God acceptably with reverence and godly fear: for our God *is* a consuming fire" (Heb. 12:26–29). As Berkeley first pointed out, the Hebrews passage itself alludes to Haggai 2:6–7: "For thus saith the Lord of hosts; Yet once, it *is* a little while and I will shake the heavens, and the earth, and the sea, and the dry *land*; and I will shake all nations, and the desire of all nations shall come; and I will fill this house with glory, saith the Lord of hosts." Both passages address themselves to the same idea: that which is ephemeral will pass away in the wake of that which will endure. In Haggai, what will pass away is the belief in and commitment to the old Temple as it is superseded by the new, which in turn will possess a glory far surpassing the old. In Hebrews, what will pass away is the belief in and commitment to the old dispensation as it is superseded by the new, which in turn will provide a means of ultimate salvation. What the author of Hebrews does, then, is reinterpret and recast Old Testament prophecy to accord with New Testament ideology. In his analysis of the allusions, Berkeley feels that the Old Testament context has a greater bearing on *Lycidas*. He argues that in the use of "Yet once more," Milton, like those who go about to reconstruct the Temple, suggests his trepidation at performing a task that is beyond him and for which he is too immature, when in fact he is able to produce a construct far surpassing anything of its kind. Wittreich, on the other hand, emphasizes the importance of the New Testament context as it prefigures the apocalyptic point of view established by St. John the Divine in the Book of Revelation. With Wittreich, I incline toward the New Testament perspective and all that it implies.

In the framework of *Lycidas*, the counterpart of "Yet once more" is to be seen, of course, initially in the pronouncement "smite no more" (131) and ultimately in the consolation "Weep no moe"(165). Like "Yet once more," "Weep no more" is indebted not only to classical and Renaissance pastoral elegy but also to specific passages of Scripture, such as Isaiah 30:18–19 and 65:17–19, on the one hand, and Revelation 7:16–17 and 21:1–5, on the other. Through those passages, "Weep no more" becomes a formulary in its own right, one that signifies the remission of wrath and the promise of joy.[19] With its two counterbalancing formulas ("once more"–"no more"), *Lycidas* opens with one scriptural declaration and culminates in another, the first anticipating the second, the second recalling and reformulating the first. There is nothing new in this juxtaposition: *Lycidas* accords structurally with a multitude of classical and Renaissance pastoral elegies that employ the same architectonic device. What is interesting, however, is the extent to which that device functions in *Lycidas* to bring into play an entire complex of nuances embodied in the formulaic language of Scripture, and particularly in the language that characterizes the prophetic books. It is this aspect of the formulaic diction of *Lycidas* that I shall now explore: the unique significance of "once more" and "no more" as scriptural formulas.

A word first about formulas. Although recent practitioners of "formula criticism" would have us believe otherwise, the concept of the scriptural formula is not new.[20] Indeed, it flourished in Milton's own time in the many scriptural thesauri that his age produced. Anticipating modern dictionaries such as the Botterweck and Ringgren *Theologisches Wörterbuch zum Alten Testament* and the Kittel *Theologisches Wörterbuch zum Neuen Testament*,[21] Renaissance thesauri distinguish what might be called "key" words and phrases that occur with formulaic consistency throughout both the Old Testament and the New. As might be expected, two such key phrases for the Renaissance (as well as for the twentieth century) are "once more" and "no more." According to Thomas Wilson, for example, both phrases fall under the heading of what his *Christian Dictionary* calls "*the chiefe Words dispersed generally through Holy Scripture of the Old and New Testament, tending to increase Christian knowledge.*"[22] Other Renaissance compendia follow suit. Those that deal with the phrases in their original Semitic and Greek contexts are particularly careful to indicate precisely what theological ideas accrue to them as they are repeatedly used throughout Scriptures. So the seventeenth-century exegetes Salomon Glass and Jacques Gousset in their respective works (*Philologia sacra* and *Commentarii Linguae Ebraicae*) provide extensive commentaries on such key phrases as "*a'od achat m'at he*" ("Yet once it is a little while") and "*eti hapax*" ("Yet once") that underlie the "once more" formula, on the one hand, and "*lo . . . a'od*" ("not . . . any more) and "*ou me . . . eti*" ("not at all . . . [any] longer") that underlie the "no more" formula, on the other.[23] Although we shall discuss these formulas in more detail later, suffice it to say that during Milton's time, they formed the basis of a theological perspective as sensitive to the formulaic significance of key terms as any that the twentieth century has produced.

For our purposes, twentieth-century formula criticism is useful as it elaborates upon the significance of formulaic repetition, particularly in the Old Testament. Rooted in what the formula critics see as the oral formulaic character of specific texts, this kind of repetition gives rise to what they call formulaic systems, defined "as a group of phrases having the same syntactical pattern, the same metrical structure, and at least one major lexical item in common."[24] It is not my intention here to explore the complex characteristics of such systems, and there is as much bickering about the fine points in Old Testament formula criticism as there is in the allied disciplines that allegedly got there first.[25] What I do find significant, however, is the way in which certain formulas common to one text (Isaiah, for example) are assimilated into the framework of another (Micah, for example), either through automatic recourse to a stockpile of such formulas or through conscious borrowing and adaptation. From the second point of view, the formula critics have found that "literate poets resort to the fixed word pair much as the oral poets do."[26] In other words, the use of set formulas can be a characteristic of the most sophisticated poetic practices. Such is true not only of the Hebrew Scriptures but also of the Greek. There Old Testament formulas are reformulated and provided with a context specifically in keeping with the New Testament frame of mind.[27]

Appropriately, this phenomenon is most graphically demonstrated by the author of Hebrews himself. Invoking Haggai 2:6–7 ("Yet once, it *is* a little while"), the author of Hebrews maintains, "This *word*, Yet once more, signifieth the removing of those things that are shaken, as of things that are made, that those things which cannot be shaken may remain" (Heb. 12:27). The point is that the author of Hebrews has taken a phrase (*"a'od achat m'at he"* in the original) and made a formula of it: *"to de eti hapax, deloi"* literally, "But the Yet once, signifies." More precisely, the author of Hebrews has reformulated what was already formulaic, since *"a'od m'at"* ("Yet a little while") itself had the status of a formula by the time the old Testament prophet adopted it for his own use.[28] It is this act of formulating or reformulating (giving meaning to meaning) that the author of Hebrews both engaged in and alluded to with the term *"deloi"*[29] In doing so, he provided his own hermeneutic of the formula.

Formulaic language, that hermeneutic implies, reformulates what was previously understood to be embodied in a particular signifier (a word or a phrase) and infuses it with new meaning. More than that, it removes those layers of meaning it considers impermanent and lays bare what it considers lasting.[30] It is a radical hermeneutic that the author of Hebrews embraced. As indicated in his use of the term "*deloi*," this kind of formulaic language is essentially revelatory and finally apocalyptic: "Yet once more I shake not the earth only, but also heaven. . . . For our God is a consuming fire" (Heb. 12:26, 29). For the author of Hebrews, the formula itself thereby "signifieth the removing of those things that are shaken, as of things that are made, that those things which cannot be shaken may remain."

What is immediately striking about the New Testament context is the way in which the author of Hebrews appropriates for his own purposes the Old Testament phrase signifying "*yet once, it is a little while*" (Hag. 2:6–7) and creates a formulary, "*eti hapax*," "yet once more," with its own unique signification.[31] The precise nature of that signification is eschatological: it embodies, quite dramatically, the portent of the *parousia*, the Second Coming, at the Last Judgment. This, of course, is exactly how the Renaissance saw it. "Yet once more," says David Dickson, signifies "*That Heaven and Earth shall passe away and be chaunged, at the power of CHRIST'S uttering His Voyce: That these chaungeable Heavens and Earth beeing removed, Hee may make a New Heaven, and a New Earth, wherein His Subjects and His Kingdome over them, may remayne for ever setled*," all of which will occur at the "Day of Judgement."[32] For John Diodati, the phrase "Yet once more" betokens "an universall and finall change and annihilation of the state and form of all the creatures, at Christs last appearing in judgment, which shall be the accomplishment of his kingdome."[33] In Milton, "Yet once more" assumes a no less apocalyptic bearing. In fact, it is associated by Milton, at various stages, with the entire redemptive mission of Christ, culminating in the Last Judgment and the enjoyment of heavenly bliss by those who are saved.

This can be established if we trace the course of the phrase throughout Milton's work. Let us begin with *Christian Doctrine*. There, "Yet once more" characterizes the coming of the Messiah, whose advent, foretold by Haggai (2:6–7) as *adhuc semel* (*yet once*), "will shake" "all nations" (15: 282–83). In the *Fair Infant* elegy, Milton mythologizes the event in a reference to Astraea as a type of Christ who "cam'st to visit us once more" (50–53). The true coming of the Messiah, of course, provides for the redemption, as the Son himself describes it in *Paradise Lost*: "Once more I will renew / His lapsed powers . . . /

Upheld by me, yet once more he shall stand / On even ground against his mortal foe" (III.175–79). The coming of Christ in man's form, however, is not alone sufficient to fulfill the redemptive mission. There is, as Milton says in *The Passion*, "Yet more; the stroke of death he must abide" (20) in the crucifixion, after which the resurrected Christ shall return at the Last Judgment. In keeping with the eschatological dimension, that event is appropriately signified in *Paradise Lost* by the *"eti hapax"* formulary. Proclaiming with a trumpet blast God's judgment that man must be expelled from paradise, Milton then adopts the typological perspective of the author of Hebrews (12:19, 26) by suggesting that the sound of the trumpet, as likewise "heard in *Oreb*" with the giving of the Laws, will "once more" "sound at general Doom" (XI.72–75; cf. *Nativity* ode 157–64). Following the Judgment, "The World shall burn, and from her ashes spring / New Heav'n and Earth, wherein the just shall dwell" (*PL* III.333–35). "After all thir tribulation long" (*PL* III.336), the redeemed shall receive the kingdom, a state Milton in Sonnet 23 longs to enjoy, as "yet once more" he "trust[s] to have / full sight" of his "late espoused saint" "in heaven without restraint" (1, 7–8). The formulary has come full circle in its depiction of the redemptive mission, and with it the eschatology that characterizes the Messiah. Assuming the status of a *topos*, defined by the author of Hebrews, it becomes an expressive device that underlies what Frank Kermode in *The Sense of an Ending* calls "eschatological fictions, fictions of the End." Those fictions always have before them the imminence of finality: they reenact the apocalypse in small.[34]

That *Lycidas* belongs to this mode of "end-determined fictions" may be seen in the way that Milton modulates the "Yet once more" formulary throughout the poem. He does so by enacting a minor apocalypse at the very outset of *Lycidas*, in that initial five-line unit cited earlier (1–5). If Milton invokes the pastoral elegiac tradition "Yet once more," he does so in a decidedly destructive manner. He calls upon its conveotions (its foliage, its growth, its seasonal revolutions) not with the assurance of a Theocritus or a Sannazaro to signal the onset of a lament through a suitable form, but to dramatize, in his own unpreparedness, both the untimeliness of Lycidas' death and the insufficiency of traditional form to sustain the impact of his vision. What results is an undermining of convention by means of convention: in the very act of calling up the pastoral elegiac tradition with repeated insistence ("Yet once more . . . and once more"), Milton "shatters" it. The formulary, to use one of our own current formularies, becomes "self-consuming." That event is perfectly in keeping, of course, with the signification attributed to "Yet once more" by the author of

Hebrews: "this *word*," we recall, "signifieth the removing of those things that are shaken as of things that are made, that those things which cannot be shaken may remain" (12:27). It hardly needs to be reargued that from the Miltonic point of view, "those things that are shaken" are none other than the pagan world embodied in pastoral form, whereas "those things which cannot be shaken" are none other than the Christian world embodied in the new pastoral form of *Lycidas*.

In the process of creating this form, the swain undergoes a "*paideia*"[35] whereby he learns of the transition implicit in his own formulary. Calling upon the "*Sicilian* Muse" (133) to inspire his "*Dorick lay*" (189), he is made aware finally of the inefficacy of the pagan world, with its well-fed "flocks," its "rural ditties," dancing "Satyrs" and "fauns," its "low" "valleys," "mild whispers," its "shades and wanton winds, and gushing brooks" (29–35, 136–37). Lycidas' death gives rise to the "canker[ed]" "rose," the sick "herds," frozen flowers, and shrunken "streams" (45–47, 133). "No more," laments the swain, "shall" the "willows" and "hazel copses" "be seen" (42–43). With the failure of the pagan world to protect its children, the swain is made aware of "a higher mood" (87), characterized by "all-judging Jove / As he pronounces lastly on each deed" (82–83) and "the dread voice" (132) of St. Peter as he warns of "that two-handed engine" which "Stands ready to smite once and smite no more" (129–30).

As it touches our "trembling ears" (77) or "shatters" our "frail thoughts" (153), the eschatology of the reference is unmistakable. We are reminded of the inevitability of the *parousia* in a reversal of the formulary from "once more" to "no more." This is the *alpha* and the *omega*, the judgment that is absolutely final: "for the powers of heaven shall be shaken. And then shall they see the Son of man coming in a cloud with power and great glory" (Luke 21: 26–27). But implicit in the *parousia* is the promise of redemption for those who are saved. Through "the dear might of him that walkt the waves" (173), the swain is comforted by a vision of the Messiah. In apocalyptic terms, he learns that Lycidas inhabits not the pagan kingdom where Orpheus is dismembered (57–63) and one's "bones" are "hurld" (155) throughout the universe, but "the blest kingdoms" with "other groves and other streams" where the resurrected body is cleansed and comforted (174–77). There Lycidas' "tears" are wiped "for ever from his eyes" (180).

"Yet once more" thereby embodies its own consolation: it leads inevitably to its own reversal in the climactic declaration, "Weep no more, wofull shepherds weep no more" (165). With this declaration, the pastoral elegiac tradition, undermined at the outset, gives rise to a new pastoral form based upon "those things which cannot be shaken." If "those things that are shaken" are the pagan world embodied in pastoral form, "those things which cannot be shaken" are the Christian world embodied in the new pastoral form of *Lycidas*. As a reflection of the movement from those things that are shaken to those things that cannot be shaken, the transition from the "once more" formula to the "no more" formula is, as I hope to show, fundamental not only to the action of *Lycidas* but also to the formulaic disposition of scriptural language. It is particularly within the prophetic contexts of this language that the transition becomes meaningful.

According to Robert Culley, a major aspect of scriptural formula resides in phonetic iteration: once pronounced, the formula reverberates through repeated patterns of sound, orchestrated to recall the formula as originally uttered. The technique is basic to the phonetic constitution of *Lycidas*, in which such rhetorical devices as epanalepsis figure prominently.[36] From the formulaic perspective, these devices are implicit in the *or* sound of "once *more*," which reverberates throughout the poem as in an echo chamber. We hear *or* repeatedly in the phonetic insistence of "Laur*els*" (1), "bef*ore*" (5), "m*orn*" (26, 187; var. "*mourn*" 41), "*horn*" (28), "*o'*regrown" (40), "*thorn*" (45), "rem*ors*less (50), "*bore*" (58, 110), "*roar*" (61), "*goary*" (62), "*shoar*" (63, 153), "*sport*" (65), "*nor*" (54, 55, 79, 80; var. "*ore*" 170), "promont*ory*" (94), "st*ory*" (95), "*dore*" (130), "*floar*" (167), "*morn*ing" (171), "gl*ory*" (180), "*Dor*ick" (189), as well as in the iteration of "*more*" itself, repeated seven times throughout the poem. In the process, "once more" becomes "no more," at first imperceptibly in the lament "the willows, and the hazel copses green / Shall now *no more* be seen" (42–43; my italics), then disturbingly in the prophetic denunciation "But that two-handed engine at the *dore* / Stands ready to smite *once* and smite *no more*" (130–31; my italics). In that denunciation, the "*eti hapax*" that initiates the poem is transformed: "once more" becomes "no more." A new formula has emerged. Its initial appearance is disturbing, just as the "yet once more" is at first disturbing. Both betoken a shaking of the heavens and the earth; both betoken an apocalypse. But just as "once more" embodies its own consolation, the reward of "a kingdom, which cannot be moved," "no more" ultimately emerges in a consolatory form: "Weep no more, wofull shepherds weep no more" (165).

In this sense, *Lycidas* subscribes to what Claus Westermann has called the "basic forms of prophetic speech." Underlying scriptural prophecy, Westermann maintains, is the announcement of judgment, on the one hand, and of salvation, on the other. Prophetic utterance is structured according to the categories of "judgment proclamation" and "salvation proclamation," each with its own formulas.[37] Among those formulas are the ones of most immediate concern to us, "once more" and "no more." In its own way, each embodies the dialectic of judgment and salvation essential to prophetic speech. That such is true of the scriptural contexts of the "once more" formula as "*a'od achat ma'at he*" (Hag. 2:6–7) and "*eti hapax*" (Heb. 12:26–27) we have already seen. It is the "no more" formula in its scriptural setting that must engage us now.

Let us begin with the "no more" formula as an expression of the judgment proclamation. The *locus classicus* for the use of "no more" in this form is Revelation 18:21–24:

> And a mighty angel took up a stone like a great millstone, and cast *it* into the sea, saying, Thus with violence shall that great city Babylon be thrown down, and shall be found *no more* at all. And the voice of harpers, and musicians, and of pipers, and trumpeters, shall be heard *no more* at all in thee; and no craftsman, of whatsoever craft *he be*, shall be found *any more* in thee; and the sound of a millstone shall be heard *no more* at all in thee; And the light of a candle shall shine *no more* at all in thee; and the voice of the bridegroom and of the bride shall be heard *no more* at all in thee: for thy merchants were the great men of the earth; for by thy sorceries were all nations deceived.[38]

Although Saint John the Divine does not proclaim directly that "no more" "signifieth" any meaning in particular, his "*deloi*" is implicit in the formulaic context his prophetic denunciation creates with the constant iteration of "*ou me . . . eti.*" In that way, it recalls the "*eti hapax*" of the author of Hebrews. The recollection, in fact, is both verbal and thematic, verbal because of the repeated adverb "*eti*" and thematic because of the significance of the destruction of the kingdom (that is, the "removing of those things that are shaken" [Heb. 12:27]) embodied in the "*ou me . . . eti*" formula. In keeping with this formulaic pattern, *Lycidas* itself, of course, reflects precisely that concern with which kingdoms will endure and which will not. Those that will not, because they are both corrupt and transitory, will be "removed" by "that two-handed engine the dore" (130). So it must be before "the blest kingdoms meek of joy and love" (177) are attainable. One of the primary features of both judgment proclamation and salvation proclamation, as might be expected, is the role of the kingdom in prophecy. Whether as "*he basileia*" or as "*malchut,*" the kingdom itself becomes the object either of castigation or of fulfillment that underlies the basic forms of prophetic speech.[39] Such is no less true of Saint John the Divine than of the author of Hebrews. For our purposes, the primacy of the kingdom is figured forth most compellingly in the "once more"–"no more" dialectic that engages us here. Implicit in the *"ou me . . . eti"* of Saint John the Divine, it is equally discernible in the Old Testament prophetic formulations upon which the *"ou me . . . eti"* formula is based.

According to the James Hope Moulton, the formula, which occurs repeatedly in Revelation (sixteen times) and is almost a distinguishing characteristic of that book, has its roots in Semitic originals, particularly among the prophets. There it is rendered *"lo . . . a'od"* ("not . . . any more"), as in Ezekiel 26:13, with Tyre as the object of judgment proclamation: "And I will make cease the noise of your songs; and the sound of your harps shall not be heard any more [*lo . . . a'od*]."[40] Especially as it incorporates various renderings of *"yasaf"* ("more," "again"), the formula becomes very emphatic, as in Ezekiel 36:12–15, with Idumea as the object of judgment proclamation:

> Yea, I will cause men to walk upon you, *even* my people Israel; and they shall possess thee, and thou shalt *no more* bereave them *of men.* . . . Therefore thou shalt devour men *no more*, neither bereave thy nations *any more*, saith the Lord God. Neither will I cause *men* to hear in thee the shame of the heathen *any more*, neither shalt thou bear the reproach of the heathen *any more*, neither shalt thou cause thy nations to fall *any more*, saith the Lord GOD.[41]

This passage is of particular interest because in it the "no more" formula undergoes a transformation in the movement from judgment proclamation (against the heathens) to salvation proclamation (on behalf of the Israelites). In scriptural terms, it is particularly this latter aspect with which we are already familiar.

The seminal passages for that aspect may be found, of course, in Revelation. There is consummated what the author of Hebrews calls the "receiving" of a "kingdom which cannot be moved" (Heb. 12:28). Accordingly, Saint John the Divine proclaims: "They shall hunger *no more*, neither thirst *any more*; neither shall the sun light on them, nor any heat. For the Lamb which is in the midst of the throne shall feed them, and shall lead them unto living fountains of waters: and God shall wipe away all tears from their eyes" (Rev. 7:16–17; italics mine). "And there shall be *no more* death, neither sorrow, nor crying, neither shall there be *any more* pain: for the former things are passed away" (Rev. 21:4; italics mine), These passages, we recall, harken back to Isaiah: "Thou shalt weep no more" in Jerusalem (Isa. 65:19). Even more compelling, however, is Jeremiah, who incorporates a rendering of *"yasaf"* into the *"lo . . . a'od"* formula: "Therefore they shall come and sing in the height of Zion . . . ; and they shall not sorrow any more at all" (Jer. 31:12). In these cases, as in others, the "no more" formula that underlies the salvation proclamation becomes the occasion for celebrating the redemption of those chosen to participate in the renewed Jerusalem. As vehicle for both salvation and judgment, this formula gives shape and meaning to prophetic utterance. Through it, that utterance carries a resonance that distinguishes it as the uniquely charged language of the prophet, performing the same function as its counterpart, "once more." Each gives rise to the proclamations of judgment, on the one hand, and salvation, on the other, that characterize the basic forms of prophetic speech.

Like "Yet once more," "Weep no more" thereby becomes a formulary in its own right, one that signifies the remission of wrath and the promise of joy. We recall Milton's translation of Psalm 85: "God of our saving health and peace, / Turn us, *and chide no more*" (13–16). Significantly, the phrase *"chide no more"* is Milton's own. It points toward a time predicted by the Son, when he says to the father in *Paradise Lost*: "wrauth shall be no more / Thenceforth, but in thy presence Joy entire" (III.264–65). The eschatology of hope formulated here is fundamental to the idiom of religious poetry. Who can forget the climactic effect of the refrains in Donne's *A Hymne to God the Father*? The appeal for forgiveness implicit in "When thou hast done, thou hast not done, / for I have more" culminates in the realization of mercy: "Thou hast done, / I have no more."[42] Although the circumstances surrounding the use of language (notably the punning) differ markedly between the appearance of the formulary in this poem and in *Lycidas*, the idiom is the same. "No more," like "once more," exists in an eschatological environment that suggests the redemptive mission of Christ. In *Lycidas*, that environment is enhanced by a pagan pastoral tradition of formularies that the Christian tradition comments upon and finally supersedes in the creation of a new form. That form embodies a language of its own, a language that can be understood only through a knowledge of the full range of its significations.

Within the scope of the foregoing discussion, I have attempted to illuminate two areas of signification, the pagan and the biblical. I wish to close this aspect of the analysis with the mere suggestion of a third.

In the movement toward the eschatology established by the biblical context, *Lycidas* concerns itself in no small degree with the political dimension, culminating in the denunciation of the clergy by him who "Last came and last did goe" (108). With his "two-handed engine" as Miltonic weapon, "the Pilot of the *Galilean* lake" (109) becomes the exponent of an ideology whose political repercussions were to take England by storm in the ensuing years. Such an outlook prompted William Haller to look upon *Lycidas* as a revolutionary political document: "The performance of Prynne, Bastwick and Burton and of Lilburne, the dialectics of John Goodwin, and the appearance of *Lycidas*," maintains Haller, "showed that revolution was ready to burst forth."[43] Rhetorically, it has been demonstrated that *Lycidas*, among Milton's early poems, anticipates the polemical strategies of his antiprelatical tracts.[44] It is therefore no accident that Milton later drew upon Hebrews 12:26–29 in *Areopagitica* to characterize the Reformation as a time "when God shakes a kingdom with strong and healthful commotions to a generall reforming" (4:350). The sentiment displayed here is, of course, basic to the Nonconformist outlook. It appears fully articulated in a sermon preached by John Owen a few months after the beheading of Charles I. Entitled *The Shaking and Translating of Heaven and Earth* (April 19, 1649), the sermon elaborately glosses "Yet once more" as a formulary signifying the fulfilling of the Reformation in England with the coming of the Messiah, whose kingdom, Owen says, is "even at the doors!"[45] The political bearing of Owen's interpretation is unmistakable: "The Lord Jesus Christ, by his mighty power, in these latter days, as antichristian tyranny draws to its period, will so far shake and translate the political heights, governments, and strength of the nations, as shall serve for the full bringing in of his own peaceable kingdom;—the nations so shaken becoming thereby a quiet habitation for the people of the Most High."[46] From the political point of view, "Yet once more" became, in some respects, the rallying cry of Nonconformist sentiment. To what extent that sentiment is present in Milton's use of the formulary in *Lycidas* lies beyond the scope of this analysis. Judging by the political overtones Milton creates through the figure of St. Peter, such sentiment would appear to be present at least potentially. If so, it adds an even further dimension to the pagan and biblical significations of the formulary already established. As such, it suggests even further the extent to which "Yet once more," like "Weep no more," demonstrates the richness and complexity of Milton's verbal art and how that art is to be understood.

If the foregoing discussion has been successful in addressing what has been defined as the revelatory dimension of *Lycidas*, that dimension, as earlier discussed, finds its counterpart in the amatory dimension. Despite the great amount of attention devoted to *Lycidas* in recent years, the amatory dimension of the poem remains largely unexplored.[47] As the editors of the *Variorum Commentary* make clear, the amatory is signaled at the outset of Milton's poem with the reference to "myrtle" (2) as the plant of Venus. A symbol of love poetry, the myrtle is to be distinguished from the "laurel" (1), the plant of Apollo, and "ivy" (2), the plant of Bacchus, also invoked by Milton at the outset of his poem. All three plants, of course, are intertwined in the poet's crown.[48] All are likewise drawn from a landscape that was intimately associated wth the classical world. As a poem that moves from the classical world to the Christian, however *Lycidas* transforms pagan landscape into a landscape with a foliage all its own:

> So *Lycidas* sunk low, but mounted high,
> Through the dear might of him that walk'd the waves
> Where other groves, and other streams along,
> With *Nectar* pure his oozy Lock's he laves,
> And hears the unexpressive nuptial Song,
> In blest Kingdoms meek of joy and love.   (172–77)

In that transformation, the amatory dimension of *Lycidas*, signaled in the reference to the myrtle, is consummated in the "unexpressive nuptial Song" that the drowned poet, now in "the blest Kingdoms," is allowed to hear. Building toward that consummation through a network of amatory allusions and nuances, *Lycidas* becomes Milton's own "unexpressive nuptial Song." It is this transformation from pastoral as pagan love song to pastoral as Christian love song—indeed, Christian epithalamium—that I should like to explore more fully.

From the perspective of the Renaissance theoreticians, the amatory nature of classical bucolic verse is perceptively delineated in Scaliger's *Poetices*. "Pastoral poetry has many themes," says Scaliger, "but love (or *materia Amatoria* seems to have been the earliest." "Both youth and maidens," he continues, "acted as shepherds, and were thus not only thrown much together, but easily inflamed by the example of the flocks." Deifying amorous delights in Venus, youthful shepherds were "easily enticed into love" by their "nude or lightly clad condition, for though the virgins were clothed, yet their ordinary garments showed the bare thigh." Scaliger goes on to distinguish various species of "alluring song" ("*cantiuncularum* "), including the poetic monologue or *monoprosopos* and the poetic dialogue or *oaristys*. Both forms, he concludes, can be traced to the *Idylls* of Theocritus.[49]

There the amatory pastoral assumes a number of compelling forms, including a burlesque of the whole idea with Theocritus' casting of the monstrous Cyclops, Polyphemus, as spurned pastoral lover. Thus, in *Idyll XI*, for example, Polyphemus, struck by the shaft of Venus, woos the disdainful nymph Galatea, who only rebuffs his advances.[50] Other instances of the pastoral lover whose advances are rebuffed are discernible in *Idyll III*, addressed to the cruel Amaryllis. The speaker of *Idyll III* is certainly one lover who never gets to "sport with *Amaryllis* in the shade," much as he might enjoy the prospect. On the contrary, he threatens to leap into the waves and commit suicide for lack of love (28–29). If pastoral poetry has its source in amatory verse, as Scaliger contends, it is *amor* of a very unrewarding kind.

When pastoral poetry, in turn, is fused with elegy to form pastoral elegy, the destructive qualities of *amor* prevail. Theocritus' first *Idyll* is a case in point. As James Holly Hanford has demonstrated in his thorough study of the underpinnings of Milton's pastoral elegies, both *Lycidas* and the *Epitaphium Damonis* are profoundly indebted to Theocritus' first *Idyll*, the very "archetype of the pastoral elegy."[51] In the first *Idyll*, Thyrsis of Aetna laments the death of Daphnis, "the ideal hero of pastoral song."[52] Recently wedded to a nymph, Daphnis is betrayed by her infidelity, which becomes the occasion of his subsequent death.[53] In the spirit of *Lycidas*, Daphnis is sent "down the stream," as the waters wash over his head (139–40). Theocritus' first *Idyll* is significant because it introduces the amatory element not simply as a source of grief but as a motive for a self-annihilation that is actually realized rather than merely threatened, as in *Idyll III*. That motive is compounded, moreover, by the taunts to which Daphnis is subjected in the person of Venus herself (98–101). Particularly relevant, however, is the nuptial dimension of the *Idyll*. That dimension provides its own unique way of suggesting the destructive qualities of *amor* as pastoral phenomenon.

The idea is not limited only to Theocritus. Bion's *Lament for Adonis*, for example, draws upon similar associations. Although not itself a pastoral in the strictest sense, the *Lament for Adonis* becomes assimilated into the pastoral elegiac tradition, most notably through Moschus's *Lament for Bion*. For our purposes, Bion's *Lament for Adonis* is especially interesting because it conceives of the Venus-Adonis for relationship not only in the amatory terms normally associated with the myth but, what is most remarkable, in distinctly *nuptial* terms. Accordingly, in Bion's version, Venus is depicted as being "widowed" by the death of Adonis. In response to that death, "Hymenaeus quenched every torch at the doorposts and he scattered the nuptial wreath and no more did he sing, 'Hymen, Hymen,' no more his own song, but 'Alas for Adonis,' he chants, even more than the bridal song.''[54] What Bion laments, then, is not only a blighted relationship between two lovers but, of all things, a destroyed marriage.

This amatory—and, by extension, nuptial—dimension extends into the later pastoral elegiac tradition. In his tenth eclogue, for instance, Vergil drew upon Theocritus' first *Idyll* to bemoan the fate of Cornelius Gallus, spurned by the love of Lycoris (actually, Gallus's mistress, the actress Cytheris). Although love here is portrayed as cruel and destructive,[55] there is no suggestion of the nuptial relationships implicit in Theocritus and Bion. For that, we must move to the Renaissance and the piscatory eclogues of Jacopo Sannazaro. In the first piscatory eclogue, the figure of Lycidas laments the death of Phyllis, whom he was to wed: "Why," Lycidas asks,

> should I tarry longer in unhappiness in order that,
> stretched out on this vile seaweed, I might see only
> dried shrubs and abandoned shores and cast my words
> upon a thankless tomb? Is this . . . the wedlock, these
> the happy nuptials that I am to celebrate? Is it thus
> that Venus grants me the joys of the wished nuptial
> torch?[56]

One might suggest from these examples that the pastoral elegy gives rise to a kind of perverse epithalamium, one in which the nuptials are either violated or never fully consummated. Milton's *Lycidas* is a product not only of the amatory sources of the pastoral elegy but of the epithalamic qualities that pastoral elegy comes to assume, and upon which Milton bestows new meaning and a new life.

The amatory dimension of *Lycidas* is discernible in the network of nuances and allusions that permeate its texture. Invoking the plant of Venus, Milton casts his poet-shepherd in the role of lover. As we have seen, the practice is an ancient one, traceable to Theocritus' archetypal poet-shepherd Daphnis. Unlike the poet-shepherds of Greek and Roman pastoral, however, Milton's poet-shepherd bestows his affection not upon nymphs and naiads but upon the craft of poetry itself. It is for the sake of that craft that he worships his own disdainful mistress, the "thankless Muse" (66). It is she (or the Muses in general) to whom the poet-shepherd appeals: "Hence with denial vain, and coy excuse" (18).[57] For the poet-shepherd can have none of that if his poem of seduction is to succeed.

But the poet-shepherd that Milton conceives is convinced at the

outset that he will be a very bad lover. Accordingly, he invokes the
materia Amatoria (to use Scaliger's phrase) of pastoral in the following
manner:

> I com to pluck your Berries harsh and crude,
> And with forc'd fingers rude,
> Shatter your leaves before the mellowing year.   (3–5)

The lines accord with the amatory dimensions of the pastoral elegiac
tradition itself. In sexual terms, the poet's love song violates the very
traditions of amatory verse it is to draw upon. The language of
plucking berries and shattering leaves before the mellowing year, in
fact, is reminiscent of that which Milton had earlier used to different
(but related purpose) in *The Fair Infant* elegy. There the death of
Milton's niece assumes the form of a metaphorical ravishing by which
that "fairest flower" (the niece) is "blasted" (that is, "untimely
pluck'd")[58] before the mellowing year by that rather clumsy lover
winter, who unwittingly but rudely destroys her: "For he being amorous of that lovely die / That did . . . [her] cheek envermeil, thought to
kiss / But kill'd alas, and then bewayl'd his fatal bliss" (1–7). Inten-
sifying this commonplace idea of "killing" as sexual act, Milton alludes
to the "rape" of Orithyia by Boreas (or Aquilo) and creates a myth in
which Aquilo desires a new conquest in the form of a "wedding" or
coupling with the "fair infant" of Milton's elegy, an act that results in
her unfortunate death (8–14).

The great fear that plagues the poet-shepherd of Milton's *Lycidas* is
that he too will be clumsy, harsh, and crude, that in drawing upon the
traditions of pastoral elegy he will botch things miserably, that he will
in the end be a very bad lover indeed; and in fact, Milton's poem does
initially have about it the quality of a *carpe rosam* that has gone sour:

> As killing as the Canker to the Rose,
> Or Taint-worm to the weanling Herds that graze,
> Or Frost to Flowers, that their gay wardrop wear,
> When first the white Thorn blows:
> Such, *Lycidas*, thy loss to Shepherds ear.   (45–49)

What Milton's poet-shepherd lacks, of course, is the knowledge that
he will gain at the end, the knowledge of what it means to write the
love song that *Lycidas* finally proves itself to be. He must proceed,
however, even at the expense of "plucking the berries harsh and
crude" and "shattering the leaves before the mellowing year." Only
by doing so will he gain the requisite knowledge that he lacks.

It is no accident that in *Ad Patrem* Milton looked upon poetry as the product of a sexual relationship with knowledge (*scientia*), here depicted as seductress: "Sweeping the clouds apart," she "comes to be viewed, and, naked, she inclines her bright face to my kisses, unless I should wish to flee, unless I should find it too burdensome to taste her kisses" (90–93). At the risk of failing utterly, the poet-shepherd of *Lycidas* takes upon himself the burden of learning what it means to write a poem in the pastoral-elegiac vein, that most amatory of forms. What he produces is a consummate love poem, an "unexpressive nuptial Song" of unparalleled beauty. He does so, however, only after an encounter with love relationships that have failed miserably. For Milton, these relationships constitute the classical heritage of *amor*. As such, they are endemic to the landscape from which the pastoral elegy emerges. A litany of those relationships runs throughout *Lycidas*.

Instances abound. Milton's allusions to "*Arethuse*" and "*Alpheus*" (32) are a case in point. "The nymph Arethusa, bathing in the river Alpheus was," we recall, "pursued by the river god, and, that she might escape his embrace, was transformed by Diana into a stream."[59] In his *Lament for Bion*, Moschus invokes precisely this story of pursuit and transformation. At the same time, he alludes to another myth that is important to the amatory dimension of Milton's poem, that of Apollo and Hyacinth.[60] In *Lycidas*, the AI, AI (alas, alas) of that unfortunate relationship appears "inwrought" in the attire of *Camus*.[61] Through the love of Apollo and Hyacinth, Milton provides male-male relationship as a counterpart to the male-female relationships that populate his poem. This variation is hardly alien to the pastoral tradition, as Vergil's well-known second eclogue (suggesting the homoerotic relationship between Corydon and Alexis) will attest.[62] In either case (male-male or male-female), the amatory element is destructive.

In *Lycidas*, the idea is discernible as early as the reference to the mourning of the "echoes" (41), a reference that calls up associations of Echo, as a mountain nymph, lamenting her unrequited love for Narcissus.[63] As Ovid says, "She hides in woods and is seen no more upon the mountainsides; but all may hear her, for voice, and voice alone, still lives in her."[64] Behind Milton's references to Echo lurks the Venus-Adonis relationship as well. In Bion's *Lament for Adonis*, for example, Echo cries, "Lovely Adonis is dead" in response to the cries of Venus, an idea repeated in Ronsard's *Adonis*.[65] Thereafter the litany continues in the poet-shepherd's calling upon the nymphs: "Where were ye Nymphs when the remorseless deep / Clos'd o're the head of your lov'd *Lycidas*?" (50–51). The apostrophe to the nymphs has its ultimate source in Theocritus' first *Idyll*: "Where were ye, Nymphs, oh where, while Daphnis pined? / In fair Peneus' or in Pindus' glen?" (66–67).[66] Had the nymphs been present, Theocritus implies, Daphnis' death by water might have been averted. When we remember both the amatory and the nuptial circumstances surrounding that death, we can see how important to Milton's poem the convention of calling up the nymphs becomes.

If we agree with the *Variorum* editors that the nymphs Milton calls upon find their counterpart in the Muses (those very beings the poet-shepherd himself woos),[67] then we must conclude that the nymphs would have been helpless even if they *had* been present. For immediately after invoking the nymphs Milton makes exactly the same point: "Ay me," the poet-shepherd laments,

> I fondly dream!
> Had ye been there—for what could that have don?
> What could the Muse her self that *Orpheus* bore,
> The Muse her self for her inchanting son
> Whom Universal nature did lament,
> When by the rout that made the hideous roar,
> His goary visage down the stream was sent,
> Down the swift *Hebrus* to the *Lesbian* shore.
>
>   (56–63)

As the *Variorum* editors remind us, the reason that the Bacchantes attacked Orpheus in the first place was because they were "enraged by his devotion to his dead wife."[68]

From the nuptial point of view, then, we come full circle. Daphnis dies because his wife has been unfaithful to him; Orpheus, because he was faithful to his wife. In the first place, the nymphs are not present to save the aggrieved groom; in the second, the Muse Calliope, the counterpart of the nymphs, cannot save her recently married son, even though she *is* present.[69] Once again, *amor*, as represented in the classical myths that Milton draws upon, fails in all respects. All that the pastoral elegy can do, Milton would agree, is to lament that failure, pretty much as Hymen does in Bion's *Lament for Adonis*, when, rather than singing a "bridal song," he intones an epithalamium of death.

It is precisely this aspect of *amor* that Milton had originally thought to make the focus of his famous flower passage. In the earliest draft of *Lycidas* in the Cambridge Manuscript, Milton had written the following lines:

Bring the rathe primrose that unwedded dies
colouring the pale cheeks of uninjoyed love
and that sad floure that strove
to write his own woes on the vermeil graine
next adde Narcissus that still weeps in vaine . . . to strew the
laureat herse & c.[70]

The idea of decking the body in this manner finds its source in Bion's
Lament for Adonis. There Adonis, bereft of his nuptial wreath, is laid
to rest in the same bed he had shared with Venus: "The bed yearns for
Adonis, dismal though his fate," laments the poet. "Cast on him
wreaths and flowers. With him all things have died, even as he, and the
flowers are all withered."[71] It is no doubt this context that Milton had
in mind in his earliest version of the flower passage, a version that
reflects both the amatory and nuptial dimensions of his source. Although in the revised version Milton chose not to emphasize those
aspects that point directly to either "uninjoyd" or "unwedded" love,
the Venus-Adonis context still remains to suggest the way in which the
passage was at first conceived and should now be read.

Because *Lycidas* is a poem that embodies the Christian perspective,
however, it necessarily transcends the amatory environment of pagan
pastoral from which it is drawn. As Christian pastoral, it concludes
with a vision of *amor* that is eternal rather than transitory, celestial
rather than earthly, creative rather than destructive. It is, after all, a
poem whose landscape is that of "other groves, and other streams,"
where, we recall, Lycidas "hears the unexpressive nuptial Song. / In
the blest Kingdoms meek of joy and love" (174–77).

The reference is one that conflates a number of biblical passages,
particularly two from Revelation. The first passage (Revelation 14:3–4)
addresses itself to the redeemed in heaven and the new song only they
are able to hear: "And no man could learn that song but . . . [those]
which were redeemed from the earth" and "follow the Lamb wither-
soever he goeth." The passage was a crucial one for Milton, who
speaks in *An Apology* of the "high rewards of ever accompanying the
Lambe, with those celestiall songs to others inapprehensible" (3: 306).
These are of a kind with what Milton in *Ad Patrem* calls "a never dying
melody [*immortale melos*]" and "a song beyond all describing [*inenar-
rabile carmen*]" (38). Such songs are comprised of the "unexpressive
notes" (116) of Milton's *Nativity* ode and are the foundation of "that
undisturbed Song of pure concent" (6) that unites us with the "celestial consort" (27) of Milton's *At a solemn Musick*. This "celestial
consort" is both a *concentus* or concert and a *consortium* or marital

union. In both senses, the "consort" distinguishes the new song the redeemed are able to hear in Revelation 14:3–4.[72] This, of course, is the "nuptial Song" referred to in *Lycidas*.

The specific meaning of that song, in turn, is made clear in Revelation 19:7, the second passage in question: "Let us be glad and rejoice . . . : for the marriage of the Lamb is come, and his wife hath made herself ready." Of this passage, Milton says in *Christian Doctrine*: "The love of Christ [*Amor Christi*] towards his invisible and spotless Church is described by the appropriate figure of conjugal love [*amore coniugali*]" (16: 64–65). It is by means of just such a figure that Milton calls upon Christ as groom in *Animadversions*: "Come forth out of thy Royall Chambers, O Prince of all the Kings of the earth, put on the visible roabes of thy imperiall Majesty . . . for now the voice of thy Bride calls thee, and all creatures sigh to bee renew'd" (3: 148). The sense of renewal that Lycidas experiences in the "blest Kingdoms" is very much in keeping with Milton's appeal to Christ in *Animadversions*.

The ideal is one that engaged Milton not only in *Lycidas* but in *Epitaphium Damonis* as well. There the nuptial dimension assumes an orgiastic fervor all its own, as Damon "consummates, eternally, immortal nuptials [*immortales hymenaeos*], where there is singing, where the lyre revels madly, mingled with choirs beatific, and festal orgies run riot, in bacchante fashion, with the thyrsis of Zion" (217–20). If the "immortal nuptials" that consummate *Lycidas* are much more subdued than this, they nonetheless underscore the significance of Milton's poem as an "unexpressive nuptial Song" of the most exalted kind. Superseding all previous pastoral elegies, Milton forges a new song, one in which transitory unions give way to a wedding that can never be dissolved. *Lycidas* is Milton's epithalamic celebration of that event.[73]

As the foregoing discussion has attempted to demonstrate, *Lycidas* is a profoundly self-conscious and self-reflexive document, one that establishes an ongoing dialogue with its forebears. Drawing upon the conventions of those forebears (both classical and biblical), *Lycidas* refashions earlier *topoi* and recreates them in a form that is *sui generis*. This unique quality of Milton's poem is demonstrated at the very outset with its opening declaration of subject, a declaration that reverberates throughout the poem as a whole. In the process of that reverberation, two dimensions in particular emerge, the revelatory and the amatory. Embodied in the patterns of phrasal formulation and verbal repetition, on the one hand, and in the complex networks of allusion, on the other, these two dimensions function not only to disclose hidden meanings, but to redefine generic expectations. In its capacity to perform both functions, *Lycidas* is a poem at once traditional and revolutionary. In it, form and convention assume renewed significance. It is this sense of renewal that underscores Milton's fundamental outlook as a poet.

CHAPTER SIX

The Dialogic Imagination

IN his criticism of *Paradise Lost*, a deservedly obscure eighteenth-century schoolmaster by the name of John Clarke once took Milton to task for introducing God and the Son as "Actors in his Poem." "A Poet," observed Clarke, "may contrive Scenes of Action, and find speeches for his Fellow Mortals of the highest Degree," but that poet dare not "bring down the most High into a Scene of Diversion, and assign him his Part of Acting and Speaking."[1] Although Clarke made no mention of specifically what "Scene of Diversion" he had in mind, we may safely assume that the dialogue in Heaven in Book III is an excellent candidate. Few scenes in *Paradise Lost* have occasioned as much difficulty as that one.

Responding to the scene, critics have traditionally objected not only to Milton's handling of character delineation but to his treatment of theological doctrine. In both respects, they have taken issue with Milton's attempt to render God and the Son dramatically. Those troubled by character delineation have customarily leveled their barbs at the figure of God. Pope's quip that "God the Father turns a School-Divine"[2] implies as much the failure of drama as the impropriety of attempting drama under such circumstances in the first place. These are exactly the issues that underlie more recent criticism of the scene. William Empson's charge that Milton's God is reminiscent of Uncle Joe Stalin represents the crude extreme to which a criticism of Milton's dramaturgy is liable to extend.[3] Complementing the criticism of Milton's delineation of God is that which calls into question the theology his Deity espouses. This criticism faults Milton for his failure to make his theology palatable. That failure, argue the proponents of such a view, is the result not only of the theology itself but of the manner in which it is transmitted. For these critics, the theology is transmitted in a way that suggests nothing more than the flat presentation of dogma by an unpleasant and pedantic figure who has His "yes-man" sitting at His right-hand side ready to assent to anything his Father might have to hand down.[4] What results for those who hold this view is a scene that is decidedly undramatic in its transmission of theology. For them, dogma has usurped drama.

In reponse, critics like Irene Samuel have attempted to reclaim the integrity of the scene by arguing that it is incorrect to "read the scene as a mere presentation of doctrinal assertions conveniently divided between Father and Son." Reacting to the scene in that way, readers "have incautiously misconstrued as dogma what Milton intended as drama."[5] This emphasis upon drama invites an interpretation of Father and Son not as mouthpieces for the expression of an unpalatable theology, but as fully conceived characters participating in a dramatic interchange. Perceptive as Samuel's argument is, however, her insights have not won as many converts as might be expected. Jackson Cope, for example, maintains that the so-called drama Samuel discovers is really not drama at all. Rather, what she misconstrues as drama is actually a kind of ritual enactment of dogma reinforced through the employment of rhetorical schemes from one set speech to the next.[6] Such a view is in keeping with J. B. Broadbent's observation that the scene is founded upon an "impregnable rhetoric of dogma" through which "corridors of verbal mirrors" do nothing but reflect "unbodied concepts."[7]

One does not need either Cope or Broadbent, however, to call into question the dramatic point of view that Samuel endorses. Ironically, Samuel does that herself. In precisely the essay in which she argues for a dramatic reading of the dialogue in Heaven, she compromises her own point of view by maintaining that Milton's God as Transcendent Being speaks tonelessly and dispassionately. Representing "the toneless voice of the moral law," Milton's God, avers Samuel, "speaks simply what is." In other words, one finds a curious turnabout in Samuel's essay. While maintaining that the scene must be read dramatically, she deprives the dialogue of just that drama which would otherwise bring it to life. She does so because the moment it is conceived as true drama, those characters who participate in it become liable to the very judgments that prompted such critics as William Empson to level his charges in the first place. If God is removed from the arena of drama, then such charges no longer obtain. God is conceived not as character but as principle: "Total Being," "Primal Energy," the "Voice of Reason," to invoke Samuel's epithets.[8] One cannot have it both ways: either the scene is conceived dramatically, or it is not. The decision to interpret the scene one way or the other makes all the difference for an understanding of Milton's epic and the theology it embodies.

In his reading of the scene, Stanley Fish, for example, opts to interpret it totally as nondrama. Transforming the scene from dialogue into monologue, Fish conceives of Milton's God as a Being who makes logical, accurate, and objective pronouncements in a kind of divine vacuum. This Being, says Fish, "does not argue, he asserts, disposing a series of self-evident axioms in an objective order, 'not talking to anyone in particular but meditating on objects.'" If the reader takes exception to what God says, "the fault (quite literally)" is his own, not God's. Almost as an afterthought, Fish does concede, albeit parenthetically, that God is "technically address[ing] the Son"; nonetheless, God "is not in any sense . . . initiating a discussion."[9] Like the God of Irene Samuel, the God of Stanley Fish is relieved of any of the responsibilities that constitute dramatic verisimilitude. Totally removed and fully aloof, He effectively assumes the role of an abstraction void of dimensionality. He is cleansed of the taint of drama: He simply is.

In effect, what Fish does is argue for a Ramistic interpretation of Milton's God, which, considering the profound influence of Ramism upon Milton, is quite understandable. As Fish documents, the phrase "not talking to anyone in particular but meditating on objects" comes from Walter J. Ong's pioneering study *Ramus, Method, and the Decay of Dialogue.*[10] According to Father Ong, the Ramist mentality is fundamentally antidialogic: "in the characteristic outlook fostered by the Ramist rhetoric," observes Father Ong, "speaking is directed to a world where even persons respond only as objects—that is, say nothing back." Markedly hostile toward drama, Ramus supported an educational reform that included the abolishing of plays.[11] Ramus's attitude, in turn, was particularly congenial to the English Puritans. In its own way, the closing of the theaters in 1642 represents ample testimony to the influence of this outlook in the political sphere. From the aesthetic perspective, the outlook is equally compelling. So Father Ong observes that "when the Puritan mentality, which is here the Ramist mentality, produces poetry, it is at first blatantly didactic, but shades gradually into reflective poetry which does not talk to anyone in particular but meditates on objects."[12]

The statement returns us once again to Stanley Fish, who says of Milton's God that "the tonal qualities usually ascribed to his voice are accidental, the result of what the reader reads into the speech rather than what is there. The form of his discourse is determined by the nature of the thing he contemplates rather than by the desire to project a personality (ethos) or please a specific audience (pathos); its mode is exfoliation; that is, the speech does not build, it unfolds according to the rules of method."[13] As far as I am concerned, nothing could be further from the truth. To remove Milton's God to a realm of abstraction void of dimensionality, to cleanse Him of the taint of drama, to conceive Him simply as that which is denies Him those essential characteristics that constitute Milton's rendering of God as a fully realized being in *Paradise Lost*.

This is a being who may disturb us, who may even repel us; but He is a being nonetheless. His proper environment is that of drama; His proper discourse that of dialogue, not monologue. As such, Milton's conception of God is in harmony with what Mikhail Bakhtin implies is "the dialogic imagination," according to which the word as uttered "encounters an alien word . . . in a living, tension-filled interaction."[14] It is this "living, tension-filled interaction" that underscores the celestial dialogue in *Paradise Lost*. If Milton's rendering of God's causes us discomfort, so be it. The answer to this discomfort is not to consign the Deity to the realm of abstraction. The appropriate response, paradoxically, is that of God's critics, who are inclined to argue with Him, to impugn His motives, to be offended by what He says and how He says it, to engage Him in debate, to struggle with Him, to see Him struggling with Himself.[15] It is the critics of Milton's God who provide the greatest insight into how the Deity of *Paradise Lost* is to be understood. For knowingly or not, these critics at the very least credit Milton with the courage, if not the audacity, to have conceived God dramatically. This, as I shall argue, is how Milton did conceive God, and along with Him the Son in Book III of *Paradise Lost*. There Milton provides a full account of what he terms in *Christian Doctrine* "the drama of the personalities in the Godhead" ("*et personalitatum illud totum drama advocem*") (14: 196–97).[16] Although disinclined to discuss that drama in his theological tract, Milton gave it full play in the epic.

If one examines the dialogue in Heaven closely, he will discover there what amounts in fact to a five-act drama. In Act I (80–134), the Father foretells the fall of man but promises grace; in Act II (144–66), the Son responds to his Father's promise in a way that causes the Father in Act III (167–217) to delineate His intentions further by calling for a volunteer to sacrifice himself on behalf of man. That request, in turn, sets the stage for the Son's act of accepting his sacrificial vocation in Act IV (227–65). This gesture is followed by the Father's praise of the Son and prognostication of the future in Act V (274–343).[17] The action, of course, is essentially comedic: although it begins tragically, it resolves itself in an assertion of the *felix culpa* upon which the epic as a whole is based.[18] From the comedic perspective, the Son's *anagnorisis* or recognition concerning the nature of redemption and his role in becoming the means by which God brings it about is followed by a *peripeteia* or reversal in the action: "So Heav'nly love shall outdo Hellish hate, / Giving to death, and dying to redeem, / So dearly to redeem what Hellish hate / So easily destroy'd" (III.298–301).[19] The five-act structure of the dialogue that encompasses this mimesis, furthermore, is framed by a prologue and an epilogue. If the prologue is represented by the poet's "Hail" that inaugurates Book III (1–55), the epilogue is represented by the "Hail" of the assembled hosts that surround the throne as witnesses to the dialogue (372–415). As such, both prologue and epilogue embody their own doxologies, one human, the other angelic. To the angelic "Hail" that closes the dialogue, the poet joins his own voice: / "Hail Son of God, Saviour of Men, thy Name / Shall be the copious matter of my Song / Henceforth, and never shall my Harp thy praise / Forget, nor from thy Fathers praise disjoin" (III.412–15). Framed by prologue and epilogue, the five-act drama is thereby brought full circle.

If Milton found a discussion of "the drama of the personalities in the Godhead" unsuitable to his theological tract, then the re-creation of the drama as epic event became entirely appropriate to the action of *Paradise Lost*. Such is only natural, given Milton's predisposition to accommodate sacred matter to the demands of secular form. *Pace* John Clarke, Milton saw nothing amiss in "bring[ing] down the most High into a Scene of Diversion, and assign[ing] him his Part of Acting and Speaking." Doing so, in fact, was entirely in accord with his interpretation of the biblical text, which for Milton represented a veritable storehouse for dramatic reenactment. All one need do is glance at Milton's plans for dramas in the Cambridge Manuscript to verify this fact. If those plans provide insight into the dramatic underpinnings of Milton's epics, they suggest the extent to which his closet drama is a fully realized product of this dramaturgical perspective. Defending that perspective in the preface to *Samson Agonistes*, Milton accordingly found himself in agreement with those who viewed the Book of Revelation as a tragedy, divisible into "Acts distinguisht each by a Chorus of Heavenly Harpings and Song between."

The idea is enunciated as early as *The Reason of Church-Government*, in which Milton revealed his inclination to view the events of Scripture in dramatic terms. Ranging over the entire field of literary precedent available to him in the fulfillment of his own future endeavors, he enthusiastically endorsed a reading of Scripture consistent with the practice of conceiving the biblical text as the highest form of drama, one comparable even to the "Dramatick constitutions" of

Sophocles and Euripides. Embedded in Scripture could be found drama of all kinds. So Milton observed that "Scripture affords us a divine pastoral Drama in the Song of Salomon consisting of two persons and a double Chorus . . . and [that] the Apocalyps of Saint John is the majestick image of a high and stately Tragedy, shutting up and intermingling her solemn Scenes and Acts with a sevenfold Chorus of halleluja's and harping symphonies" (3: 237–38). In keeping with such views, Milton proposed in *The Reason of Church-Government* "to celebrate in glorious and lofty Hymns the throne and equipage of Gods Almightiness" (3: 238).[20]

By the time Milton came to formulate the celestial drama through which this occurrence would be made possible, he was prepared to stage an event that would represent the culmination of all those dramatic plans earlier set down in the Cambridge Manuscript. He was prepared, that is, to fulfill his role as dramatist by writing what John Demaray has so aptly called the "theatrical epic."[21] In its own way, the dialogue in Heaven in *Paradise Lost* is as much a fully conceived drama within that "theatrical framework" as any Milton ever wrote. "Shutting up an intermingling her solemn Scenes and Acts," the dialogue in Heaven is a "Dramatick constitution," to use Milton's phrase, that portrays as vividly as one can possibly imagine the conflicts, the struggles, the passionate interchanges, and the reconciliations of "the drama of the personalities in the Godhead." To gain a fuller appreciation of how the dialogue was originally conceived and how it is to be understood, then, one might well begin with Milton's early plans for a drama on the Fall. An examination of those plans will suggest something of the literary bearing that the dialogue would come to assume in *Paradise Lost*. This understanding, in turn, will provide a greater awareness of how Milton fashioned God and the Son as dramatic characters.

As the plans in the Cambridge Manuscript make clear, Milton definitely had in mind some sort of celestial dialogue as part of his projected dramas. Although a dialogue between Father and Son is not specifically mentioned, a debate among the figures of Justice, Mercy, and Wisdom certainly is. In the second draft of his plans, or example, Milton included "Justice, Mercie, and Wisdome" among the "Persons" of his proposed drama, and in the third draft, he fleshed out his intentions by conceiving Justice, Mercy and Wisdom as "debating what should become of man if he fall." (The third draft is particularly apposite, for it not only projects a debate among Justice, Mercy, and Wisdom but subscribes to a five-act structure framed by a prologue and a choric epilogue.) As outlined in the fourth draft, Justice and

Mercy reappear to admonish man and comfort him after he falls (18: 229–32).

The inclusion of Justice, Mercy, and Wisdom in his dramatic plans suggests Milton's indebtedness to the medieval tradition that allegorizes Psalm 85:10: "Mercy and truth are met together; righteousness and peace have kissed each other."[22] Dating back at least as far as the twelfth century, the allegory depicts Mercy, Truth, Righteousness (or justice), and Peace as the Four Daughters of God debating over the soul of man in the dramatic setting of a celestial parliament. Although the occasion of the various parliaments ranged in time from the Creation to the Last Judgment, the debates among the Daughters consistently focused upon what would become of the soul of man. Presided over by God, these debates normally resolved themselves in the offer of the Son to atone for man's sins as an expression of divine grace. As a result of that offer, the Four Daughters were reconciled. If the allegory of the Four Daughters of God enjoyed wide currency during the Middle Ages, it left its mark on the Renaissance as well.[23] For our purposes, the importance of the allegory lies in the uniquely dramatic character it bestows upon the conception of the celestial parliament. In its traditional formulation, the celestial parliament was transformed into an arena of emotionally charged conflict, with the future of the human race at stake. Even a cursory overview of medieval and Renaissance renderings of the allegory will suggest how fully it lent itself to drama of the most spirited sort.

In what is probably its earliest Christianized form, Hugo of St. Victor's *Annotations on the Psalms* (ca. 1120 A.D.) depicted Truth and Mercy not simply meeting but in effect contending with one another over the soul of man. According to Hope Traver, Hugo might have been influenced in this regard by a tenth-century midrash, which has Mercy and Truth not merely meeting but "thrusting" at one another, and Justice and Peace not kissing but "fighting" together.[24] The spirit of contentiousness underscores the allegory from the very beginning, and the drama implicit in this contentiousness informs the debates to a greater or lesser degree throughout the Middle Ages and the Renaissance. So in the play of the Salutation and Conception from the *Ludus Coventriae* (ca. 1468), there is a parliament in Heaven in which the Four Daughters debate over the salvation of man. "Should he be saved?" asks *Justitia*, and then responds to her own question with "Nay! nay! nay!" Following this harsh and emotional judgment, *Misericordia* observes, "Sister Righteousness, you are too vengeable!" The debate is not resolved until *Filius* offers himself as a sacrifice for man in a Council of the Trinity, after which the Virtues are finally reconciled.[25] The emotionally charged atmosphere discernible here extends into the celestial parliaments portrayed in such Renaissance works as Giles Fletcher's *Christ's Victory and Triumph* (1610) and Joseph Fletcher's *The History of the Perfect-Cursed-Blessed Man* (1628).[26]

As one greatly influenced by this tradition, Milton might well be expected to be responsive to its dramatic implications. Accordingly, the concept of debate that one finds so much a part of the plans in the Cambridge Manuscript is likewise present in the dialogue in Heaven in *Paradise Lost*. So pervasive is its presence, in fact, that Barbara Lewalski sees it as the means by which Milton structures the drama as a whole. For Lewalski, each of the speeches in the drama accords with the office of one of the Four Daughters: "God's first speech . . . sets forth the truth of things—Satan's escape, his impending success in the temptation, man's Fall, the doctrines of free will, sufficient grace, and personal responsibility for choice"; the Son's response, in turn, "pleads the case for mercy to mankind, but appeals also to God's justice to prevent the triumph of Satanic evil"; the Father's next speech voices "the stern demands of justice," but at the same time restates His intention to renew and save mankind and ends with a call for charity; the Son's response emphasizes the "peace assured, / And reconcilement" he will achieve for man, along with an affirmation that he will "satisfy God's justice by his death and so allow the divine mercy to flow to man." These four speeches (each represented by one of the Four Daughters) culminate in the Father's concluding speech which "celebrates the Son for reconciling all these elements in love."[27] What we have seen as the five-act structure of the drama, then, subscribes for Lewalski to the tradition of the Daughters of God. Although this reading might seem a bit too paradigmatic, it does suggest the extent to which Milton assimilates the concept of the Daughters to his dramaturgical outlook. More telling for our purposes, however, is the way in which Milton appropriates the sense of emotionally charged conflict so characteristic of the Four Daughters tradition in order to delineate the figures of Father and Son as fully conceived characters.

In the triumphant song of jubilee that fills the eternal regions after the completion of the dialogue, the angelic hosts provide their own dramatic cue to the intensity of this conflict. Hymning both Father and Son, the angels declare:

> No sooner did thy dear and onely Son
> Perceive thee purpos'd not to doom frail Man
> So strictly, but much more to pitie enclin'd,

> He to appease thy wrauth, and end the strife
> Of Mercy and Justice in thy face discern'd,
> . . . offerd himself to die
> For mans offence. (III.403–10; my italics)

These lines are revealing not simply because of the way in which they acknowledge the tradition of the Four Daughters, but because of the way in which they suggest how the dialogue is to be read. What they suggest is that this conflict occurs not only between characters, but within characters as well. What Milton offers us, in short, is a kind of psychodrama through which inner turmoil comes to the surface in rather disturbing and unsettling ways.[28] When applied to the figure of man as a character, such psychodrama is perfectly acceptable. (We witness it, for example, in the figure of Adam when, after he has fallen, he is tossed "in a troubl'd Sea of passion" [X.718].) When applied to the figure of God as a character, however, such psychodrama tends to make us uncomfortable. God struggling with Himself is somehow unbecoming, unGodlike, as it were. Milton, of course, was perfectly aware of the risks he was taking in portraying God in this manner. Doing so, however, represented for him not merely a testimony to his own powers as a poet, but an assertion of his faith in the kind of God he felt called upon to portray.

In order to support so radical an outlook, Milton sought justification once again in the Holy Scriptures. On the basis of his reading of those Scriptures, he maintained in *Christian Doctrine* that "our safest way is to form in our minds such a conception of God, as shall correspond with his own delineation and representation of himself in the sacred writings. For granting that both in the literal and figurative descriptions of God, he is exhibited not as he really is, but in such a manner as may be within the scope of our comprehensions, yet we ought to entertain such a conception of him, as he, in condescending to accommodate himself to our capacities, has shown that he desires we should conceive." We may be certain, Milton assures us, "that sufficient care has been taken that the Holy Scriptures should contain nothing unsuitable to the character or dignity of God, and that God should say nothing of himself which could derogate from his own majesty." Nonetheless, if the Scriptures indicate that "it repented Jehovah," "let us believe that it did repent him." Moreover, if the Scriptures say that "it grieved the Lord at his heart," "let us believe that it did grieve him." Finally, if it be said that "he feared the wrath of the enemy," "let us not believe that it is beneath the dignity of God . . . to fear in that he feareth." So Milton concludes: "For however we may attempt to soften down such expressions by a latitude of interpretation, when applied to the Deity, it comes in the end to precisely the same" (14: 33–35).[29] Far from attempting to "soften down such expressions," Milton affords them full play in the dialogue in Heaven in *Paradise Lost*. An analysis of the first two speeches in that dialogue should suggest the extent to which the dialogue as a whole embodies "the drama of the personalities in the Godhead."

A sense of conflict is present from the very outset of the dialogue. It is, in fact, what distinguishes the Father's opening speech and underscores His character. If the Father's speech culminates in the assurance that His glory shall excel "in Mercy and Justice both" but that "Mercy first and last shall brightest shine" (III.132–34), it is not so much the reconciliation of the two as it is the struggle through which that reconciliation is achieved that distinguishes the divine presence from the beginning, and throughout the speech as a whole. The speech itself begins from the perspective of observation. "High Thron'd above all highth," God "ben[ds] down his eye, / His own works, and their works at once to view" (III.56–59). Surrounded by "the Sancti-ties of Heav'n" and accompanied "on his right" by His "onely Son," He beholds "from his prospect high" past, present, and future (III.77–78). His address to His Son is in response to the foreknow-ledge that such a prospect affords. It is with the nature of this response that the present analysis will be concerned.

The address begins dispassionately enough. Commenting upon Satan's act of presuming to break the bounds of his captivity, God traces the course of the Adversary from Hell, through Chaos, to the "Precincts of light," as he heads "Directly towards the new created World," there "with purpose to assay / If him by force he can destroy or worse, / By som false guile pervert" (III.80–92). Such attempts at "desperate revenge," God has already assured His audience, shall do nothing but "redound / Upon his [Satan's] rebellious head." Despite these assurances, however, the tone of detachment with which God's speech begins undergoes a transformation as the Deity moves from the present prospect to the immediate future in the exercise of His foreknowledge. What follows an introductory section of dispassionate observation and commentary is a passage of righteous indignation, moral outrage, and self-justification. In Satan's attempt to pervert man, God proclaims, the Adversary will be successful:

> For man will heark'n to his glozing lyes,
> And easily transgress the sole Command,
> Sole pledge of his obedience: So will fall

Hee and his faithless Progenie: whose fault?
Whose but his own? ingrate, he had of mee
All he could have; I made him just and right,
Sufficient to have stood, though free to fall.

(III.92–99).

Far from being a passage in which a "toneless" Deity speaks "simply what is" or disposes "a series of self-evident axioms in an objective order," this is an impassioned, emotionally charged utterance imbued with a sense of genuine conflict (or, to use the telling word of the angelic hosts, "strife").

The language in which that utterance is cast is harsh and uncompromising: it grates, it repels, it provokes. The word "ingrate" itself is enough to cause any reader to bristle. The discomfort we feel in response to the use of that word is intensified, moreover, by our awareness that "ingrate" is applied to unfallen beings who have not even had the opportunity to be ungrateful yet, just as the word "faithless" is applied to offspring who have not even had the opportunity to be born yet. If God beholds "past, present, and future" in a timeless realm of "foreknowledge absolute," His utterance treats future events as if they had already transpired. Collapsing temporal distinctions in this manner intensifies the severity of the pronouncements and thereby causes the distress that a foreseeing Deity experiences to be that much more disturbing. Verbal repetition ("sole Command," "sole pledge"), followed by verbal variation ("so will fall," "whose fault?"), does nothing to alleviate the harshness of this impression. Nor is that harshness confined to the first speech alone: "He with his whole posteritie must die, / Die hee or Justice must" (III.209–10) is one of a number of examples that might be cited to suggest the presence of such harshness in later utterances as well.

If we find God's language sharp and cutting, however, we must remember that it proceeds from a Deity who has already been betrayed once by reprobate "Ethereal Powers" and "Spirits" (III.100–01), and who knows that He is soon to be betrayed again by His new terrestrial creations. "He had of me all he could have" is as applicable to what has already transpired as it is to what will yet once more transpire in the near future. Portrayed as one who "foreseeing spake" (III.79), God is thereby dramatized as a wrathful and aggrieved parent who looks before and after only to find betrayal. The result of this knowledge is an ire, a defensiveness, an anguish that gives rise to a language at once tortuous and torturous: "Not free, what proof could they have givn," "What pleasure I from such obedience paid?," "nor can justly accuse / Thir maker," "As if Predestination over-rul'd / Thir will," "they themselves decreed / Thir own revolt, not I," etc. (III.100–19). This is hardly a language of detachment, of equanimity. It is rather troubled speech, a language of pain. If Milton was courageous enough, even audacious enough, to dramatize his Deity in this manner, we as readers should not attempt to tone down what the dramatist has taken such great pains to portray according to his understanding of what constitutes the *ira Dei*.[30] It is no accident that Milton has his own God refer to Himself later in the dialogue as "th'incensed Deitie" (III.187). If God refers to Himself as "incensed," we ought at the very least acknowledge that Milton's God knows what He is about.

It is in this spirit, then, that we are to read the concluding portion of the speech. In these lines, we find a full expression of God's attitude toward His creations, their behavior, and the decrees that He has issued to govern their behavior:

> So without least impulse or shadow of Fate,
> Or aught by me immutablie foreseen,
> They trespass, Authors to themselves in all
> Both what they judge and what they choose; for so
> I formd them free, and free they must remain,
> Till they enthrall themselves: I else must change
> Thir nature, and revoke the high Decree
> Unchangeable, Eternal, which ordain'd
> Their freedom, they themselves ordain'd their fall.
>
> (III.120–28)

What Milton presents us with here and throughout the speech as a whole is a Deity who undergoes the "strife" of one fully aware of the demands that His own decrees have placed both upon Himself and His creations, and who is therefore at pains to justify those demands and unwilling to compromise them. Knowing what the past has brought and the future will bring, this is a Deity who is put to the expense of attempting to justify the ways of God not only to His creations but, by virtue of the setting in which that justification is rendered, to Himself as a dramatically conceived character. *Paradise Lost* is an epic in which God justifies the ways of God to God. It is an epic in which God talks to Himself, that is, in which God responds as Accommodated Being to what He as Absolute Being is.[31] In this respect, He, like His own creations, is "Author to Himself in all / Both what He judges and what He chooses." As "Author to Himself," He not only accepts the responsibility of abiding by His own decrees, but assumes the role of one fully conscious of what those decrees entail both for Himself and for His creations. Having become "Author to Himself" in this manner, He appears to us as Accommodated Being. By its very nature, His presence in that role is dramatic: it embodies that personality, that ethos, through which Accommodated Being makes itself known. If Absolute Being is beyond perception, Accommodated Being is manifested in that dramatic portrayal called "God." It is this portrayal that we as audience witness in the dialogue in Heaven in *Paradise Lost*. What we witness in this portrayal is nothing less than an *agon* through which Milton's God as *Deus agonistes* struggles with His own theology.

If we find that struggle unsettling and disturbing, Milton would maintain that this is exactly as it should be. An encounter with *Paradise Lost* and the theology it embodies is not meant to be a comforting experience, one that encourages the sort of complacency that Milton decries in *Areopagitica* as the mark of "a fugitive and cloister'd vertue, unexercis'd & unbreath'd" (4: 311). "A man may be a heretick in the truth," Milton observes in that same tract; "and if he beleeve things only because his Pastor sayes so, or the Assembly so determins, without knowing other reason, though his belief be true, yet the very truth he holds, becomes his heresie" (4: 333). So in an encounter with *Paradise Lost*: conflict is at the heart of it; conflict is its very soul, the very source of its being. To encounter Milton's epic is to grapple with it. It is the drama of that combat that Milton portrays through his delineation of God in Book III of *Paradise Lost*. If this is true of Milton's delineation of God, it is no less true of his delineation of the Son, In that delineation, we come to appreciate as never before what Milton means by "the drama of the personalities in the Godhead." To understand that drama, however, one must come to terms as fully as possible with the Son's response to his Father's first speech.

Despite this, one of the pronounced curiosities of Milton criticism is its unwillingness to give that response its due. Readers have almost invariably made hash of what the Son says. Those critical of the Son's response misread with a certain perverseness. Excising the first ten lines or so from the response as a whole, J. B. Broadbent accuses the Son of simply "weav[ing] lyrical patterns" with his Father's speech "as if to beautify brutality."[32] John Peter blames the Son for being guilty of "tactful bribery."[33] Those who defend the Son, on the other hand, do him more harm than good. Almost as if afraid to give the Son his due, Allan Gilbert, for example, sees the Son as "a prudent courtier, beginning with deference his speech to the monarch . . . and then endeavoring to persuade him [the monarch] not to go too far in his punishment of disloyal man."[34] At the very least, these assessments have the virtue of crediting the Son with some kind of dramatic presence, an alternative Stanley Fish, we recall, deprives him of almost entirely. Not only does the Son enjoy a dramatic presence; however; he infuses the scene with a sense of energy and excitement previously unknown to the traditions of celestial debate through which Milton fashioned his dialogue in Heaven.

The Son's rejoinder to his Father begins courteously enough. It praises his Father for concluding His "sovran sentence" with the promise that "Man should find grace" (III.144), the means by which the conflict between Justice and Mercy will finally be reconciled. As the embodiment of divine compassion, infinite love, and immeasurable grace (III.141–42), the son is understandably joyful at the prospect that "mercy first and last shall brightest shine." He communicates that feeling of joy in a language of assent that runs over six lines:

> O Father, gracious was that word which clos'd
> Thy sovran sentence, that Man should find grace;
> For which both Heav'n and Earth shall high extoll
> Thy praises, with th'innumerable sound
> Of Hymns and sacred Songs, wherewith thy Throne
> Encompass'd shall resound thee ever blest.
>
> (III.144–49)

Were his response to conclude at this point, then the sense of conflict that so underscores the Father's speech would remain confined to that speech alone. This is not the case; that sense of conflict becomes part of the Son's rejoinder as well. Six lines of praise are followed by seventeen lines of challenge that call into question the very promise of grace that the first six lines made a point of extolling. In effect, the first six lines perform the task finally not of extolling but of anticipating what amounts to a series of animadversions that are as extreme in their implied censure as any that Milton himself ever marshaled during his polemical career:

> For should Man finally be lost, should Man
> Thy creature late so lov'd, thy youngest Son
> Fall circumvented thus by fraud, though joynd
> With his own folly? that be from thee farr,
> That farr be from thee, Father, who art Judge
> Of all things made, and judgest onely right.

> Or shall the Adversarie thus obtain
> His end and frustrate thine, shall he fulfill
> His malice, and thy goodness bring to naught,
> Or proud return though to his heavier doom,
> Yet with revenge accomplish't and to Hell
> Draw after him the whole Race of mankind,
> By him corrupted? or wilt thou thy self
> Abolish thy Creation, and unmake,
> For him, what for thy glorie thou hast made?
> So should thy goodness and thy greatness both
> Be questiond and blaspheam'd without defence.
>
> (III.150–66)

Rhetorically, the animadversions assume the form of two sets of questions (III.150–53, 156–64), the first set of which is followed by an answer (III.153–55) that serves as much to admonish as to affirm, and the second set of which is followed by an answer (III.165–66) that serves at once to challenge and to warn. In outline, the first set of questions looks like this:

> Should man "finally be lost"?
> Should man "fall circumvented thus by fraud"?

Answer: "That be from thee farr, / That farr be from thee, Father." Implication: If that be far from one who "judgest onely right," why do His judgments provoke the kinds of questions that cause His own Son to raise the possibility that these judgments might lead to the loss of God's "creature late so lov'd" in the first place?[35] Rather than settling the matter, the answer provides a transition into the second set of questions. This set is potentially even more damaging (certainly more unrelenting) than the first. In outline, the second set of questions looks like this:

> Shall Satan triumph?
> Shall Satan obtain his end?
> Shall Satan fulfill his malice?
> Shall Satan accomplish his revenge?
> Will you allow yourself to be frustrated, Father?
> Will you allow your goodness to be undermined?
> Will you abolish your creation?

Unlike the answer to the first set of questions, the answer to the second set is not an assertion of the unlikelihood that the answer might possibly be "yes," but a warning that if the answer is indeed "yes" (the very real possibility is implied here), then God's "goodness and . . . greatness both" would be justifiably "questiond" and, what is even more devastating, "blaspheam'd without defence" (III.165–66). Consider the implications of the Son's challenge. Warning his Father that if His Decree is not executed in a manner consistent with His promise of mercy, the Son charges that his Father's actions would render Him defenseless against whatever justifiable accusations (either in the form of questioning or outright blasphemy) His actions might provoke. One senses in the challenge that the Son himself would be foremost among the reprobate in excoriating the Father, should the Father fail to heed His son's warning.

The intensity of the drama at this point could not be greater, an intensity that the language of the challenge does much to reinforce: "So should thy goodness and thy greatness both / Be questiond and blaspheam'd without defence." Recalling the whole series of questions that build to a crescendo in the Son's response, the word "questiond" encapsulates the response as a whole. (The Son in effect has been questioning God's goodness and greatness all along.) At the same time, the word "questiond" threatens future acts of questioning in response to which any claims of divine goodness and greatness would be rendered totally ineffectual.

Moving from the word "questiond," the challenge culminates in the astounding word "blaspheam'd." To have the Son proclaim that his Father's actions might be justifiably "questiond" is one thing; to have him proclaim that they might be "blaspheam'd without defence" is quite another. Blasphemy, as Milton was quick to point out in *Christian Doctrine*, runs counter to the spirit of the Ten Commandments ("thou shalt not take the name of the Lord thy God in vain" [Ex. 20:7]). As an "impious or reproachful mention of God," blasphemy for Milton is a sin of the greatest magnitude.[36] Milton knew from the Gospel of Matthew that whereas "all manner of sin shall be forgiven," blasphemy against the Spirit of God is absolutely unforgivable: "Whoever speaketh a word against the Son of man," says Jesus, "it shall be forgiven him: but whosoever speaketh against the Holy Ghost, it shall not be forgiven him, neither in this world, neither in the world to come" (Matt. 12:31–32). In Revelation, blasphemy is the sin of the Beast, which carries the name of blasphemy upon its heads: "And he opened his mouth in blasphemy against God, to blaspheme his name, and his tabernacle, and them that dwell in heaven" (Rev. 13:1, 6). Closer to his own time, Milton no doubt remembered the figure of Capaneus in the inferno of Dante's *Commedia*. Railing ceaselessly against God, this most disdainful and scowling of blasphemers is doomed to an eternity of fire and burning sand (I.xiv.43–75).

In *Paradise Lost*, blasphemy, of course, is what Satan is charged with: "O argument blasphemous, false and proud!," exclaims Abdiel upon hearing the rebellious words of the Adversary; "Words which no ear ever to hear in Heav'n / Expected, least of all from thee, ingrate / In place thy self so high above thy Peers. / Canst thou with impious obloquie condemn / The just Decree of God [?]" (V.809–14). If one recalls this charge in the context of the Son's response to his Father's Decree after the defeat of the impious rebels, one cannot help being struck by the dramatic irony in Abdiel's words. Assuming that the fiery and zealous servant of God is among the assembled host when not Satan but the Son of God has uttered his challenge, one is prompted to ask: "What must Abdiel be thinking now?" "Who is the ingrate, after all?" "Will the real adversary please step forward?"

"So should thy goodness and thy greatness both / Be questiond and blaspheam'd without defence." In an epic that purports to justify the ways of God to men, Milton creates a circumstance in which the very theology upon which that justification is founded threatens to undermine its own cause. I know of no other instance in the history of either dramatic or epic poetry in which a poet has undertaken such risks. When Milton referred to his "adventrous Song" as one that "pursues / Things unattempted yet in prose or Rime" (I.13–16), he knew only too well whereof he spoke. By having the Son challenge the Father in these terms, Milton deliberately placed himself in a situation "compasst round" with all kinds of dangers. His purpose, however, was not to be provocative simply for the sake of being provocative. If Milton writes incendiary drama, it is because the theology of his poem must be constantly testing itself, constantly subjecting itself to challenges of the most extreme sort. Through the dramatization of his theology, Milton gives us his own version of Jacob's combating with God; he conceives of God's own Son as a figure who is not afraid to wrestle with his Father "until the breaking of the day." Embodied in the Son is the name that God bestowed upon Jacob after their combat: "Thy name," says God to Jacob, "shall be called no more Jacob, but Israel: for as a prince hast thou power [lit. 'have you contended'] with God . . . and hast prevailed" (Gen. 32:24–30).

As startling as the Son's defiance of the Father appears to be, the spirit of contentiousness is accordingly not without biblical precedence. When the God of Isaiah declares, "Come now, and let us reason together" (Isa. 1:18), his use of the word "reason" is derived from a Hebrew term (*yachach*) that suggests the idea of arguing, debating, and contending as much as it does the act of reasoning. What is true for Isaiah is similarly true for the Old Testament in general. In fact, the idea of contending with one's God is part of the fabric of Old Testament theology. God's faithful are forever engaged in controversy with Him, whether in the manner of Job, who wishes to arraign God in a court of law (Job 13:6, 40:2), or of Jeremiah, who is prompted to dispute with God concerning the nature of God's ways (Jer. 12:1).[37] As Merritt Y. Hughes has shown, the Psalmist himself is hardly reluctant to reprimand God when the occasion calls for such chastisement. Significantly, this act of chastisement in the Psalms occurs within the context of the reconciliation of mercy and truth, righteousness and peace of Psalm 85 that is the basis of the allegory of the celestial debate we have been exploring. In the very next Psalm, comments Hughes, "David strengthens his prayer for divine mercy in a public calamity by reminding God of his vaunted pre-eminence among all gods. Later, in the same tone of reverence and intimacy, he praises God because justice, mercy, and truth share his throne. But he also warns God that Israel's reverses destroy confidence in his will and power to keep his covenant to preserve it as a kingdom forever, and that the sneers of its enemies threaten his prestige in the world."[38]

Psalm 86, of course, is part of the earlier group of Milton's Psalm translations (Ps. 80–88), rendered in 1648 during the Civil Wars. As a group, these Psalms shed a good deal of light not only upon the concept of a debate within a celestial council but upon the idea of the faithful servant's act of admonishing his Lord. So Psalm 82, a *locus classicus* in its own right,[39] depicts God within "the great assembly" of celestial beings (1–3). There, according to Milton's rendering, God "judges and debates" (4). Significantly, the word "debates" is not in the original; it is Milton's own interpolation. In Psalm 87, Milton envisions God within His holy mountain and provides a rendering of the Psalm that suggests the posture of one who not only praises his Lord but admonishes Him as well:

> City of God, most glorious things
> Of thee abroad are spoke;
> I mention Egypt, where proud Kings
> Did our forefathers yoke,
> I mention Babel to my friends,
> Philistia full of scorn,
> And Tyre with Ethiops utmost ends. (9–15).[40]

None of this implied bitterness is in the original; one can only imagine what "glorious things" are said of the City of God by its various enemies, who either yoked the Psalmist's forefathers or are full of scorn in reaction to the Psalmist's God and His City. Certainly, as a political document, Milton's translation admonishes those in authority during the Civil Wars to remember the enemy, particularly to avoid coming once again under the power of "proud Kings." But as a personal document in a time of trouble, Milton's rendering contains an implicit call to God to recognize the adherence of His faithful, a recognition that is fulfilled in the promise that Sion shall be established eternally.

If the Psalms (especially as portrayed through Milton's own translations) suggest something of the biblical background that underlies the Son's rejoinder to the Father in Book III of *Paradise Lost*, the most immediate source for that rejoinder is to be found in three crucial biblical passages, drawn respectively from Genesis, Exodus, and Numbers. Whereas in Genesis 18 Abraham argues against the wholesale destruction of the Sodomites, Moses in Exodus 32 and Numbers 14 argues against the wholesale destruction of the Israelites. As John E. Parish and Merritt Y. Hughes have respectively argued, the language through which the dialogue in Heaven (and in particular the Son's first speech) is formulated alludes directly to these biblical passages.[41] Thus, the Son's locution "that be from thee farr, / That farr be from thee, Father, who art Judge / Of all things made, and judgest onely right" (III.153–55) derives from Abraham's statement to God: "That be far from thee to do after this manner, to slay the righteous with the wicked: and that the righteous should be as the wicked, that be far from thee: Shall not the Judge of all the earth do right?" (Gen. 18:25). Moreover, the questions that follow upon the Son's "that be from thee farr," namely "Or shall the Adversarie thus obtain / His end . . . shall he fulfill / His malice [?]," etc.—these questions find their counterpart in Moses' words to God both in Exodus and in Numbers. So in Exodus, Moses admonishes God: "Lord, why doth thy wrath wax hot against thy people, which thou hast brought forth out of the land of Egypt with great power, and with a mighty hand? Wherefore should the Egyptians speak, and say, For mischief did he bring them out to slay them in the mountains, and to consume them from the face of the earth? Turn from thy fierce wrath and repent of this evil against thy people" (Ex. 32:11–12). In Numbers, Moses' words are likewise to the point: "Now if thou shalt kill all this people as one man, then the nations which have heard the fame of thee will speak, saying, Because the Lord was not able to bring this people into the land which he sware unto them, therefore he hath slain them in the wilderness" (Num. 14:15–16).

It is in the spirit of such challenges to authority that Milton in *The Doctrine and Discipline of Divorce* invokes the Genesis 18 account of Abraham's confrontation with God: "Therefore Abraham ev'n to the face of God himselfe, seem'd to doubt of divine justice if it should swerve from the irradiation wherewith it had enlight'ned the mind of man, and bound it selfe to observe its own rule" (3: 445). When it appears not "to observe its own rule," Milton counsels the kind of healthy defiance reflected in Moses' challenge to God. For that purpose, Milton invokes Exodus 22:10 to support the following statement that appears in *Christian Doctrine*: "Hence our knowledge of God's will, or of His providence in the government of the world ought not to render us less earnest in deprecating evil [*mala deprecanda*] and desiring good [*bona petenda*], but the contrary" (17: 101, 102). The kind of "evil" Milton would have us "deprecate" is none other than God's own desire to consume the Israelites, a desire that Moses persuades God to overcome.[42] With its indebtedness to the Abrahamic and Mosaic sources, such is the spirit embodied in the Son's response to the Father in Book III of *Paradise Lost*.

If the foregoing suggests something of the biblical perspectives that Milton drew upon to fashion his dialogue, these perspectives can only begin to provide a sense of the complexity of the dialogue itself. So multifaceted is the dialogue, in fact, that an exclusive reliance upon the biblical perspective runs the risk of encouraging us to overlook the extent to which the dialogue radicalizes even the Bible. In this respect, the Son's challenge to the Father ("So should thy goodness and thy greatness both / Be questiond and blaspheam'd without defence") represents a case in point. No amount of digging into backgrounds (biblical or otherwise) will produce an unequivocal source for the Son's challenge. Nowhere does Abraham, Moses, or David venture such an affront to God. This is Milton's doing, and Milton alone must stand accountable for it.

Once we realize how extensively Milton radicalizes dialogue in his portrayal of his "Dramatick constitution," we shall have gained an invaluable insight not only into the character of his dramaturgy but into the nature of his theology. The character of his dramaturgy is clear enough. As we have discussed, Milton is content with no middle flights: he pursues only "things unattempted yet in Prose or Rime" (I.16), and those "things unattempted" include the contents not only of secular literature but the most sacred of books as well. When Andrew Marvell, in his commendatory poem *On Paradise Lost* wrote "the Argument / Held me a while misdoubting his [Milton's] Intent, / That he would ruin . . . / The sacred Truths to Fable and old Song," Marvell included among his list of "sacred Truths" "Messiah Crown'd, Gods Reconcil'd Decree" (3–8), just the subjects that engage us here.[43] In his poetic reformulation of those subjects, Milton did not hesitate to take chances, even at the risk of undermining sacred truths. Although he held the Bible as the repository of these truths in the highest esteem, his ultimate guide was the Spirit of God within him. So he maintained in *Christian Doctrine*: "The Spirit which is given to us is a more certain guide than Scripture, whom therefore it is our duty to follow" (16:279). This is as much a declaration of aesthetic independence as it is of doctrinal independence. It accounts in part for the dramaturgical extremes to which he is willing to go when the occasion calls for such extremes.

His radicalizing of dialogue, however, is not confined to his dramaturgy. It likewise extends to (and is an expression of) his theology. The Logos for Milton contains a quality that is essentially combative. The Son may be God's "word, . . . [His] wisdom, and effectual might" (III.170), but the Son's personality (his *essentia*, to use Milton's theological terminology) is his own. It is this quality that renders the dialogue in Heaven so compelling, for when all is said and done, the purpose of the dialogue is the proving of the Son, the establishing of his identity, an event that cannot occur before the Son has been given the opportunity to manifest his true nature. If that event involves the act of issuing the most extreme of challenges, it also implies a willingness to accept the most awesome of responsibilities: that of offering oneself as a sacrifice for man.

Viewed in the context of the interchange between Father and Son, the dialogue in Heaven that graces Book III of *Paradise Lost*, then, represents a moment of high drama in Milton's epic. It is a drama of fully delineated characters engaged in the kind of dialogue that Milton no doubt had in mind when he endorsed a reading of Scripture consistent with the practice of conceiving the biblical text as the highest form of drama, one comparable even to the "Dramatick constitutions" of Sophocles and Euripides. The dialogue in Heaven is just this sort of "Dramatick constitution." As a "drama of the personalities in the Godhead," that dialogue draws upon all the resources available to it in its portrayal of the divine interchange. Resorting to the traditions of the celestial parliament that date from the Middle Ages and the Renaissance, it derives its spirit from the combativeness and contentiousness implicit in the biblical models. But it ventures beyond these models to fashion for itself an event that extends the frontiers of drama to a point at which the very theology upon which *Paradise Lost* is founded threatens to undermine its own cause. In the jargon of contemporary critical parlance, one might say that the dialogue in Heaven provides the occasion by which Milton's epic threatens to deconstruct itself. Whether or not such an occurrence actually takes place—and I would argue that it does not—the dialogue offers ample evidence of Milton's willingness to push drama to its limits. In so doing, Milton succeeds in pursuing "things unattempted yet in Prose or Rime." As one of the most compelling of "Dramatick constitutions," the dialogue in Heaven in Book III of *Paradise Lost* fulfills this intention admirably.

CHAPTER SEVEN

The Theology of Strength

AS a glance at any concordance to *Samson Agonistes* will immediately confirm, the one substantive word that Milton uses more frequently than any other in his drama is "strength."[1] So often does this word, along with its cognates, appear, that it rings like a leitmotif that harmonizes the drama as a whole.[2] Such a circumstance is only natural, if not inevitable, considering the subject of the drama itself. If the term "strength" did not appear frequently in a drama about what the Bible considers the world's strongest man, where would it appear? This point seems self-evident, but in acceding to it we run the risk of overlooking dimensions of the drama that are not at all obvious. Those dimensions have to do with the precise nature of Milton's portrayal of strength as a category of value in *Samson Agonistes*, and the relationship between that portrayal and the form that strength assumes in his other writings. The purpose of the discussion that follows, then, is to explore the meaning of strength in *Samson Agonistes*.

As I hope to demonstrate, there emerges in Milton's drama what might be called a theology of strength, one both related to and distinct from strength as a theological category in the other writings. In order to suggest precisely what is meant by the phrase "theology of strength" and how that concept functions in Milton, I shall need to establish the appropriate biblical and exegetical backgrounds, as well as Milton's recourse to them. Accordingly, I shall begin with a detailed account of the way in which strength emerges as a category of value in the Old and New Testaments. From the perspective of the biblical milieu, I shall suggest the bearing of that category on Milton's writings in general. Having established these larger contexts, I shall then return to the Bible and focus my discussion specifically on the nature of strength in the Samson narrative and related biblical material, followed by a glance at the exegetical traditions to which this material gave rise. Moving from these backgrounds, I shall conclude with a discussion of the way in which Milton delineated Samson as the embodiment of strength both in the prose and poetry in general and in

Samson Agonistes in particular. Such an investigation should help not only to elucidate the complex issue of strength as a fundamental category in Milton's thought, but further to illuminate the action of Milton's closet drama as a work in which strength assumes a unique and compelling significance.

In the Old Testament, strength reflects an entire range of meanings. With its primary source in the notion of *gabhar* and its synonyms, strength in its most fundamental form has to do with the power and awfulness of God.[3] In that form, strength and power become interchangeable expressions of the same idea. *Gabhar* implies at once strength and power.[4] As an attribute, strength is either implicit in the idea of power, or it is bestowed by God, the source of power, upon those empowered or strengthened as a result of this divine bestowal. To understand the meaning of strength from the theological point of view, then, is to appreciate the significance of *gabhar* in all its forms. From the Old Testament perspective, the "realization of Yawheh's power involved ascriptions of 'cosmic majesty' even at an early date. The Song of Deborah pictures how before this great and terrible One the earth trembles, the heavens drop, the mountains quake" (Judg. 5:4). Under God's power, "the stars in their courses" (Judg. 5:20) and the sun in the heavens (Josh. 10:12) come to the help of Israel.[5] The primary manifestation of divine power occurs with the overwhelming of the hosts of Pharaoh at the Red Sea, an event celebrated in the Song of Moses: "Thy right hand, O Lord, is become glorious in power: thy right hand, O Lord, hath dashed in pieces the enemy" (Ex. 15:6, 13; 32:11). This, of course, is the decisive event in Israel's history. "When the righteous of the Old Testament are reminded of the power of God, they think of the act of God at the Red Sea which completed the Exodus."[6] As the result of such an event, God's very name is associated with His might.[7] Intimately associated with God's power is His wisdom. In fact, as an Old Testament concept, "all power has its root in wisdom."[8] In Job, the association is so fundamental as to be formulaic: "With him *is* wisdom and strength, he hath counsel and understanding," and "With him *is* strength and wisdom; he hath understanding and insight" (12:13, 16).[9] These are the primary attributes possessed by those who are faithful to God and adhere to His ways.

The concept of power as the means by which God enacts such miraculous occurrences as making the heavens drop, the mountains quake, and the seas part is likewise crucial to the New Testament outlook. "On the basis of the miraculous beginning of His existence Jesus is equipped with special power and is the Bearer of power." As a result of this power (*dynamis*), he is able, for example, to perform such miraculous acts as casting out unclean spirits (Luke 4:36). By means of his *dynamis*, Jesus not only performs miracles but effects salvation (cf. Luke 8:43–48). "As the essence of God is power, so endowment with power is linked with the gift of His Spirit." Endowment with the Spirit bestows upon Jesus "a definite personal authority which He has, in substantial terms, the *dynamis* to exercise."[10] So Acts 10:38: "God anointed Jesus of Nazareth with the Holy Ghost [*pneumata agio*] and with power [*dynamei*]: who went about doing good, and healing all that were oppressed of the devil; for God was with him." In the New Testament, then, the Old Testament concept of *gabhar* assumes a Christocentric bearing as *dynamis*. In either case, it underscores the biblical emphasis upon what Rudolf Otto calls the "overpoweringness" of God as one who bestows His divine strength upon others.[11]

From the perspective of Milton's own writings, this view of strength as a manifestation of God's power and awfulness is all-pervasive. Addressing the nature of God's omnipotence in *Christian Doctrine*, Milton invokes such texts as 2 Chronicles 20:6 ("in thine hand is there not power and might") and 1 Timothy 6:15 ("the only Potentate, the King of kings and Lord of lords") as a given. God's name, observes Milton, is *El Shadai*, that is, God Almighty (14: 47–49). Residing in the very "substance of God [*substantia Dei*]" is a "bodily power [*vis corporea*]" that God bestows at will upon His chosen (15: 24–25). Such an act is effected by means of God's Spirit, which is an emissary of "the virtue [*virtutem*] and power [*potentiam*] of the Father." Milton's prooftexts here include Romans 1:4 (Jesus Christ is "declared to be the Son of God with power, according to the spirit of holiness") and Acts 10:38 ("God anointed Jesus of Nazareth with the Holy Ghost and with power"), among others. "For thus the Scripture teaches throughout," Milton avers- "that Christ was raised by the power of the Father [*patris virtute suscitatum*], and thereby declared the Son of God" (14: 365–67).[12]

It is this view of divine power as that which not only characterizes the Deity but is bestowed by the Deity upon His chosen that suffuses Milton's poetry. The psalm translations are a case in point. There Milton at once celebrates "the strength of the Almighties hand" (4), as in his translation of Psalm 114, and exhorts God to "awake. . . [His] strength" and to save His faithful by His "*might*" (11–12), as in his translation of Psalm 80. For Milton, the notion of God is synonymous with His power: He is, as Milton declares in his translation of Psalm 80, the very "God of *strength*" (3).[13] It is this strength, in turn, that

God bestows upon His Son in *Paradise Lost*, when He sends His Son out to defeat the rebel angels on the third day of the War in Heaven: "Into thee such Vertue and Grace / Immense I have transfus'd," the Father says to the Son, "that all may know / In Heav'n and Hell thy Power above compare" (VI.703–05). This statement is then followed by the declaration of divine power: "Go then thou Mightiest in thy Fathers might, / Ascend my Chariot, guide the rapid Wheeels / That shake Heav'ns basis, bring forth all my Warr, / My bow and Thunder, my Almightie Arms / Gird on, and Sword thy puissant Thigh; / Pursue these sons of Darkness, drive them out / From all Heav'ns bounds into the utter Deep: / There let them learn, as likes them, to despise / God and *Messiah* his anointed King" (VI.710–18). It is at this pivotal point that *Paradise Lost* resolves itself into an epic of power. In the transfusion of divine power from one being to the next, Milton provides the occasion by which the theological issues having to do with the nature of divine strength as delineated in *Christian Doctrine* assume poetic form. Specifically, at the very center of his epic, Milton portrays the way in which the *vis corporea* that resides in the *substantia Dei* is passed on from the Father to His Son in an act of divine commission. Infused with the *vis corporea*, the Son goes forth in the "Chariot of Paternal Deitie" to overwhelm the rebel angels.[14] Whereas the Son puts forth only "half his strength," the rebel angels, on the other hand, experience the withering of all their strength, as they are left drained of their "wonted vigour," "Exhausted, spiritless, afflicted, fall'n (VI. 850–53).[15] From the perspective of both his theological tract and his poetry, this, then, suggests Milton's understanding of the nature of divine strength or power as a category that finds its antecedents in both Old Testament and New Testament formulations.

This, however, is not the only view of strength that Milton discovered in the biblical text. In fact, as Milton was well aware, there emerges in both the Old Testament and the New a view of strength that is decidedly paradoxical. According to that view, the concept of strength undergoes a profound transvaluation that spiritualizes it and reconceives it in a new form. From the Old Testament point of view, such a reconceptualization already begins in the prophecy of Jeremiah. There one finds "a renunciation of everything that is called *gibbor* [mighty] in the physical or any other visible sense." "If one is a *gibbor*, 'mighty man,' he is not to glory in his *gebhurah*, 'might,' or his riches or his own wisdom, but in that he understands and knows God, who alone practices steadfast love, justice, and righteousness in the earth. In these things God delights" (cf. Jer. 9:22).[16] In Zechariah, moreover, one discovers what amounts to an act of spiritualization that effectively reverses all previous understandings of the significance of divine power: "Not by might (*b'chayyil*), nor by power (*b'koach*), but by my spirit (*b'ruchiy*), saith the Lord of hosts" (4:6).[17]

Uncompromising in its reconceptualization of the meaning of power, this point of view finds full expression in the New Testament. There it assumes its own unique rendering. Founded upon a paradoxical reversal in the relationships customarily ascribed to strength and weakness as categories of value, that reversal is made most dramatically evident in the Pauline epistles. "Be strong in the Lord, and in the power of his might," admonishes Saint Paul in the Epistle to the Ephesians. In keeping with such prophets as Jeremiah and Zechariah, the kind of strength that Paul has in mind is of the spiritual, not the physical, sort. For Paul, this is the very attire of the Christian warrior: "Put on the whole armour of God, that ye may be able to stand against the wiles of the devil. For we wrestle not against flesh and blood, but against principalities, against powers, against the rulers of the darkness of this world, against spiritual wickedness in high places." Arming himself against such foes, the Christian warrior dons the equipage of spiritual combat: his loins girt about with truth, his upper torso protected by the breastplate of righteousness, his feet shod with the gospel of peace, his hands grasping the shield of faith and the sword of the spirit, his head adorned with the helmet of salvation (Eph. 6:10–17), he is fully prepared, as one strong in the Lord and in the power of His might, to enter lists with the devil. The transvaluation already initiated in the Old Testament finds renewed expression here.

St. Paul, however, extends that transvaluation to its most radical point by actually reversing the terms of the equation: it is a sublime weakness, coupled with a sublime foolishness, rather than an imposing strength, coupled with a daunting wisdom, that dominates in Pauline thought. Such a reversal represents the theological focus of the Epistles to the Corinthians. Preaching the significance of the cross to those who suffer for Christ's sake, Paul maintains that to the unfaithful who perish, the cross is foolishness, but unto those who are saved, it is the power of God. Implicit in this power is a sublime foolishness, a remarkable weakness that only those who acknowledge Christ's ways can understand. Accordingly, "the foolishness of God is wiser than men; and the weakness of God is stronger than men," for "God hath chosen the foolish things of the world to confound the wise; . . . and the weak things of the world to confound the things which are mighty" (1 Cor. 1:18–28; cf. 3:18–19). Those who understand this mystery are able to declare, "We *are* fools for Christ's sake . . . ; we *are* weak, but ye *are* strong; ye *are* honourable, but we *are* despised" (1 Cor. 4:10; cf.

2 Cor. 1:5). In that sublime state of foolishness and weakness, the Christian, like Christ, makes himself a "servant unto all, that . . . [he] might gain the more" (1 Cor. 9:19; cf. Phil. 2:7). From the perspective of such an outlook, the most profound expression of this remarkable transvaluation is to be found in 2 Corinthians 12:9–10, the *locus classicus* of the Pauline rendering:

> And he [God] said unto me, My grace is sufficient for thee: for my strength is made perfect in weakness [*he-gar dynamis mou en astheneia teleioutai*]. Most gladly therefore will I rather glory in my infirmities, that the power of Christ may rest upon me. Therefore I take pleasure in infirmities, in reproaches, in necessities, in persecutions, in distresses for Christ's sake: for when I am weak, then am I strong.[18]

The act of perfecting strength in weakness is one that fully subverts all previous renderings of strength as a category of value in the biblical text. Here the transvaluation assumes its most radical and compelling form. The extent to which this transvaluation pervaded Milton's own thinking will be seen upon further investigation.

In this regard, 2 Corinthians 12:9–10 represents a case in point. It is a truth universally acknowledged that this text was among Milton's favorites. So taken was he with the reassurance offered by it that he inscribed the text as a kind of self-reflexive motto in the autograph albums of Christopher Arnold in 1651 and John Zollikofer in 1656 (18: 271).[19] To know me, Milton seems to be implying, is to know the full meaning of the Pauline paradox by which strength is perfected in weakness, a perfection that allows the true Christian to glory in his infirmities. Imbued with the power of Christ, the Christian may then declare, "When I am weak then am I strong" (2 Cor. 12:10). The paradoxical notion of perfecting strength by means of weakness is so crucial to Milton's outlook that it appears time and again in his works. As early as *The Reason of Church-Government*, Milton had celebrated the "mighty weakness of the Gospel," which throws down the "weak mightines" of all worldly values (3: 246). The oxymoronic codifications implicit in the distinction between "mighty weakness" and "weak mightines" suggest the extent to which the Pauline transvaluation has permeated Milton's thinking. Drawing upon the full scope of that transvaluation, Milton conflates a number of comparable instances in which it occurs: "For who is there," he asks, "that measures wisdom by simplicity, strength by suffering, dignity by lowlinesse, who is there that counts it first, to be last, something to be nothing, and reckons himself of great command in that he is a servant?" When God determined to subdue the world and hell at once, Milton observes, He might well have "drawn out his Legions into array, and flankt them with his thunder." Instead, God "sent Foolishness to confute Wisdom, Weaknes to bind Strength, Despisednes to vanquish Pride." For Milton, this is the very "mistery of the Gospel made good in Christ himself" (3: 243).[20]

It is this profound sense of mystery in which Milton later took refuge when defending himself against the personal assaults of his enemies in the *Second Defence*. Responding to those who would castigate him not only as a blind man but as a weak, bloodless, shriveled little animal, Milton is at pains to defend his physical appearance as well as his moral stature.[21] Despite his blindness, he says, he possesses that same spirit (*animus*) and strength (*vires*) that he always had. At one time, in fact, he thought himself a match for any man, even one far superior in strength. Armed with his sword, he felt that he was secure from any insult that might be offered him. In his present state of physical blindness, however, he has learned that wisdom which comes with internal sight. Far from being concerned at being classed with the blind, the afflicted, the sorrowful, and the weak, he possesses a renewed hope that because of these very infirmities, he has a nearer claim to the mercy and protection of God (8: 59–73). Recalling the Pauline antecedents, he declares:

> There is a way, and the Apostle is my authority, through weakness [*per imbecillitatem*] to the greatest strength [*ad maximas vires iter*]. May I be one of the weakest, provided only in my weakness that immortal and better vigour be put forth with greater effect; provided only in my darkness the light of the divine countenance does but the more brightly shine: for then I shall at once be the weakest [*infirmissimus*] and most mighty [*validissimus*]; shall be at once blind, and of the most piercing sight [*caecus eodem tempore et per specacissimus*]. Thus, through this infirmity should I be consummated, perfected [*hac possim ego infirmitate consummari, hac perfici*]; thus through this darkness should I be enrobed in light. (8: 72–73)

In this instance, Milton's blindness, as an occasion for opprobrium on the part of his enemies, becomes for him a source of comfort through the validation provided by the New Testament text. The more infirm one is, the more he can take refuge in that sublime Pauline transvaluation by which one's strength is perfected in weakness. Suffused with the light of the divine countenance, Milton has been able to penetrate "the mistery of the Gospel made good in Christ himself." His is a "mighty weakness" able to overcome a "weak mightines." That is the source of his illumination, the foundation of his strength. Of a decidedly spiritual nature, this mighty weakness eschews the worldly, the physical, the strong in favor of the otherworldly, the spiritual, the weak. With the Apostle, it proclaims, "my strength is made perfect in weakness. Most gladly therefore will I rather glory in my infirmities, that the power of Christ may rest upon me." Taking pleasure in sufferings and persecutions for Christ's sake, Milton is able to declare, "when I am weak, then am I strong."[22]

If such an outlook informs Milton's prose works, it is no less apparent in his poems. It is on the basis of the Pauline principle that such poems as *Paradise Lost* and *Paradise Regain'd* are written. At the conclusion of his colloquy with Michael in *Paradise Lost*, for example, Adam demonstrates that despite his earlier spiritual blindness, he has attained new sight. Representing a new spiritual enlightenment, this sight has bestowed upon him the sum of wisdom founded once again upon the profound paradox implicit in the Pauline text. The force of this text is made apparent in Adam's observation that God accomplishes great things by means of small things, subverts strong things by means of things deemed weak, and overcomes worldly wisdom by means of divine meekness (XII.565–69).[23] Implicit in such an idea is a theology of "subversion" (to use Milton's term), one that undermines prevailing worldly values in order to foster an otherworldly perspective. It is for this reason that Michael earlier corrects Adam's impression that when the Messiah and Satan do battle, their combat will be of a physical kind: "Dream not of thir fight, / As of a Duel, or the local wounds / Of head or heel: not therefore joyns the Son / Manhood to God-head, with more strength to foil / Thy enemie; nor so is overcome / *Satan*" (XII.386–91). Rather, he who comes as man's savior performs his feats of strength not by destroying Satan but by destroying Satan's works in man and in man's seed through that obedience which man himself initially failed to fulfill (XII.394–97). As Michael is aware, this willingness to fulfill the law on the part of the Messiah results in that supreme sacrifice by which the Son as savior comes "in the Flesh / To a reproachful life and cursed death, / Proclaiming Life to all who shall believe / In his redemption" (XII.405–408). From the Pauline perspective delineated above, this represents the full import of what Milton calls the "mighty weakness of the Gospel."

For Milton, that "mighty weakness," of course, is most fully manifested in the suffering servant depicted as a *Christus patiens*.[24] Underscoring the theology of *Paradise Lost*, this idea is fundamental to *Paradise Regain'd*. There the Pauline transvaluation receives its fullest expression. Recalling Michael's admonition to Adam in *Paradise Lost*, God, at the outset of *Paradise Regain'd*, proclaims that His Son will undergo combat in the wilderness not by taking up arms but by laying down the rudiments of his warfare, as a result of which "His [the Son's] weakness shall o'recome Satanic strength" (I.157–61). The outcome of this event is the final discomfiture of Satan as the Son remains standing upon the pinnacle of the tower in Book IV. Milton draws upon two allusions to portray this event. The first is that which concerns the battle between Hercules and Antaeus: "As when Earths Son *Antaeus* . . . in *Irassa* strove / With *Joves Alcides*, and oft foil'd still rose, / Receiving from his mother Earth new strength, / Fresh from his fall, and fiercer grapple joyn'd, / Throttl'd at length in th' Air, expir'd and fell; / So after many a foil the Tempter proud, / Renewing fresh assaults, amidst his pride / Fell whence he stood to see his Victor fall" (IV.562–71). In keeping with the Pauline implications explored thus far, the allusion demonstrates the way in which strength is subverted by means of weakness. This act of subversion, however, extends not only to what the allusion implies but to how it works. What it implies is that in overcoming Satan, Jesus is like Hercules, who overcame Antaeus. Hercules, however, overcame Antaeus not through an exercise of divine weakness but through a demonstration of God-given strength. The allusion, then, subverts its own cause: by portraying the way in which God-given strength overcomes earth-given strength, it demonstrates instead the way in which strength is made perfect in weakness, that is, the way in which divine weakness overcomes worldly power.

If this subversive dimension is true of the first allusion, it is no less true of the second. In that allusion, Oedipus is portrayed as answering the riddle of the Sphinx: "And as that *Theban* Monster that propos'd / Her riddle, and him, who solv'd it not, devour'd; / That once found out and solv'd, for grief and spight / Cast her self headlong from th' *Ismenian* steep, / So strook with dread and anguish fell the Fiend" (IV.572–76). In this allusion, the issue is not strength but knowledge. From the Pauline perspective (and, as we have seen, in Milton's understanding of it), the two (strength and knowledge) are nevertheless intimately related: "The foolishness of God is wiser than men; and the weakness of God is stronger than men" (1 Cor. 1:25). As with the first allusion, the subversiveness of the Pauline transvaluation extends not only to what the allusion implies but to how it works. What it implies is that in overcoming Satan, Jesus is like Oedipus, who overcame the Sphinx by solving the riddle. But whereas Oedipus responds in a manner that demonstrates his knowledge of this world and its ways, Jesus responds in a manner that reveals his knowledge of God's ways. If for Oedipus the answer to the riddle of the Sphinx is "man" and all that man represents, for Jesus the answer is "God" and all that God represents. In Pauline terms, Jesus' answer is one that completely confounds everything that worldly wisdom (and therefore worldly strength) implies: "But God hath chosen the foolish things of the world to confound the wise; and God hath chosen the weak things of the world to confound the things which are mighty" (1 Cor. 1:27). Man's ways are not God's ways: embodying the "mighty weakness of the Gospel," as opposed to the "weak mightines" of this world, God's ways are the ways of faith, the ways of foolishness, the ways of weakness.

Once again, we are reminded of Milton's observations in *The Reason of Church-Government*. When God determined to subdue the world and hell at once, He might well have "drawn out his Legions into array, and flankt them with his thunder." Instead, God "sent Foolishness to confute Wisdom, Weaknes to bind Strength, Despised-nes to vanguish Pride." For Milton, this is the very "mistery of the Gospel made good in Christ himself." More than any other poem in Milton's canon, *Paradise Regain'd* is a testament to the force of these observations. As such, Milton's poem is the supreme embodiment of all that is implied by the concept of a *Christus patiens*, which derives its impetus from a theology of strength that completely transvalues or "subverts" accepted formulations. As we have seen, it is precisely these formulations that Milton, in accord with Pauline antecedents, was himself at pains to subvert in his own reponses to his antagonists in the polemical writings. Particularly because of its placement in the 1671 volume, *Samson Agonistes* represents a fitting commentary on the entire Pauline outlook to which *Paradise Regain'd*, among the other writings, is so indebted. In order to understand the import of that commentary, we must turn specifically to the Samson narrative in the Old Testament itself. There we shall discover the principles upon which Milton bases the theology of strength that underlies his closet drama and that, in turn, comments upon the various meanings that strength as a category of value comes to assume in Milton's *corpus* as a whole.

In Judges 13–16, the source of the Samson narrative, the primary word used for strength as a manifestation of God's power is *koach*. While Samson's great strength pervades the entire narrative, the primary focus of its delineation as *koach* is Judges 16, the chapter in which Delilah successfully interrogates the strong man about the source of his strength. It is accordingly to the meaning of the term *koach* that we must attend in order to understand its nature both as a biblical concept in general and with respect to the Samson narrative in particular. As a biblical concept in general, *koach* appears numerous times in the Old Testament.[25] In its various formulations, it suggests the ability to endure (Job 6:12), but more commonly it expresses potency, that is, the capacity to produce. This idea may be expressed in sexual terms (Job 40:16; Gen. 49:3), or it may express the product of the earth's potency (Gen. 4:12; Job 31:39; etc.). As a specifically theological term, *koach* suggests the nature of God's omnipotence. His *koach* is manifested in creation (Jer. 10:12, 32:17), in the events of the Exodus (Ex. 9:16, 15:6), in His capacity to subdue His enemies (Job 36:19) and to deliver His people (Isa. 63:1). Compared with His power, human strength is nothing (2 Chron. 20:6; Job 37:23; Ps. 33:16; Amos 2:14).[26] From a biblical perspective, then, *koach* implies endurance, sexual and generative potency, the capacity to perform miraculous acts, the power to overcome enemies, and thence the ability to deliver from bondage. With its source in God's own omnipotence, it is synonymous with the attribute of *gabhar*, that underscores the biblical notion of power in its various forms.[27] It is precisely such an exalted view of power that comes to be associated with the figure of Samson in the Judges narrative. Samson is not merely a strong man, a charismatic figure possessing inordinate physical strength; he is a "deliverer" (cf. Judg. 13:5), one through whom God's power might become a source of freedom, renewal, even redemption for others.[28] As one upon whom the divine *koach* has been bestowed, Samson is moved by the Spirit of God (cf. Judg. 13:25: *ruach Adonai*) to perform remarkable acts. In this capacity, he defeats God's enemies and manifests God's might in all its forms.

As the Judges account makes clear, Samson's *koach* has another dimension as well. From the very beginning, we are told by the angel who comes to announce his birth that Samson "shall be a Nazarite unto God from the womb" (Judg. 13:5).[29] It is the peculiar fact of Samson's distinction as a Nazarite that causes his *koach* to assume the status of that which is uniquely holy, uniquely set apart, and in fact bound up in some mysterious way with the particular vows of the Nazaritical calling.[30] The betrayal of the secret of this mystery, finally, is the occasion of Samson's undoing: "Then he [Samson] told her [Delilah] all his heart, and said unto her, There hath not come a razor upon mine head; for I *have been* a Nazarite unto God from my mother's womb: if I be shaven, then my strength will go from me, and I shall become weak, and be like any *other* man" (Judg. 16:17). Not in any overt sense an acknowledged part of the legal strictures surrounding the Nazaritical code, this association of *koach* with the Nazaritical vow having to do with the preservation of one's hair appears here in the Judges narrative for the first time.[31] As such, the association represents a remarkable act of mythologizing on the part of the narrator.[32] In its association with Nazaritical injunctions that must be kept a secret, *koach* is at once not only mythologized but sacralized. As such, it causes the Samson narrative to become a vehicle for the reconception of *koach* as a divine category with its own unique significance and its own quite remarkable codes of conduct. These codes, furthermore, are not confined to Samson alone. As suggested by the elaborate injunctions that are placed upon his mother in preparation for his birth, they are as much a part of his generation as they are of his earthly behavior. The sanctity that underscores Samson's *koach*, moreover, is intensified by the theophanic nature of the angelic figure that announces his birth and the fact of the Nazaritical environment into which he will be born. Surrounding this angelic figure, of course, are both the generative sense of a power to impregnate what was formerly barren and the supreme mystery that prohibits a knowledge of the divine secrets (Judg. 13:3–5, 17–20). All this is implicit in the *koach* that infuses Samson as Nazarite.

The fact that Samson ultimately betrays his Nazaritical vows and violates the sanctity of God's power does not compromise the notion of *koach* itself. Despite his transgressions, Samson's *koach* returns even in the reflourishing of his hair (Judg. 16:22). As a testament to this, God, in response to Samson's request for a renewal of his strength, overwhelms the enemy in a final demonstration of *koach* even more devastating than any that had been realized before: "And he [Samson] bowed himself with *all his* might [*b'koach*]; and the house fell upon the lords, and upon all the people that *were* therein. So the dead which he slew at his death were more than *they* which he slew in his life" (Judg. 16:28–30). If Samson himself does not survive this ultimate act, the power of God certainly prevails. In this respect, the Samson narrative becomes a myth of the nature of divine strength, its sources, its qualities, its effects, and the possibility of its ultimate renewal even after it has been violated. As a text for the transmission of this myth, the Samson narrative gives rise to its own unique concept of strength as a distinctly theological category. The figure of Samson himself becomes the vehicle through which this concept is realized.

It is from this perspective that strength as a category of value was understood in the traditions of interpretation, both Judaic and Christian, associated with the Samson narrative from the very beginning. From the Judaic point of view, Josephus represents a case in point.

Commenting upon the Samson narrative in *The Jewish Antiquities*, Josephus consistently emphasizes Samson's strength as a divine attribute through which the Philistines would be afflicted (V.277–78).[33] As a figure whose very coming is announced by an angel from God, Samson is sent to manifest God's strength over the enemy (V.283–84). So important is this concept of divine strength to Josephus that he even derives the etymology of the name "Samson" from the word "strong" or "mighty" (*iskyros*) (V.285).[34] Although this is a mistaken (or at the very least an extremely loose) etymology, it does emphasize the thrust of Josephus' reading. As he notes, Samson errs in divulging the secret of strength to Delilah, or in Josephus' rendering, "Dalala" (V.306–14).[35] Despite Samson's error, Josephus nonetheless praises him "for his valour, his strength, and the grandeur of his end," as well as for the "wrath which he cherished to the last against his enemies" (V.317).[36] In short, it is clearly strength as a category of value that prevails in Josephus' rendering. Above all else, strength as a means of effecting God's divine purpose is what is most important. For Josephus, Samson the *iskyros* ultimately lives up to the full significance of his name.

The emphasis that Josephus places upon Samson's strength is hardly unique to the Judaic tradition. In the Talmudic and Midrashic commentaries, for example, Samson's superhuman strength is constantly stressed. The very dimensions of his body are seen to be gigantic. He is said to have "uprooted two great mountains, and rubbed them against each other." These feats he was able to perform as often as the spirit of God moved in him. Whenever this happened, the outpouring of his strength was manifested in his hair, which began to move and emit a bell-like sound that could be heard from great distances.[37] Suggesting the commonplace association of Samson as *Shimshon* with the sun as *shemesh*, the tractate *Sotah* (10a) of *The Babylonian Talmud* maintains that "Samson was called by the name of the Holy One . . . ; as it is said, *For the Lord God is a sun and a shield* [Ps. 84:12]." As God shields the world, "so Samson shielded Israel during his generation."[38] In this respect, strength is what the *Talmud* refers to as Samson's "distinguishing feature."[39] If such is the case, it is just this feature on account of which Samson incurred punishment, for he was weakened through that person whose very name means "weakness," that is, Delilah.[40] It is because of this inability to overcome weakness that Samson as a bastion of strength must, according to Talmudic and Midrashic traditions, finally be faulted.[41] In both traditions, Samson's great strength is seen as a means of his downfall. His inability to withstand the onslaughts represented by the temptations of Delilah as an emblem of weakness leads to the abuse of his strength, an abuse from which he never fully recovers. Despite such negative appraisals, he still remains a symbol of one whose strength, as long as it remains intact, may be looked upon as a sun and a shield that protected Israel against its enemies. At the forefront of Talmudic and Midrashic commentary, then, is the all-important category of strength as a concept through which one might understand the nature of God's ways embodied in His chosen. As a manifestation of God's own power and protection, Samson is one in whom strength is his "distinguishing feature."

If the foregoing suggests something of the Judaic interpretation of strength as an all-important category in the Samson narrative, the idea is of no less importance to the Christian point of view. In fact, it is of such immense importance that it is canonized as a staple of New Testament teaching. Its canonization, moreover, occurs within that very context provided by the Pauline transvaluation of strength discussed earlier. In this context, however, it assumes a form distinctly its own, as will be seen in an analysis of the Epistle to the Hebrews, the source of New Testament teaching about the meaning of strength as embodied in the figure of Samson. Because of the authority that was ascribed to this epistle as a distinctly Pauline document from the time of the early church onward, its treatment of strength as a category of value is most appropriately considered from the Pauline perspective established above.[42] As indicated, that perspective is one in which the Old Testament concept of strength as *gabhar* (and, by extension, *koach*) undergoes a transvaluation that subverts traditional formulations and replaces them with a new set of values. According to this new set of values, one is to perfect strength in weakness, to glory in infirmities, to take pleasure in sufferings and persecutions. Only under such circumstances may one revel in what St. Paul terms the "foolishness" and "weakness" of God (1 Cor. 1:25). It is from the perspective of this transvaluation, indeed, this subversion, that one is invited to consider the treatment of strength in the Epistle to the Hebrews as a "Pauline" (or pseudo-Pauline) document.

The *locus classicus* for such a consideration, of course, is Hebrews 11, the one New Testament text that addresses itself specifically to the nature of strength as the distinguishing characteristic of the figure of Samson. As is common knowledge, Hebrews 11 alludes to Samson in this manner at the climactic moment of a long and detailed celebration of those Old Testament figures empowered by their faith to work wonders.[43] Having celebrated a number of such figures, the author of Hebrews then turns to those warriors and prophets through whom wonders of all sorts were effected:

And what shall I more say? for the time would fail me to tell of Ged'e-on, and of Ba'rak, and *of* Samson, and *of* Jeph'tha-e; *of* David also, and Samuel, and *of* the prophets: Who through faith subdued kingdoms, wrought righteousness, obtained promises, stopped the mouths of lions, Quenched the violence of fire, escaped the edge of the sword, out of weakness were made strong [*enedynamothesan apo astheneias*], waxed valiant in fight [*egenethesan iskyroi en polemow*], turned to flight the armies of the aliens [*parembolas eklinan allotrion*]. (11:32–34)[44]

Given the Pauline perspective established thus far, the foregoing passage is remarkable, for in effect what it does is reinstate the primacy of the Old Testament understanding of strength within a New Testament context. The Pauline transvaluation of strength as a theological category thus reasserts itself in a manner that concurrently embraces both the sense of divine power as Old Testament imperative and the sense of divine weakness as New Testament imperative. It is in both senses that Hebrews 11 in general, and the above passage in particular, must be understood. From the New Testament outlook established above, Hebrews 11 extols those who willingly endured hardship and suffering as an expression of their faith in God. Their doing so, of course, made them types of Christ, the consummate embodiment of such suffering. In the words of the author of Hebrews, these Old Testament elders chose "rather to suffer affliction with the people of God, than to enjoy the pleasures of sin for a season; Esteeming the reproach of Christ greater riches than the treasures" of this world (Heb. 11:25–26).[45] In this respect, they anticipate the Christian soldier who takes pleasure in infirmities, in reproaches, in necessities, in persecutions, in distresses for Christ's sake. Imbued with the power that Christ would later bestow upon his own heirs, they evinced that faith through which strength is made perfect in weakness. Suffering in effect for Christ's sake, they might then have declared, "when I am weak, then am I strong."

As compelling as such an idea is in Hebrews 11, however, the spiritualization of power in that epistle does not hesitate to accommodate the Old Testament notion of *gabhar* (and its counterpart *koach*). This accommodation is precisely what characterizes the passage having to do with Gideon, Barak, Samson, Jephtha, David, and Samuel cited above (11:32–34). If these figures work wonders through faith, they do so in a manner that is dependent as much upon the Old Testament sense of divine overpoweringness as it is upon the New Testament sense of suffering for Christ's sake. Such is true of each of the figures named: all are heroes and warriors in their own right. The author of

Hebrews associates with them not only the ability to endure but the power to subdue kingdoms, to engage in battle, to overcome enemies. In the phrases adopted by the author of Hebrews to describe their accomplishments ring the triumphs of Israel's military victories. As far as Samson in particular is concerned, one thinks especially of the subduing of kingdoms, the stopping the mouths of lions, waxing valiant in fight, and turning to flight the armies of the aliens. Most of all, however, the phrase *enedynamothesan apo astheneias* suggests the renewed power (*dynamis*) bestowed upon Samson, who rises from utter weakness to new strength and slays more in his death than he had slain in his lifetime (Judg. 16:30).[46] The author of Hebrews thus reinstates the primacy of strength or power as an Old Testament category, while propounding a *kerygma* fully in keeping with the New Testament emphasis upon suffering for Christ's sake. The Samson narrative thereby serves as a bridge to both worlds, that of the Old Testament and that of the New. In both, it is the idea of strength or power and the manifold implications of this idea that are uppermost in the author of Hebrews' allusions to the Samson story.

If such is true of the author of Hebrews, it is no less true of the traditions of Christian exegesis for which the nature of strength in the Samson narrative assumed major importance. As early as St. Augustine's *Sermo de Samsone*, one finds an elaborate allegorical commentary on the significance of strength, as opposed to weakness, in the Samson narrative. As might be expected, the interpretation proceeds along typological grounds. Whereas Samson in his strength signifies Christ the Son of God, in his weakness he prefigures Christ the Son of Man. The strength that resides in Samson's hair, moreover, is a figure of Christ "sustained by the prophecies of the Old Testament; and Samson's hair growing again prophesies the conversion of the Jews."[47] Among the Church Fathers, Samson is customarily associated in his strength with Hercules. "In the latter part of the third century, Eusebius of Caesarea mentioned in his *Chronicorum Canonum* that the life of Samson had been compared by some with the life of Hercules, and in the following century Philastrius [in his *Liber de Haeresibus*] gave it as his opinion that the Greeks had stolen the concept of Samson from the Old Testament and named it Hercules." In fact, throughout the patristic period Samson and Hercules were so frequently compared in both their strength and their exploits that "their association became a stock-feature of nearly all hermeneutic, homiletic or poetic references to Samson." As a result, few writers ever thought of one without invoking the other.[48] In this respect as in others, the exegetical concern with the meaning of strength in its various forms among the Church Fathers and those who followed in their wake extends throughout the Middle Ages and into the Renaissance.[49]

Especially among the Renaissance expositors, it flourished as a subject of discourse in elaborate commentaries on the significance of strength as a distinguishing characteristic of Samson. Approaching this issue in his *Commentarius in Ioshue, Iudicum, et Ruth*, Cornelius a Lapide, for example, provides what amounts to a four fold interpretation of strength as a category of value. In Lapide, strength (particularly as it resides in Samson's hair) is interpreted according to the literal, allegorical, tropological, and anagogical senses of Scripture. "In the literal sense this feature of the story means that the strength of any Nazarite lies in his faithfulness to his vows, of which his unshorn locks are a badge; in the allegorical sense, Samson herein was a figure of Christ, who is our head; in the tropological sense, the hair of Samson denotes the cogitations and intentions of Man, sound thoughts springing from a sound mind; and, finally, in the anagogical sense, the hair signified that Samson's strength was supernatural, a special gift of God, and it kept him mindful that such special endowments were his only so long as he was free from sin."[50] Lapide is only one among a number of Renaissance exegetes for whom strength in its various forms is the basis for understanding the Samson narrative.

Equally important in this regard is the seventeenth-century expositor William Gouge, whose *Commentary on the Whole Epistle to the Hebrewes* is remarkable for the extent to which strength figures in it as a central concern.[51] Invoking the customary association of Samson's name with that of the sun, Gouge then suggests the direction his entire commentary is to take: Samson as the sun was a fit name, he observes, "for by reason of his unparalleld strength, his fame shined thorowout the world. Never was there such a man heard of for strength."[52] Gouge next proceeds to engage in a full anatomy of the meaning of strength in the Samson narrative. Under the general heading "*Of Samsons Excellencies*," he anatomizes strength in the following manner. Samson's special excellencies were two: his great strength and his right use thereof. The greatness of his strength, in turn, was manifested in two ways: by the things he did and by the means and manner of his doing them. Among the things he did, Gouge mentions Samson's tearing of the lion, his slaying multitudes, his carrying away the gates and posts of a city, his breaking of cords, and finally his pulling down at once two strong pillars of a great house and "the roof whereof could bear three thousand people." "For the things which he accomplished," Gouge says, "they were such, as thereby nothing seemed too strong for him: he vanquished, and removed whatsoever stood against him." The means and manner of his accomplishing these things was simple: he accomplished them with his own hands. As Samson's excellency was manifested by the greatness of his strength, it was likewise demonstrated "by the right use thereof," namely, by deploying it singly and at his own hazard against the enemies of God and his Church.

Through this discourse on Samson's "special excellencies," Gouge arrives at the following conclusion about the nature of Samson's divine strength:

> In God is all power: he can derive it to whom he pleaseth, and in as great measure as seemeth good to himself. So as a divine power shall be manifested in human weaknes. A great encouragement this is, against all sorts of enemies, and against all their assaults: especially spirituall. In these doth God most usually, manifest his greatest power.[53]

The conclusion is significant, for what it does is to draw upon the all-important idea delineated in Hebrews 11:34 ("out of weakness were made strong" [*enedynamothesan apo astheneias*]) in order to suggest that Samson as human was the recipient of divine power for the sake of carrying out superhuman feats of strength. At the same time, however, Gouge adds that "great encouragement" fostered by the Pauline concept of the Christian warrior, who, in fending off the assaults of the spiritual enemies, effectively fulfills the paradoxical idea of perfecting strength in weakness (*he-gar dynamis mou en asthemeia teleioutai*). Among those who combat spiritual enemies, Gouge observes, God manifests his "greatest power." In keeping with the message of the author of Hebrews, Gouge's reading of the Samson narrative thereby embraces both notions of strength as a theological category, a fact allows him to glory in the feats of strength that Samson performs as Old Testament figure, and to accommodate both that figure and his great strength to a New Testament reading.

This accommodation is further reinforced by Gouge's discourse on the significance of "Samsons *strength lying in his Hair*," the subject of the next section. Although hair itself, Gouge observes, is not a natural cause of strength, "yet to *Samson*, in particular his hair was a sign, yea, and a means of his extraordinary strength, and that by Gods voluntary appointment." For this reason, "God Sanctified *Samson* from his Mothers wombe to be a *Nazarite*," and in keeping with the law of the Nazarites, "the Lord charged that no Rasor should come upon his head." Among other things, this rite both implied ceremonial purity and was a special sign of the Nazarite's dedication to God. As a reflection of Samson's own inward piety, the allegiance to this Nazaritical vow in particular demonstrated the sacred nature of Samson's strength. In violating this vow, Samson became not only impure but weak: God's spirit departed from him. When he repented, however, the spirit returned, a sign of which was that the hair had already begun to grow again.[54] It is to this event that Gouge addresses himself in the next section, "*Of* Samsons *recovery*." "Though *Samsons* fall were very great," Gouge observes, "yet it is said, *that the hair of his head began to grow again after he was shaven*. Which was a sign of the Spirits return unto him." The return of the spirit, Gouge continues, "was yet further manifested by the extraordinary strength wherewith he was endued. It was no less than before, if not greater. For the last evidence of his strength was the greatest: more was done thereby than all his life before." For Gouge, the final act of Samson was "the greatest, and best. It was the greatest evidence of his faith; and the most profitable to Gods Church."[55]

In Gouge's treatment of the Samson narrative, one fact is especially clear: the narrative itself revolves around the nature of strength as theological category. Coupled with this is a reading that sees in the Samson narrative not only the loss of strength, but its return in a form even more compelling than before its loss. In that return, it manifests itself as an overwhelming expression not only of God's responsiveness to the plight of His deliverers but of His willingness to reinstate those deliverers as the vehicles of His power. It is for this reason that Gouge does not hesitate to see in Samson a typology of the Redeemer, and it is this aspect that he explores at length in the section entitled "*Of Samson being a Type of Christ*." Among the many parallels that Gouge cites between Samson and Christ, what is especially emphasized is Samson's great strength. Christ too for Gouge is a figure of extraordinary strength. Just as Samson in his strength tore the lion and fought the Philistines, Christ "exercised his strength upon the Devill, who is a roaring *Lion*" and rescued God's people from their enemies. Moreover, just as Samson in his strength was victorious at his death, Christ was even more so at his.[56] These and other parallels round out Gouge's portrayal of Samson as strong man. It is a portrayal fully in keeping with the traditions of commentary that focus upon the nature of strength in the Samson narrative as a theological category of unique significance.[57] Although additional examples could be cited, the foregoing should be sufficient to suggest the milieu from which emerged Milton's treatment of the Samson narrative in his prose and in his poetry. In both, the nature of strength as a category of value is of uppermost importance.

As early as *The Reason of Church-Government*, Milton adopted the Samson narrative in order to construct an allegory of the way in which the strength of the king and the commonwealth is liable to be undermined by those prelatical enemies determined to weaken them as a way of furthering their own ends.[58] At the forefront of the allegory is the figure of "that mighty Nazarite *Samson*." Disciplined from his birth in the Nazaritical precepts and practices that would keep him strong, Samson "grows up to a noble strength and perfection with those his illustrious and sunny locks the laws waving and curling about his godlike shoulders." As long as he keeps his locks about him "undiminisht and unshorn," his strength remains intact: "he may with the jaw-bone of an Asse, that is, with the word of his meanest officer suppresse and put to confusion thousands of those that rise against his just power."[59] But the moment he succumbs to the Delilah-like "strumpet flatteries of Prelats," they "wickedly shaving off all those bright and waighty tresses of his laws, and just prerogatives which were his ornament and strength," he is blinded and made to grind in the prison house of his Philistian prelates. Even this situation is not irremediable, however. Recalling the fact that Samson experienced renewed strength with the growth of his hair even after he had fallen, Milton foresees the nourishing again of the "puissant hair" ("the golden beames of Law and Right") of his allegorical Samson, whose locks "sternly shook, thunder with ruin upon the heads of those his evil counsellors," although, Milton concedes, "not without great affliction to himselfe" (3: 276–77).

In his allegorical depiction of the prelatical attempt to undermine king and commonwealth, Milton focuses on both the solar and the Nazaritical dimensions of Samson's strength as manifested in the unshorn hair. From the solar perspective, Milton calls upon the commonplace association of Samson as sun figure (*Shemesh*) whose strength and authority are resplendent in "those bright and waighty tresses of his laws." When he betrays his solar authority and his "sunny locks" are cut, he is left in darkness: "those Philistims put out the fair, and farre-sighted eyes of his natural discerning." The solar perspective, in turn, is reinforced by the Nazaritical. From this perspective, Milton invokes that dimension of the narrative in which strength assumes a cultic bearing. As ceremonially sacred, strength becomes the distinguishing feature of one who as Nazarite is set apart or separated (*nazir*) to God, and thereby crowned with the blessings of God. Drawing upon earlier commentary, Renaissance exegetes characteristically associated the concept of *nazir* (that which is set apart) with the concept of *nezir* (that which is crowned).[60] As Nazarite, Samson is crowned with the strength that resides in his locks. With the violation of his Nazarate, Samson loses this distinguishing regal feature: the "prelatical rasor" berefts him of "his wonted might." From both the solar and the Nazaritical perspectives, however, Samson's strength returns. Newly empowered, he sternly shakes "the golden beames of Law and Right" with devastating results to those who misled him (and, by extension, with unavoidable affliction on himself). The foregoing political allegory demonstrates the extent to which Milton was inclined to draw upon the Samson narrative as an *exemplum* of the nature of divine strength, its unfortunate loss and its eventual triumphant (if devastating) resuscitation. As medium of divine empowerment, strength, in Milton's interpretation of the Samson narrative, assumes a mythological (solar) and a sacred (cultic) bearing, both of which contribute to Milton's delineation of political power and prelatical corruption in *The Reason of Church-Government.*

Milton's antiprelatical tract, however, is not the only example of the use of Samson as a symbol of divine power. The reference in *Areopagitica* has been cited so often as to be almost legion. For our purposes, however, its importance resides in the additional emphasis it places upon renewed strength as in effect restorative in its force. Once again, the figure of Samson is invoked in order to reinforce a political statement. In this case, it is Milton's vision of a resuscitated England imbued with that Reformation fervor that Milton sees stirring in his compatriots who have cast off "the old and wrincl'd skin of corruption" in order to overcome their "pangs and wax young again, entring the glorious waies of Truth and prosperous vertue destin'd to become great and honourable in these latter ages." It is within the context of this sense of rebirth that Milton proclaims:

> Methinks I see in my mind a noble and puissant Nation rousing herself like a strong man after sleep, and shaking her invincible locks: Methinks I see her as an Eagle muing her mighty youth, and kindling her undazl'd eyes at the full midday beam; purging and unscaling her long abused sight at the fountain it self of heav'nly radiance; while the whole noise of timorous and flocking birds, with those also that love the twilight, flutter about, amaz'd at what she means, and in their envious gabble would prognosticat a year of sects and schisms. (3: 344)

From the point of view of the traditions examined thus far, the vision brings into play an entire range of associations that augment and enhance the concept of strength embodied in the figure of Samson. Drawing upon the biblical narrative, the vision alludes most immediately, of course, to Judges 16:13–14, which recounts Samson's awakening out of his sleep still a strong man, despite Delilah's third attempt to bind him by weaving together the seven locks of his head. In the reference to Samson's "shaking" his "invincible locks," however, the vision includes both the subsequent loss of strength after the shaving of his hair (Judg. 16:19–20: "And he awoke out of his sleep, and said, I will go out as at other times before and shake myself. And he wist not that the Lord was departed from him") and its eventual resuscitation (Judg. 16:22: "Howbeit the hair of his head began to grow again after he was shaven"), followed by that final demonstration of remarkable prowess (Judg. 16:30: "And he bowed himself with *all* his might: and the house fell upon the lords, and upon all the people that *were* therein. So the dead which he slew at his death were more than *they* which he slew in his life").[61]

It is this very idea that is anticipated in *The Reason of Church-Government* with the reference to the nourishing again of the "puissant hair" of Samson, whose locks "sternly shook, thunder with ruin upon the heads" of the enemy. What the Samson of *Areopagitica* experiences, however, is the kind of regenerative "shaking" that betokens renewal and resuscitation. In political terms, this occurs "when God shakes a Kingdome with strong and healthfull commotions to a generall reforming" (cf. Hag. 2:6–7; Heb. 12:26–29) (4: 350). Further reinforcing the resuscitative dimension are the references to the serpent-like casting off one's "old and wrincl'd skin of corruption" in order to overcome one's "pangs and wax young again" and the eagle-like "muing" or renewing of one's "mighty youth."[62] This act of renewal is accompanied by a "kindling" of one's "undazl'd eyes at the full midday beam" and a "purging and unscaling" of one's "long abused sight at the fountain it self of heav'nly radiance."[63] Both references take into account the experience of vigor that comes with the renewal of one's strength: overcoming the pangs of torment that accompany corruption, one becomes young again in might; and, purifying sight from the darkness that surrounds it, one is able to see again as he has never seen before. Like a bird of God, he is able to behold the sun, the fountain of celestial radiance. He is, in effect, reborn in the sun. All this is implicit in the return of strength from weakness. From the perspective of the Samson narrative, the idea constitutes, in effect, Milton's reading of Hebrews 11:34: "out of weakness were made strong [*enedynamothesan apo astheneias*]." If the foregoing suggests the way in which strength as a category of value is crucial to Milton's treatment of the Samson narrative in his prose works, the extent to which such an idea underlies his account of

Samson in his closet drama may now receive the attention it warrants. The discussion of Milton's Samson and the theology of strength will appropriately turn, then, to *Samson Agonistes* itself.

As Michael Krouse long ago demonstrated, the idea of power or strength is crucial to the very conception of Milton's rendering of Samson as an *agonistes*. In that capacity, Samson fulfills his role both as one who demonstrates his prowess in athletic combat and as one who undergoes a spiritual trial or who experiences suffering in an arena devised for such a purpose. Undergoing this *agon*, the athlete (*athletes*) is purified and enlightened. He becomes a "champion" (*certator*) for the cause. The term *agonistes* thereby embodies a number of meanings, among them the idea not only of an active physical encounter but of spiritual torment sustained for purgative or educative purposes. The experience as a whole, moreover, is provided with a site, an arena, or a theater (implicit in the term *agon*) in which the drama occurs. Often associated in classical drama with the trials of Hercules, the concept became appropriated by the Christian exegetical traditions to suggest the experience of the *Christus patiens* and the *Christus victor*. In these roles, Christ as *agonistes* or *athletes* was a model for his saints to follow.[64] As already discussed, it is just such an idea that is implicit in the Pauline epistles, especially those that extol the warrior who, "strong in the Lord, and in the power of his might," wrestles against "rulers of the darkness of this world" and "spiritual wickedness in high *places*" (Eph. 6:10–18). Such a wrestling, we recall, is not of the physical sort, "not against flesh and blood." To be strong in the Lord and in the power of His might is to perfect strength in weakness, that is, to undergo a spiritual form of suffering. Important as this form of combat is to the concept of *agonistes*, however, the other form is equally important. It is here that we remember the passage from Hebrews: "out of weakness were made strong [*enedyna-mothesan apo astheneias*], waxed valiant in fight [*egenethesan iskyroi en polemow*], turned to flight the armies of the aliens [*parembolas eklinan allotrion*]" (11:32–34). From the Pauline perspective, *agonistes* implies both strength *in* weakness and strength *out of* weakness. As a drama that takes into account the full range of meanings associated with the concept of strength, *Samson Agonistes* must be understood in precisely these terms, as will be seen upon an analysis of the drama itself.

The drama's paramount concern with strength in all its forms is signaled from the very outset. Samson's first speech, in fact, represents a meditation on the meaning of strength and its significance to one who has abused it. Lamenting both the fact and the outcome of that

abuse, Samson recalls the announcement of his birth and the Nazaritical circumstances surrounding his breeding (23–28). His Nazarate,
reinforced by the angelic announcement "prescribing" it, causes his
"Heav'n-gifted strength" to assume an especially sacral character.
Now fallen, Samson is painfully aware that in violating the conditions
of his Nazarate by divulging the source of his strength, he has not only
betrayed God's trust in him but subjected that which is holy to that
which is profane and common (30–36).[65] As a result, he finds himself
in a state of uncleanness, exacerbated by the fact that as a prisoner of
the profane Philistines, he is put to the labor of a beast in a common
dungeon. As if this were not enough, his debasement is even further
intensified by the Philistines' having set aside that day to hold an
idolatrous solemnity in celebration of Dagon. As Samson himself will
later learn, this is a solemnity in which he himself is called upon to
participate through a demonstration of his strength.

Reflecting the entire drama's concern with the issue of strength,
Samson's first speech embodies not only the foregoing concerns but
others as well. Acknowledging his own responsibility in the debasement of his strength, Samson accordingly asks,

> Whom have I to complain of but my self?
> Who this high gift of strength committed to me,
> In what part lodg'd, how easily bereft me,
> Under the Seal of silence could not keep,
> But weakly to a woman must reveal it,
> O'recome with importunity and tears,
> O impotence of mind, in body strong!
> But what is strength without a double share
> Of wisdom? Vast, unwieldy, burdensom,
> Proudly secure, yet liable to fall
> By weakest suttleties, not made to rule,
> But to subserve where wisdom bears command. (46–57).

This part of the speech brings to the fore what has already been
discussed as the biblical association of strength and wisdom. Because
all power has its root in wisdom, those who are truly strong are truly
wise. At issue once again is the Jobean idea: "With him [God] *is*
wisdom and strength, he hath counsel and understanding," and "With
him *is* strength and wisdom; he hath understanding and insight" (Job
12:13, 16). A blind man now "in power of others," Samson is viewed
as a fool (77–78). The object of reproach and scorn, he stands as an
example of what happens when "impotence of mind" is coupled with a

"body strong." As a result of that unfortunate coupling, strength is overcome by weakness, and the strong is revealed to be the fool he really is. In its portrayal of the return of strength to one in the power of others, Milton's drama correspondingly recounts the experience of gaining wisdom and illumination on the part of one whose foolish actions have resulted in spiritual, as well as physical, blindness.

This, in effect, is the action of the drama, an action fulfilled only through subjecting the *agonistes* to the most strenuous of trials. In the words of *Areopagitica*, "that which purifies us is triall, and triall is by what is contrary" (4:311). Because of his success in sustaining this trial, Samson will be numbered among those who regained their strength and their wisdom too: out of weakness, he was made strong; out of foolishness, he was made wise; out of blindness, he was given sight. Casting off the old and wrinkled skin of corruption, he overcomes his pangs and waxes young again. Shaking his powerful hair, he rouses himself like a strong man after sleep. So renewed, he fulfills his destiny as *certator*, God's "faithful Champion" (1751). Before he is able to assume that role, however, he must experience the *agon* of the *athletes*: he must undergo a trial of his strength in combat with those who would undermine it even further. Only in this manner will he reclaim himself from the ignominy of one who is seen as nothing more than a defeated, blind fool "in power of others." Through a reaffirmation of faith in that Being who is both the source and the bestower of strength, Samson must liberate himself from his subjection, from his state of perceived powerlessness. Imprisoned in the dungeon of himself as well as in the dungeon of his captors, he must overcome his weakness and reassert his power in the teeth of his enemies: *Samson Agonistes* thus embodies a power struggle of the supremest sort.

If Samson's first speech sounds the motif of strength as the dominant theme of the drama, the Chorus of Danites who behold him as he "lies at random" with "languish't head unopropt" (116–18) reinforce the motif still further. Confined within their own perception of what they see in the present as opposed to what they recall from the past, the Chorus serves at this point primarily to deepen Samson's own sense of loss. The speech of the Chorus accordingly emphasizes the change that Samson has suffered as a result of his fall. Lamenting his abject present state, the Chorus invokes the glories of the past: "Can this be hee, / That Heroic, that Renown'd, / Irresistible *Samson*? whom unarm'd / No strength of man, or fiercest wild beast could withstand" (124–27). As bearers of past memories, the Chorus can do no more at this point than recount Samson's earlier exploits. He "tore the Lion, as the Lion tears the Kid, / Ran on embattell'd Armies clad in Iron, /

And weaponless himself, / Made Arms ridiculous" (128–31). All his enemies fled from him as he conquered them with "the Jaw of a dead Ass, his sword of bone" (143). With his remarkable strength he "pull'd up, and on his shoulders bore / The Gates of *Azza*, Post, and massie Bar / Up to the Hill of *Hebron*, seat of Giants old" (146–48). Such exploits rival those of Hercules, and such strength outgoes even that of Atlas, him "the Gentiles feign to bear up Heav'n" (150). Laboring under the burden of the past, the Chorus can only bewail the miseries of the present. For them, Samson becomes a *speculum*, a "mirror of our fickle state": "By how much from the top of wondrous glory, / Strongest of mortal men, / To lowest pitch of abject fortune thou art fall'n," they exclaim (164–69). Calling upon the image of Fortune's wheel, the Chorus associates high estate not with "descent of birth" or other such considerations but with that all-important attribute, strength: to be at the top of Fortune's wheel is to be strong, able to subdue the earth; to be at the bottom of Fortune's wheel is to be weak (170–75). Now at the bottom of Fortune's wheel, Samson is the pawn of mutability. In his reassertion of faith in God and his renewed awareness of the workings of Providence, he will, of course, gain the insight necessary to see beyond the Chorus's limited perception, bound as it is to the past. Even from this narrow perspective, however, Samson is able to benefit, for in moving toward a higher plain of understanding, he is able to reassess the meaning of strength and the uses to which it must profitably be put. The Chorus, in effect, becomes the occasion for the process of renovation, as Samson frees himself from the burden of the past, begins to understand the meaning of the present, and ultimately gains insight into the significance of the future and his role in helping to shape it.[66] In this way, he gains that wisdom which liberates him from the power of others.

If the act of liberation begins with the encounter with the Chorus, it continues with the encounter with Manoa. As the first of three major encounters (involving those with Manoa, with Dalila, and with Harapha, respectively), that with Manoa appropriately focuses attention on the significance of strength and the uses to which it should be put. Like the Chorus of Danites, Manoa begins by lamenting Samson's loss of strength and comparing the glory of the past with the ignominy of the present. Unlike the Chorus, however, Manoa does not attribute Samson's fall to mutability: Samson for Manoa is not simply a mirror of our fickle state. Rather, he is one who placed his trust in his own power, his "mortal strength," rather than in God (348–49). Yet even Manoa calls into doubt "heav'nly disposition" (373) in allowing the recipient of its gifts to suffer such a fate. Samson responds by accepting full responsibility for his acts in weakly betraying God's trust in him and sharing his "capital secret" with his enemy (394). In this assertion of responsibility, Samson lends both credibility and dignity to his present sufferings. At the same time, he places himself in the position of being able, in effect, to prophesy the outcome of his own drama: God, he says, "will arise and his great name assert; / *Dagon* must stoop, and shall e're long receive / Such a discomfit, as shall quite despoil him / Of all these boasted Trophies won on me, / And with confusion blank his Worshippers" (467–71). Although correctly anticipating the end of his drama, Samson is, to be sure, as yet unaware of the extent to which he himself will be the means by which God "will arise and his great name assert." Nonetheless, this step in his renovation is important in demonstrating what even Manoa himself recognizes as God's strength "miraculous yet remaining" in Samson's locks. "His might continues in thee not for naught," Manoa observes; "Nor shall his wondrous gifts be frustrate thus" (586–89).

Where Manoa errs, of course, is in assuming that the full return of strength can be realized without appropriate suffering. Manoa would "redeem," that is, ransom his son as a way of giving Samson an out, as a way, that is, of avoiding an *agon*. Pleading "self-preservation," Manoa would find the easiest way of liberating Samson from the power of others and returning his son to the comforts and safety of his house (516–20). In this manner, Manoa lives up to what his very name implies, that is, "rest" (*m'nuach*), but it is a false (and indeed impossible) rest that he offers: it is indeed the rest of escape. Already confronted by a false sabbath in the holiday festivities to Dagon, Samson is far from compounding this insult to God by endorsing one that is yet more grievous. He will not, he says, "sit idle on the houshold hearth, / A burdenous drone; to visitants a gaze, / Or pitied object, these redundant locks / Robustious to no purpose clustring down, / Vain monument of strength; till length of years / And sedentary numness craze my limbs / To a contemptible old age obscure" (566–72). Rather, as he says near the very outset of his encounter with his father, "let me here, / As I deserve, pay on my punishment; / And expiate, if possible, my crime" (488–90). Although still in the throes of darkest despair and a sense of Heaven's desertion (631–32), Samson even here begins to understand far better than before the meaning of strength, how it is bestowed, how it is lost, and how its loss is to be rectified. His pangs are thus becoming not merely a sign of his suffering (that is, suffering for the sake of suffering) but a means of gaining new wisdom. As *agonistes*, he is beginning to acquire the means of experiencing renewed strength.

If Manoa represents one step in this process, Dalila is equally important in moving the process yet another step forward. Approaching her fallen husband in the guise of seeking forgiveness, Dalila is instantly rebuffed. Samson recognizes immediately that her very presence constitutes a test of his ability to withstand her blandishments. As temptress, she has come, he observes, to "try" his "vertue," that is, his strength, or his "weakness" (754–56). She has come to prove or "assail" him, very much in the fashion of her earlier assaults. The first time she was successful. Samson is determined that she will not be so a second time; that is, he is determined to remain strong. Dalila's assaults are multifaceted, but they all develop further the drama's fundamental concern with the nature of strength and its ability to sustain itself in the face of whatever might challenge it. In this case, that challenge is weakness or the appeal to weakness in its various forms. Recalling the commonplace association of Delilah with "weakness" (*Dildelah*) in the Judaic tradition, Milton's Dalila fulfills her role admirably.

As masterful rhetorician, Dalila accordingly weaves a web of weakness to ensnare her former lover once again. First, she excuses her earlier actions by attributing her overly curious and inquisitive nature, as well as her desire to publish secrets, to all womankind: "It was a weakness / In me," she admits, but this weakness is "incident to all our sex" (774–76). This shirking of responsibility, in turn, is followed by an indictment of Samson's own weakness in not keeping secret what he should have: "Was it not weakness," she accuses, "also to make known / For importunity, that is for naught, / Wherein consisted all thy strength and safety? / To what I did thou shewdst me first the way" (778–81). From an admission of her own weakness, she then accuses all womankind, following this by casting aspersion upon Samson himself. The movement is deft, for she begins by seeming to seek forgiveness, and ends by imputing blame to the very being from whom she sought forgiveness. She thus implicates the aggrieved party in his own sin (in fact, holds him up as the motive force of that sin), with the result that he is placed in the untenable position of admitting culpability in the very act of extending forgiveness. As culpable as the aggrieved party may in fact be, true forgiveness under such circumstances is impossible, nor does the offender genuinely desire it. What she desires rather is to reenact her former coup by placing Samson once again in her power. This she would do by having him acknowledge his weakness at the precise moment of forgiving hers. Weaving a web of weakness, she seeks to entrap Samson in the same snare that was his original undoing, to make him a traitor to himself (401).

"Effeminatly vanquish't," he would be once again shorn like "a tame Weather," that is, emasculated (cf. 537–38, 562).

To effect such an emasculation, she employs a consummate rhetoric of seduction:

> Let weakness then with weakness come to parl
> So near related, or the same of kind,
> Thine to forgive mine; that men may censure thine
> The gentler, if severely thou exact not
> More strength from me, then in thy self was found.
>
> (785–89)

The appeal of her temptation is profound: it allows the offender to attribute a kind of perverse "vertue" (to use Samson's word) to his own weakness. Absolving weakness of guilt (and therefore of the need for forgiveness), it denies the efficacy and legitimacy of strength. "Weakness," it proclaims, "be thou my strength." From this web of weakness, there is only one escape: a categorical refusal to become ensnared in its traps. This is precisely the course that Samson adopts. Refusing to forgive his own past weakness, he refuses to forgive Dalila's:

> I to my self was false e're thou to me;
> Such pardon therefore as I give my folly,
> Take to thy wicked deed: which when thou seest
> Impartial, self-severe, inexorable,
> Thou wilt renounce thy seeking, and much rather
> Confess it feign'd.
>
> (824–29)

This refusal to forgive marks yet another step in Samson's rehabilitation, for it acknowledges a culpability that will not admit of excuse and a severity that will not allow of laxity. With the assertion of his determination to remain steadfast in his denial of all that Dalila represents, Samson liberates himself still further from the power of others. In the case of Dalila, this act of liberation is the result of his ability to withstand the wiles of his adversary: "I know thy trains," he says, "though dearly to my cost, thy ginns, and toyls." These "no more on me have power, their force is null'd" (931–35). In the continuing *agon* of his encounters, he has asserted his power over his enemy, and in the process deprived her of her force. Overcoming the temptation to weakness that is the very source of Dalila's strength, Samson has asserted his own strength. It is, as he says, a strength born of the wisdom of the adder (935). Having suffered the effects of its poison once, he has learned to turn its venom upon all those who might wish to harm him in the future. Such is the nature of Samson's wisdom; such is the nature of his renewed strength.

If this new strength characterizes Samson's response to Dalila as adversary, it is no less germane to his encounter with Harapha. As others have noted, the nature of that encounter is already implicit in the name that Milton chose to bestow upon a character whose roots are biblical but whose presence in the drama is surely an addition to the original narrative. Just as with Manoa and Dalila, to understand Harapha is, in the manner of Samson, to unravel the riddle embodied in Harapha's name.[67] For Harapha brings full circle the assault upon Samson's strength represented by the false rest implicit in "Manoa" and the temptation to weakness implicit in "Dalila." Fully engaged in his *agon*, Samson has been successful in the demonstration of that strength necessary to overcome the trials of Manoa and Dalila. His third, and in some respects most difficult, encounter is now with one whom the Chorus at his very onset announces as "the Giant *Harapha* of *Gath*, his look / Haughty as is his pile high built and proud" (1078–79). If the name "Manoa" implies *rest* and "Dalila" *weakness*, what then of "the Giant *Harapha*"? As is well established, at least part of the answer lies in the Chorus's own ascription, for the name "Harapha" finds its most immediate antecedents in the biblical references to *haraphah*, commonly translated as "the giant" and conceived variously as an epithet or as a proper name.[68] In either case, Milton's use of the term Harapha associates his character with those biblical giants (*rephaim*) to which Harapha proudly traces his own lineage and to which both Samson and the Chorus allude in their various references to "his Giantship" (cf. 1244).[69] As a giant, indeed, as *the* giant par excellence, Harapha embodies in both word and deed that overconfidence in one's own physical powers that is certain to lead to one's demise. It is the specter of his own previous giantism, or "raphaism," to coin a term, that Samson must overcome in order to regain the full force of the strength of which he was bereft as a result of his earlier transgression. In his encounter with Harapha, Samson must come to see that his opponent as a giant is nothing but another form of weakness. Such is only to be expected, considering the other meanings implicit in the name "Harapha." As it is used elsewhere (and often) in the Old Testament, *raphah* involves a wide range of meanings, but especially those associated with the idea of losing heart, abandoning the cause, becoming fearful, enfeebled, and weakened.[70] Implicit in the very notion of "the giant" as a tower of strength and might, then, is the concept of its opposite, weakness and cowardice, a quality that

underscores Harapha's own delineation as *miles gloriosus*. To understand the nature of *haraphah*, accordingly, is to recognize what this
putative tower of strength really is, nothing but a "baffl'd coward," a
"bulk without spirit vast" (1237–38), as Samson calls him at the
conclusion of their encounter. It is the transition from the perception
of Harapha as doughty giant to Harapha as enfeebled coward that
underscores the dialogue between Samson and Harapha throughout.
At the center of that dialogue is the issue of strength in its various
forms.

The perception of Harapha as doughty giant is reinforced from the
very outset not only by the antagonist's references to his "noble"
lineage among the warlike *rephaim* but by the Chorus's own imposing
description of him as he approaches Samson. As described by the
Chorus, he first assumes threatening proportions either as the product
of violent natural events (storm and tempest) or as a towering figure, a
"pile high-built and proud" (1061–69).[71] The description, of course,
resonates with meanings that find their counterparts in Milton's other
works. As the Chorus perceives him, Harapha recalls the dread
commander who occupies the hellish soil of *Paradise Lost*: he above
the rebel crew "In shape and gesture proudly eminent / Stood like a
Towr" (I.589–91). From a topographical perspective, Harapha is
subsumed into the symbolical landscape of *Paradise Regain'd*. Both as
tempest and as tower (IV.407–21, 545–50), he represents aspects of
what the divine *agonistes* must overcome in his own *agon*. As we recall
from our earlier discussion, this event assumes mythological proportions in the allusion to the defeat of another giant, as "*Joves Alcides*"
subdues "Earths Son *Antaeus*" (IV.560–68). In its treatment of the
combat, the allusion, however, is invoked not to extol the ability of the
agonistes to overcome his enemy through an exercise of divine
strength that manifests itself in a physical prowess greater than any
earthly power. Rather, in true Pauline fashion, the allusion demonstrates the way in which the strength of the enemy is subverted by
means of what amounts to a divine weakness. As Harapha comes forth
in tempestuous and towerlike fashion in *Samson Agonistes*, the Pauline distinctions once again come into play, but here in a new form
entirely consistent with the delineation of strength as a category of
value in Milton's drama.

Having traced his lineage to those *rephaim* renowned for their
strength and prowess (1078–80),[72] Harapha makes it clear that he has
come to survey Samson, of whose "prodigious might" and feats of
strength and battle the giant has often heard and is now determined
both to disparage and to challenge. Harapha's discomfiture begins at

the very moment he issues his implied challenge, for Samson responds by repeatedly issuing counter-challenges that reveal Harapha for the coward he really is. What results from this pattern of implied challenge and overt counter-challenge is Samson's own renewed awareness of the meaning of his strength, its origin, its nature, and its function. Samson's first counter-challenge is issued in a form that ironically parodies the Pauline call to arms in Ephesians 6: "Finally, my brethren, be strong in the Lord, and in the power of his might. Put on the whole armour of God, that ye may be able to stand against the wiles of the devil," etc. "Put on all thy gorgeous arms," Samson admonishes Harapha, "thy Helmet / And Brigandine of brass, thy broad Habergeon, / Vant-brass and Greves, and Gauntlet, add thy Spear / A Weavers beam, and seven-times-folded shield" (1116–22). So armed, Harapha, Samson implies, will be not strong but weak in the "power" of his lord, Dagon, and so lose in battle with Samson, who, though not attired in such knightly trim, will with nothing but "an Oak'n staff" dash out his brains (1123–29). In such a manner will Harapha's strength be made perfect in weakness (cf. 2 Cor. 12:9–10) and Samson's strength, by contrast, be made perfect in power.

This reversal of the Pauline *topos* establishes at the outset of Samson's encounter with Harapha precisely the way in which true strength, as distinguished from false or vaunted strength, is to be understood in Milton's drama. If Harapha constantly challenges the nature of true strength, Samson repeatedly clarifies its meaning so that there is no mistaking its dynamics. The strength that Samson has in mind is identical with the Old Testament concepts of *gabhar* and *koach*. It is a dynamic strength as a manifestation of divine force: before it, the earth trembles, the heavens drop, and the mountains quake. Realizing once again the full power of its impact, Samson undergoes that renovation through which God's faithful subdue kingdoms, stop the mouths of lions, out of weakness are made strong, wax valiant in fight, and turn to flight the armies of the aliens. In order to bring that renovation to fruition, Samson must respond as *agonistes* to the barrage of polemic that Harapha launches in order to undermine Samson's faith in his own abilities and in his God.

At the center of this barrage is once again the issue of strength. Harapha begins by claiming that the source of this strength, far from being divine, is the result of false magic: "Spells / And black enchantments, some Magicians Art / Arm'd thee [Samson] or charm'd thee strong," Harapha accuses him (1132–34). This accusation is then followed by a disparagement of Samson's Nazaritical obligation embodied in the covenant surrounding his hair as the seat of his strength

(1134–35). The accusation, along with the disparagement of the Nazarate, provides Samson with the opportunity not only to reaffirm his
faith in God's providence but to expound upon the way in which that
providence is manifested: "I know no Spells, use no forbidden Arts,"
avers Samson; "My trust is in the living God who gave me / At my
Nativity this strength, diffus'd / No less through all my sinews, joint
and bones / Then thine [Harapha's], while I preserv'd these locks
unshorn, / The pledge of my unviolated vow" (1139–42). This reaffirmation demonstrates the extent to which the fallen *agonistes* has
moved beyond his earlier cries concerning what he calls his "sense of
Heav'ns desertion" (632). On the contrary, he not only acknowledges
the indignities he must undergo as inflicted on him "justly," but
maintains that he despairs not of God's "final pardon," for this is a
God "Whose ear is ever open; and his eye / Gracious to re-admit the
suppliant" (1169–73). In its attestation to the primacy of "highest
dispensation" (61), moreover, Samson's reaffirmation likewise reveals
his renewed understanding of, and indeed wisdom concerning, the
nature of the covenant surrounding his Nazarate. No longer is he
inclined to complain (almost in Harapha-like fashion) that "God,
when he gave me strength, to shew withal / How slight the gift was,
hung it in my Hair" (58–59), nor does he view that gift of strength as
his "bane" and the source of all his "miseries" (63–64). Rather, his
response to Harapha represents, as it were, a resanctification of his
Nazarate, as well as a reprofession of his faith in God as the source of
strength and power, a *gabhar* and *koach* bestowed by the Spirit of God
(*ruach Adonai*) upon the elect and disseminated throughout all the
bodily parts.

Moving toward that point of resanctification, Samson challenges
Harapha to pray as a votary before Dagon for the strength to overcome Samson's strength, which he avows to be derived from "the
power of *Israel's* God." Having done so, Harapha may then combat
with him in order to demonstrate "whose God is strongest," Samson's
or Harapha's (1145–55). What will result, then, is a "power struggle,"
as the two champions of power, and therefore the representatives of
the power of their respective deities, will determine in outright battle
which source of power has greater force. If the theomachic implications of this challenge have their foundations in Old Testament concepts of holy war (*milchamot Adonai*),[73] their most immediate biblical
antecedents, of course, can be seen in the overthrow of the statue of
Dagon by the power emanating from the ark of the covenant after the
recently captured ark was installed temporarily by the Philistines in
the temple of Dagon (1 Sam. 5:1–4). Although the ark is in the "power

of others" (to use the language of Milton's *Samson*), it nonetheless retains that dreadful, holy capacity to overwhelm the enemy. In relation to *Samson Agonistes*, such an event looks forward in its own way to the outcome of Milton's drama. The event is pertinent here (in the Samson-Harapha confrontation) as a means of delineating precisely the way in which strength as a theological category is to be understood. Its dynamics are fundamentally those articulated in all that *gabhar* and *koach* represent as Old Testament phenomena with their roots in the most ancient of biblical notions. If those notions strike us as primitive ("whose God is stronger, thine or mine"), they are nonetheless in keeping with the archaic nature of the original Samson narrative, to which Milton's own drama is indebted in its conceptualization of strength as a category of value. Having been defied "thrice to single fight," Harapha departs discomfited, shown to be nothing but a coward (1222–37). In that departure, he fulfills his role both as a giant and as a figure of weakness, the two paradoxical concepts implicit in his name.

As others have noted, however, this is not all that is implied by the name Harapha. Because of at least an apparent association with the verb "to heal" (*rapha'*),[74] Milton's Harapha becomes, in effect, an unwitting physician to Samson's soul, a means, as it were, of purging that soul of the spiritual torments it has been made to undergo. Samson complains of those torments at the very outset of the drama: "My griefs," he cries, "not only pain me / As a lingring disease, / But finding no redress, ferment and rage, / Nor less then wounds immedicable / Rankle, and fester, and gangren, / To black mortification (617–22). Turning inward upon themselves, his thoughts, as harpy-like tormenters "arm'd with deadly stings," mangle his "apprehensive tenderest parts," "exasperate, exulcerate, and raise / Dire inflammation," which, Samson says, "no cooling herb / Or medcinal liquor can asswage" (623–27). What Samson seeks is some means of purging his griefs, purifying himself of the disease brought upon him by the throes of his own despair, the torments of his own guilt, and the "sense of Heav'ns desertion" (632). It is, of course, precisely this homeopathic process of catharsis that the drama of Samson's own reclamation entails.[75] In the encounter of like with like (to draw upon the sense of the Preface to the drama), Samson is made to undergo a "lustration" that finally cleanses him.[76] Each of the characters that Samson encounters furthers this process in one way or another. As *rapha*, Harapha the "healer" unwittingly helps to advance this process to its utmost point. Samson's constant challenges to engage Harapha in single combat demonstrate the extent to which the giant provides the occasion for the *certator's* assertion both of his own strength and of his trust in the deity who bestowed that strength upon him. By challenging (and finally overcoming) Harapha, Samson overcomes that giant within himself: he overcomes his own overweening pride ("bulk without spirit vast") and the temptation to doubt the efficacy of God's providence ("My trust is in the living God"). As a result of his encounter with Harapha, Samson emerges as one who has been even further cleansed in. the continuing process of his reclamation.

In recognition of that process, the Chorus itself is made to celebrate, in an impassioned song, the return of Samson's strength.[77] Their song encapsulates both the action and the alternatives that the *certator* must face in the implementation of the action. What is significant in this celebratory song of victory is that the Chorus's earlier perception of Samson as defeated warrior (115–75) is here reversed. Once again, power has returned to the deliverer, and those who were oppressed now enjoy a renewed source of hope: "Oh how comely it is and how reviving / To the Spirits of just men long opprest! / When God into the hands of thir deliverer / Puts invincible might / To quell the mighty of the Earth," the violent oppressor who supports tyrannic power (1268–76). At issue is the all-pervasive concept of power as it is manifested in the strength ("invincible might") bestowed upon the *certator* able to overcome the oppressor's power: in this *agon* between power and power, it is finally divine power that triumphs over the mighty of the earth.

The question, however, is precisely how this triumph will be effected. It is here that the Chorus raises the two alternatives that they feel their *certator* must face: either by engaging in that direct combat through which the champion defeats his enemy "With plain Heroic magnitude of mind / And celestial vigour arm'd" or by enduring the assaults of the enemy through an exercise of patience characteristic of saints and the trial of fortitude characteristic of the true deliverer (1278–92). Both alternatives, of course, are implicit in the concept of *agonistes* as that which characterizes the athlete, on the one hand, and the sufferer, on the other. "Either of these," comments the Chorus, "is in thy lot, / *Samson*, with might endu'd / Above the Sons of Men," although because of his blindness, Samson, the Chorus suggests, will probably be numbered among those "Whom Patience finally must crown" (1292–96).

What the Chorus fails to realize, of course, is that Samson will ultimately fulfill both roles as an expression of his strength: in him are embodied both the active and the passive implications of the concept of *agonistes*. As one who has endured the assaults of the enemy through an exercise of patience characteristic of saints and the trial of fortitude characteristic of the true deliverer, Samson has, in fact, already fulfilled in large part the passive (in the sense of *patiens*) implications of the concept of *agonistes*. As such, he is the true Pauline warrior, one who has put on the whole armor of God in order to stand against the whiles of the devil. Doing so, he has perfected strength in weakness (*he-gar dynamis mou en astheneia teleioutai*). Like the Milton of the *Second Defence*, he too may assert that there is a way through weakness to the greatest strength. "May I be one of the weakest," he is empowered to proclaim, "provided only in my weakness that immortal and better vigour be put forth with greater effect; provided only in my darkness the light of the divine countenance does but the more brightly shine: for then I shall at once be the weakest and most mighty; shall be at once blind, and of the most piercing sight. Thus, through this infirmity should I be consummated, perfected; thus through this darkness should I be enrobed in light." But Samson is destined to do more than suffer: he is destined to act. Feeling the "Consecrated gift / Of strength again returning with . . . [this] hair" (1354–55), he will fulfill the Chorus's hope for a deliverer who defeats the enemy in combat. In the language of *The Reason of Church-Government*, Samson, with his "puissant hair," will sternly shake "thunder with ruin" upon the heads of the enemy. Such an act will be supremely in accord with the Pauline idea, depicted in Hebrews 11, that Samson as warrior reemerges from a state of weakness to a state of profound strength (*enedynamothesan apo astheneias*), and in the process slays more in his death than he had slain in his lifetime (cf. Judg. 16:30).

This is an event that the Chorus, even here, anticipates through a language of apocalyptic fervor:

> He all thir Ammunition
> And feats of War defeats
> With plain Heroic magnitude of mind
> And celestial vigour arm'd,
> Thir Armories and Magazins contemns,
> Renders them useless, while
> With winged expedition
> Swift as the lightning glance he executes
> His errand on the wicked, who surpris'd
> Lose thir defence, distracted and amaz'd.

(1277–86)

The passage recalls another event in which an emissary of God, in fact the very Son of God in *Paradise Lost*, armed with celestial vigor, overwhelms the enemy and renders all their ammunition and feats of war useless. Going forth in the "Chariot of Paternal Deitie," the Son, we recall, guides the many-eyed "four fold-visag'd Four," whose own devastating glance flashes lightning and shoots forth pernicious fire among the accursed. As a result of that fearsome event, the enemy is left drained of their vigor, "Exhausted, spiritless, afflicted, fall'n" (VI.710–852). In its own way, the Chorus's prognostication in Milton's drama recapitulates that pivotal event in Milton's epic. Doing so, this prognostication sets the stage for what amounts to the final battle of the *agonistes*, which involves the ultimate demonstration of strength, a demonstration that results in the thunderous overthrow of the Philistines in their own arena of combat.

In its portrayal of Samson's renovation, an event concurrent with and signaled by the progressive return of his divinely bestowed strength, the entire drama has moved inexorably toward this point. It is a point of supreme crisis for Samson. Commanded to entertain his captors through a "show" of strength in a theatrical arena devised for this purpose, Samson would be made to join that line of sword-players, gymnasts, wrestlers, riders, runners, jugglers, dancers, antics, mummers, and mimics assembled to participate in the debased solemnities for Dagon (1323–25). As such, the great *agonistes* would be transformed into nothing but an *actor scenicus*, and his *agon* both as condition and as site would assume the form of profane "theater."[78] Once again, at issue is the nature of divine strength and the uses to which it is to be put. It is an issue with which Samson struggles mightily before appearing to accede to the command. "Shall I," he asks, "abuse this Consecrated gift / Of strength, again returning with my hair / After my great transgression, so requite / Favour renew'd [?]" (1354–57). Acknowledging the return of strength as a manifestation of divine favor and, along with this acknowledgment, emphasizing the consecrated nature of that gift, Samson reinforces the association of strength with his Nazarate by refusing to prostitute "holy things to Idols." As a Nazarite, he will not vaunt his strength in an abominable place to honor foreign gods. "Besides, how vile, contemptible, ridiculous, / What act," he asks, could be "more execrably unclean, profane?" (1358–64). The passage is crucial not only in reflecting Samson's renewed awareness of God's presence but in bestowing upon God's gifts—and notably that supremest gift of strength—the sense of sacrality that was originally undermined in Samson's first catastrophic transgression. It is not a transgression that Samson, as one who is now able to reaffirm his Nazarate, is willing to repeat. That he does reach the point of being willing once again to risk all suggests the extent to which Milton conceives of his final act as one that undermines all expectations of what is appropriate for a Nazarite to do and what is not.

The remainder of the drama is not Samson's: it is God's. Samson is merely the vehicle through which the *peripeteia* may occur. But he is a divine vehicle nevertheless. "Be of good courage," he counsels the Chorus: "I begin to feel / Some rouzing motions in me which dispose / To something extraordinary my thoughts" (1381–83). These "rouzing motions" are the very signal by which Samson, now as renovated *agonistes*, is seen to move to the point of being able to manifest God's strength over His enemies in a final act of triumphant devastation.[79] "If there be aught of presage in the mind," Samson avers, "This day will be remarkable in my life / By some great act, or of my days the last" (1387–89). The fact that it is indeed Samson's last day in no way lessens either the impact or the importance of the act itself. It is the act that matters, and Samson becomes the means of performing it. Nor, as he knows, will he dishonor Hebraic law or stain his Nazaritical vow (1385–86; 1424–26), for this act is one that transcends all law and the restrictions of all vows: it is a divine act, a sacred act, a law unto itself.

It is in these terms that one must understand the final, momentous scene, as related by the Messenger, in *Samson Agonistes*. This is a scene that embodies distinctly apocalyptic overtones.[80] In fact, the Messenger enters with the cry of one who has been witness to an apocalypse: "O whither shall I run, or which way flie / The sight of this so horrid spectacle" (1541–42). The cry invokes the entire context of Revelation 6:12–17: in that "horrid spectacle," the seer witnesses the falling of the stars from heaven as if shaken by a mighty wind and the moving of every mountain and island out of its place, as a result of which the peoples of the earth "hid themselves in the dens and in the rocks of the mountains; and said to the mountains and rocks, Fall on us, and hide us from the face of him that sitteth on the throne," for "the great day of his wrath is come, and who shall be able to stand?" In the enactment of that apocalypse in *Samson Agonistes*, the place of festivity becomes "the place of horrour" (1550).

The Messenger's account of what he witnessed is precisely an account of this transformation. Drawn as an outsider to the festival for Dagon, the Messenger ("an Ebrew")[81] relates how Samson is "brought forth" in the theater "to shew the people / Proof of his mighty strength in feats and games." Patiently obeying their behests, the *agonistes* first performs as an actor before them, heaving, pulling, drawing, breaking, "All with incredible, stupendous force, / None daring to appear Antagonist" (1596–1628). This activity, however, is nothing more than an ironic prelude to the true (but of course unanticipated) devastation that follows: the carnivallike (and therefore demeaning) quality of the "show" that Samson puts on is undertaken not for its own sake but finally as a supreme distraction, one that allows God, through his champion, to catch the enemy completely off guard and therefore to intensify the effect of the final act itself.[82] In the process, Samson, who has patiently allowed himself to be imposed upon as *ludio* and *actor scenicus*, may now reassert himself as true *certator*.

As the Messenger relates it, this is the supreme moment of the drama:

> As with the force of winds and waters pent,
> When Mountains tremble, those two massie Pillars
> With horrible convulsion too and fro,
> He tugg'd, he shook, till down they came and drew
> The whole roof after them, with burst of thunder
> Upon the heads of all who sate beneath.   (1647–52)

What is significant about the description is the way in which it associates the act with the forces of nature that transcend any conception of mere "humanness" as a distinct category. Rather than a carnivallike (and therefore ludic) show of physical strength, Samson's final and unexpected demonstration of his divine power is an act that marshals all the terrifying and superhuman qualities (trembling of the earth, dropping of the heavens, quaking of the mountains) characteristic of *gabhar*, on the one hand, and of *koach*, on the other, and applies them to this particular manifestation of the *dynamis* in all its archaic "overpoweringness," to invoke Rudolf Otto's term once again. Samson is the vehicle through which that overpoweringness is realized. The carnivallike nature of the *agon* as theater of sport and play is transformed suddenly and unexpectedly into the apocalyptic-like nature of *agon* as theater of horror and devastation. In his renewed capacity as *agonistes*, Samson becomes the means by which this *agonistic* transformation is made to occur. Through him, all the depersonalized power of angered deity comes to the fore and destroys those whose idolatrous behavior has in its effrontery slighted the divine source of that power. In this respect, the Messenger's final observation on what he has witnessed and escaped to tell about underscores the brutal irony of the event: "The vulgar only scap'd who stood without" (1559). Such devastation, this observation suggests, is finally reserved for those who truly merit it: the Philistines in their worship of Dagon. So the

Semichorus comments in its response to the Messenger's account. "Drunk with Idolatry" and "chaunting thir Idol," the Philistines are urged on with the mad desire "to call in hast for thir destroyer" and to importune their own destruction "to come speedy upon them." This death wish, says the Semichorus, is fulfilled by that "living Dread who dwells / In *Silo* his bright Sanctuary" (1669–81). The reference to "living Dread" is significant, for it depersonalizes deity as the source of power, just as Samson as the vehicle of power is himself depersonalized in that final catastrophic moment. What matters is the force, the *dynamis* itself, in its most primitive, most archaic form. *Samson Agonistes* resolves itself into a drama about the way in which that force ultimately finds release.

Finally in possession of all that is necessary to manifest this *dynamis*, Samson is celebrated by the Semichorus as a kind of holocaustal embodiment of the divine spirit (*ruach*) that has now been revived to its utmost intensity. No longer the blind, despised being he was when the drama began, Samson assumes "suprapersonal" status. He is that very sun, that very *shemesh* resplendent in his name: showing forth God's power both as *gabhar* and as *koach*, he flames at high noon in visionary splendor (cf. 1612).[83] Amid the "blaze of noon," he is no longer in darkness, no longer in eclipse (cf. 80–81); rather, he is enveloped by, and in effect the product of, light, not as that which illuminates but as that which devastates. The "fierie vertue" of his strength roused "from under ashes into sudden flame," he descends upon his prey like a winged serpent or dragon emitting fire or like an eagle, the bird of God, as it bolts its thunder on the heads of the enemy. Finally, he is likened by the Semichorus to that "self-begott'n bird," the Phoenix, which in holocaustal splendor is reborn from its own ashes, as it "Revives, reflourishes, then vigorous most / When most unactive deem'd" (1685–1705).[84] Despite Samson's own death, the conclusion of Milton's drama represents a triumphant attestation to all that the concept of divine strength is capable of signifying as theological category.

It is the realization of this idea that first Manoa and then the Chorus celebrate in their final speeches. This is "no time for lamentation," avers Manoa, for "*Samson* hath quit himself / Like *Samson*, and heroicly hath finish'd / A life Heroic," by fully revenging himself on his enemies (1708–11). It is the fulfillment of his role as avenger that distinguishes Samson in his father's eyes. He continues to be a deliverer, "and which is best and happiest yet," continues so, "with God not parted from him, as was feard / But favouring and assisting to the end" (1718–21). Moving from this perspective to the larger one that addresses itself to the nature of God's providence, the Chorus concludes with the final statement of consolation:

> All is best, though we oft doubt,
> What th' unsearchable dispose
> Of highest wisdom brings about,
> And ever best found in the close.
> Oft he seems to hide his face,
> But unexpectedly returns
> And to his faithful Champion hath in place
> Bore witness gloriously; whence *Gaza* mourns
> And all that band them to resist
> His uncontroulable intent;
> His servant he with new acquist
> Of true experience from this great event
> With peace and consolation hath dismist,
> And calm of mind all passion spent.   (1745–58)

The wisdom of the Chorus's speech provides an appropriate closure to the foregoing discussion.[85] In its reassertion of faith in "th' unsearchable dispose / Of highest wisdom," the Chorus would have us too participate in this moment of extreme assent. Such participation involves a willingness to endorse the full implications of that sudden, unexpected, and finally devastating moment when the "faithful Champion" is newly empowered to show forth his strength in an act that defies all resistance. In the reempowerment of the *certator*, one discovers the "uncountroulable intent" of a Being whose ways may be hidden but whose acts make themselves felt with an overwhelming finality. To experience those acts, indeed to survive them, leaves its witnesses with a renewed understanding of what Samson himself came to understand during the course of his *agon*. Such understanding may be dearly bought, but its effects are ultimately restorative. As "faithful Champion," Samson becomes the means by which God's servants may be "dismist" with peace and consolation, on the one hand, and that calm of mind which comes with the full "spending" of passion, on the other.

Afterword

As the foregoing chapters have attempted to indicate, Milton's preoc-
cupation with form and convention is of major importance to his
conduct as a writer and thinker. Form and convention pervade his
treatment of such enterprises as pedagogy, metaphysics, polemics,
theology, and poetics, and assume a unique bearing in both the prose
and the poetry. That bearing is one in which bodily form, on the one
hand, and generic form, on the other, are at the forefront of Milton's
thought. In his incorporation of the body as metaphor, Milton is able
to suggest the nature of his pedagogical, metaphysical, polemical, and
theological outlook. A concern with the body—its disposition, its
attributes, its attire, and its conduct—provides Milton with an unparalleled opportunity to discourse upon the relationships between things
physical and things spiritual, appearance and reality, external and
internal, corruption and purity, and immanence and transcendence,
among other issues of importance to Milton's point of view. Corresponding to this concern with bodily form is a profound interest in
generic form. Here the uncompromising sense of commitment to all
that Milton values most in the cultivation of bodily forms finds its
counterpart in what amounts to a reformulation of genre, in which,
Milton makes it clear that genre too has its disposition, its attributes,
its attire, and its conduct. In these and other respects, generic form as
Miltonic phenomenon undergoes a transformation that undermines
conventional expectations and gives rise to meanings all its own.
Whether as pastoral, as epic, or as drama, genre in Milton assumes a
new form, one in keeping with a sensibility at once committed to the
primacy of form and convention in all areas of endeavor, but at the
same time entirely radicalized to accord with an outlook that is
fundamentally nonconformist. It is this radicalized, nonconformist
outlook, finally, that provides the impetus for Milton's treatment of
form and convention throughout his works.

In keeping with a passage cited earlier, it might be appropriate to
conclude by recalling once again Milton's rendering of "discipline" in
The Reason of Church-Government:

> And certainly discipline is not only the removall of disorder, but
> if any visible shape can be given to divine things, the very visible
> shape and image of vertue, whereby she is not only seene in the
> regular gestures and motions of her heavenly paces as she walkes,
> but also makes the harmony of her voice audible to mortall
> eares. (3: 185)

From the vantage point of the foregoing study, this passage takes on
new meaning. In its concern with various aspects of form and convention in Milton's works, this study has essentially addressed itself to the
two dimensions of discipline envisioned above: that of the visible
shape and image of discipline, as she is beheld in the gestures and
motions of her heavenly paces, and that of the grand and harmonious
sound of discipline as she is heard in the modulations of her celestial
voice. Discipline for Milton embodies both aspects. As a transcendent
being, she accommodates herself to us not only in shape and image but
in sound. Those chapters that have explored the bodily implications of
form and convention as pedagogical, metaphysical, polemical, and
theological enterprises have concerned themselves with the shape and
image of discipline, as she is seen in the regular gestures and motions
of her heavenly paces. Those chapters that have explored the generic
implications of form and convention as poetic enterprises have concerned themselves with the sound of discipline, that is, with her song,
as she makes the harmony of her voice audible to mortal ears. Apt as
such a metaphor might be for what the foregoing study has attempted
to accomplish, it should not be forgotten, however, that discipline as
Milton conceives it in *The Reason of Church-Government* is only part
of the story. Equally significant is that immense and dynamic, even
strenuous, sense of effort that goes into the creation of so harmonious
a figure. Here is where the image of truth enters in. If truth, as Milton
reminds us in *Areopagitica*, was "a perfect shape most glorious to look
on" when she first came into the world, the body of this virgin was
subsequently "hewd" into a thousand pieces and scattered to the four
winds. In keeping with the friends of truth, Milton as teacher, thinker,
theologian, and writer is put to the difficult and laborious task of
attempting to "re-form" truth in preparation for the second coming of
her Master, who "shall bring together every joynt and member, and
shall mould them into an immortall feature of loveliness and perfection." Until that time, Milton advocates a "reforming of Reformation
it self" (4: 337–38, 340). As the foregoing study has argued throughout, such a "re-formation" is not an easy task. In fact, as we recall
from the allusion that culminates *Of Education* (4: 291), it will require

the very sinews that Homer gave Ulysses in order to bring that event about. In his deployment of form and convention throughout his writings, Milton goes far toward fulfilling the calling of one who has indeed been endowed with the sinews of Ulysses.

Notes

NOTES TO CHAPTER ONE

1. *The Works of John Milton*, ed. Frank Allen Patterson (New York: Columbia University Press, 1931–38), 4:291. All references (by volume and page) to Milton's prose are to this edition. References to his poetry are to *The Complete Poetry of John Milton*, ed. John T. Shawcross, 2nd ed. (Garden City, New York: Doubleday, 1971). Biblical references are to the Authorized Version.

2. See, among many examples, Sir Thomas Elyot's *The Boke Named the Gouernour* (1531), ed. Henry Herbert Stephen Croft (1883; New York: Burt Franklin, 1967) 1:60: "By the example of Ulisses," Homer "apprehended many noble vertues," especially wisdom.

3. The allusion's source is the *Posthomerica* of Quintus of Smyrna (4th century B.C.). See the *Complete Prose Works of John Milton*, gen. ed. Don M. Wolfe (New Haven: Yale University Press, 1953–82) 4:595 n. 205. Compare Homer's own account of Ulysses' wrestling match with Ajax in *The Iliad* (XXIII.690–743). Ulysses' physical prowess is replaced by rhetorical cunning in the vocal combat between Ulysses and Ajax in Ovid's *Metamorphoses* (XIII.1–398).

4. See Milton's statement in *The Reason of Church-Government*: "It were happy for the Commonwealth, if our Magistrates, as in those famous governments of old, would take into their care . . . the managing of our publick sports . . . such as may inure and harden our bodies by martial exercise to all warlike skil and performance, and may civilize, adorn and make discreet our minds by the learned and affable meeting of frequent Academies, and the procurement of wise and artfull recitations . . ." (3:239–40). For Milton's interest in exercise and gymnastics in general, see his entry "Gymnastica" in the Commonplace Book (23:205–6).

5. "The Life of John Milton," in *The Early Lives of Milton*, ed. Helen Darbishire (New York: Barnes and Noble, 1932) 32.

6. Dennis Brailsford, *Sport and Society, Elizabeth to Anne* (London: Routledge and Kegan Paul, 1969) 97.

7. In *The Complete Poetry of John Donne*, ed. John T. Shawcross (Garden City, New York: Doubleday, 1967).

8. Brailsford 95. Although physical education does find a place in Comenius (see, for example, *The School of Infancy*), it is not central to his scheme. Such reformers as John Dury, William Petty, and Samuel Hartlib, in turn, place little, if any, emphasis upon exercise as an important activity (Brailsford 92–94).

9. Brailsford 41–43, 140, 141, and passim. According to Brailsford, "school statutes and records show virtually no evidence of active provision and guidance for the physical training of their sixteenth-century pupils," although some historians would lead us to believe otherwise (41). The universities, in turn, made little or no official provision for exercise. "Oxford and Cambridge both forbade football in the latter part of the sixteenth century, and even swimming was barred to all members of the University by the Cambridge Vice-chancellor in 1571 on account of its danger." Despite these restrictions, however, sports (such as football) were engaged in (43).

10. *The Dialogues of Plato*, trans. B. Jowett, 2 vols. (New York: Random House, 1937) 2:551, 568. Future references (by volume and page number) are to this edition. See also Galen's *De Sanitate Tuenda* (1538), which is "the fullest text on physical education available in any language and the valuable basis for an English literature on the subject" (Brailsford 15).

11. Plato 2:668

12. *The Politics of Aristotle*, trans. B. Jowett (New York: Random House, 1943)

322-26. Despite his apparent endorsement of gymnastics, Aristotle is critical of "the evil of excessive training in early years" and of the idea that study and exercise complement one another: "the labour of the body impedes the mind, and the labour of the mind the body."

13. E. Norman Gardiner, *Athletics of the Ancient World* (Oxford: Clarendon Press, 1930) 72. "The Greek boy's physical education extended over twelve years or more." The most important part of that education was wrestling, as indicated in the name *Palaestra*. The counterpart of gymnastics was music (90-92).

14. See, for example, Girolamo Mercuriale's *Artis Gymnasticae* (1569) and Pertrus Faber's *Agnosticon* (1592).

15. Baldassare Castiglione, *Libro del Cortegiano*, trans. Thomas Hoby, 1561, *Three Renaissance Classics*, ed. Burton A. Milligan (New York: Charles Scribner's Sons, 1953) 278-82.

16. Elyot 1:169-72. See also 188-96, 290-306. See also Elyot's *The Castell of Helth* (London, 1548) passim.

17. Roger Ascham, *The Scholmaster*, ed. Laurence V. Ryan (Ithaca: Cornell University Press, 1967) 52-53. For additional works in the same tradition, see Gervase Markham's *The Gentlemans Academie* (1593) James Cleland's *The Instruction of a Young Noble Man* (1607), and Henry Peacham's *The Complete Gentleman* (1622), which devotes an entire chapter to the "Exercise of the Body" (ed. Virgil B. Hetzel, Folger Documents of Tudor and Stuart Civilization [New York: Cornell University Press, 1962] 135-43).

18. Richard Mulcaster, *Positions Wherein Those Primitive Circumstances Be Examined, Which are Necessarie for the Training vp of children, either for skill in their booke, or health in their bodie* (1581) 22, 51-52. Mulcaster devotes nearly half his treatise to exercise (chapters 6 through 34 and passim).

19. The idea has antecedents in Plato's statement in the *Republic* that exercise, like music, is designed to improve the soul and "stimulate the spiritual element" in man (*Dialogues* 1:674). The views runs counter to Aristotle's attitude, discussed above (n. 12).

20. John Locke, *Some Thoughts concerning Education*, 4th ed. (London, 1699) 1.

21. For the evolution of the terms *exercitatio*, *gymnasium*, and *palaestra*, see *A Latin Dictionary*, comp. by Charlton T. Lewis and Charles Short (Oxford: Clarendon Press, 1975), s.v. According to *The New College Latin and English Dictionary*, comp. by John C. Traupman (New York: Bantam, 1966), *prolusio* carries with it the meanings "sparring, shadow-boxing." *Palaestra* was used metaphorically by the Romans to signify "rhetorical academic oratory" and "elegance of composition." Rhetoricians, in turn, assembled in the gymnasium or palaestra to practice their art. (Ironically, *palaestra* can also mean "brothel.")

22. Cicero, *De Oratore*, ed. Karl Wilhelm Piderit, 3 vols. (Amsterdam: Verlag Adolf M. Hakkert, 1965) 1:112-13.

23. Donald Leman Clark, *Rhetoric in Greco-Roman Education* (New York: Columbia University Press, 1957) 61 and 177.

24. George Kennedy, *The Art of Rhetoric in the Roman World* (Princeton: Princeton University Press, 1972) 92-93.

25. In the *Second Defence*, for example, Milton depicts himself as a warrior laying low the adversary Salmasius, whom Milton "engaged . . . in single combat": with the "stylus" as a weapon he stabbed his enemy and "bore off abundant spoils" 8:13-15).

26. The Columbia edition has "wayfaring" (4:311), but I prefer the reading of the Yale *Complete Prose Works of John Milton*, 2:515, which has "warfaring" (see n. 102 there).

27. The scholarship on this subject is immense. See my chapter on warfare in *Poetics of the Holy: A Reading of "Paradise Lost"* (Chapel Hill: University of North Carolina Press, 1981).

28. See Nemean I (33-50), *The Odes of Pindar*, trans. Sir John Sandys, The Loeb

Classical Library (Cambridge: Harvard University Press, 1978). In this ode, Tiresias predicts the battle between Hercules and Antaeus as one of the many battles Hercules must wage (60–72).

NOTES TO CHAPTER TWO

1. Prolusion VI ("Against the Scholastic Philosophy"), in particular, recounts Milton's extreme distaste for metaphysics, but similar attitudes are discernible throughout the prolusions. In such poems as *De Idea Platonica* and *At a Vacation Exercise*, the subject is handled with a good deal of jocularity.

2. For an account of Milton's thorough exposure to metaphysics, see, among other works, Harris Francis Fletcher's *The Intellectual Development of John Miton*, 2 vols. (Urbana: University of Illinois Press, 1961) 2:182–90. According to Kathryn A. McEuen's notes to the Prolusions in the *Complete Prose Works of John Milton*, 2:262, Milton's performance in matters of metaphysics "is not to be underestimated. Much as Milton may have disliked the duty he was called upon to perform, he proved himself a competent disputant in good medieval fashion." In his prolusions, he "shows a grasp of the problems involved and uses the scholastic terms accurately."

3. He interrupts his fourth Prolusion, for example, to complain: "I am not sure whether I am boring you; certainly I am very boring to myself" 12:185).

4. In Prolusion IV, for instance, Milton argues that we cannot separate a property from its subject (12:181), and that quantity must not be confused with form nor quality with matter (12:185).

5. We should not, of course, be surprised to discover metaphysical principles implicit in a work of logic. Metaphysics and logic were traditionally viewed as complementary disciplines. In M. Jacobus Martinus's commonly used text *Metaphysicae Disputationes* (Wittenberg, 1606), we find the statement that metaphysics and logic have "*maximam affinitatem*": indeed, they are "*eadem scientia*" (First "*Disputatio*," sig. A2r). Actually, the conception of metaphysics may be traced back to Aristotle's use of the term *theologia* in the *Metaphysics* (Fletcher 182–83). For Francis Bacon, metaphysics (which he terms *magia*) is the study of ultimate being, but especially of form (*Novum Organum*, *The Works of Francis Bacon*, ed. James Spedding et al. [London: Longman and Co., 1857] 1:235). Compare Henry More's statement in *Enchiridion Metaphysicum* (London, 1671) 1.: "*Metaphysica est Ars recte contemplandi res Incorporeas.*"

6. Cf. *Tetrachordon* 4:101. For a full exposition of the idea that form is the cause "*per quam res est id quod est,*" see George Downame's *Commentarii in P. Rami Regii Professoris Dialecticam* (Frankfort, 1601). By way of explanation, Downame says: "*id est, quae dat proprium esse rei, ut forma hominis est, per quam homo est homo, et non aliud aliquid*" (146). For an account of Downame's relationship to Milton, see Thomas S. K. Scott-Craig, "The Craftsmanship and Theological Significance of Milton's *Art of Logic*," *Huntington Library Quarterly* (hereinafter referred to as *HLQ*) 17 (1953) 1–16.

7. In his *Logic*, Milton states: "Hence the cause in the true sense of the word is also called *principium* by Cicero (*De natura deorum* I), and more frequently among the Greeks" 11:31).

8. Thus Downame: "*Forma est quae dat esse rei*" (146). See Martinus (sig. D1v).

9. See John Wyclif, "*De Materia et Forma*," *Miscellania Philosophica*, ed. Michael Dziewicki (London: Trübner and Co., 1902) 1:163.

10. See Aristotle's discussion of the relationship between "thing" and "essence" and "form" and "matter" in his *Metaphysics*, ed. and trans. John Warrington (London: J. M. Dent and Sons, 1956) 178–80, 184–86. All future references cited parenthetically by page number are to this edition. Greek interpolations are from *Aristotle: The Metaphysics*, ed. T. E. Page, 2 vols. (Cambridge: Harvard University Press, 1933).

11. Fundamental to scholastic philosophy, the Aristotelian view finds expression in writers as diverse as Averroes, Avicenna, and St. Thomas Aquinas. In his *Commentary upon the Metaphysics of Aristotle* (trans. John P. Rowan, 2 vols. [Chicago: Henry Regnery Co., 1961] 2:533; 1:308), St. Thomas, for example, associates form with essence, and in his *On Being and Essence* (trans. Armand Maurer [Toronto: The Pontifical Institute of Medieval Studies, 1949] 27–28), he states that form as essence "signifies the determination of each thing." When St. Thomas associates form with essence, however, he refers to *forma totius* rather than *forma partis*, a distinction common to medieval writers. *Forma totius* implies the "whole essence" (including both form and matter), not just "part of the essence" (*forma partis*) uniting with matter to make up the complete essence (28, n. 7). Apparently it is not a distinction Aristotle makes, although St. Thomas claims to have found it in Aristotle. See Armand Maurer, "Form and Essence in the Philosophy of St. Thomas," *Mediaeval Studies*, 13 (1951) 165–76. "Form of the whole" and "form of the part" correspond to the scholastic classification of substantial and accidental forms.

12. Bacon, *Works* 2:121, 137. For a sobering account of Bacon's philosophical attitudes, see Virgil Whitaker, "Bacon's Doctrine of Forms: A Study of Seventeenth-Century Eclecticism," *HLQ* 33 (1970) 209–16.

13. In his *Commentary on the Metaphysics of Aristole* 2:864–65, St. Thomas accepts both Plato's theory of "the separate Forms" as "things which exist by nature" and Aristotle's theory of inherent forms as "things which comprise a particular composite substance." In Milton's own time, Downame (143–44) suggests that we are indeed able to reconcile the Platonic "*per quam*" with the Aristotelian "*esse quod quid est.*"

14. According to R.G. Collingwood, *The Idea of Nature* (New York: Oxford University Press, 1970) 64–65, the problem ultimately resolves itself. From the Platonic perspective, "when you try to state [the theory of forms] in terms of immanence you are implying transcendence, and when you try to state it in terms of transcendence you are implying immanence." That is, "Plato recognized the two elements to be logically interdependent."

15. For a lucid explanation of the whole matter, see Richard Kroner, *Speculation in Pre-Christian Philosophy* (Philadelphia: The Westminster Press, 1956) 164–65, 194–95. See also Irene Samuel, *Plato and Milton* (New York: Cornell University Press, 1947) 134.

16. Kroner 194–95. See also William B. Hunter, Jr., "Milton's Power of Matter," *Journal of the History of Ideas* (hereinafter referred to as *JHI*) 13 (1952) 552–54.

17. Greek interpolations are from *Plato: The Works*, ed. T. E. Page, 10 vols. (London: William Heinemann, 1926).

18. *JHI* 13:558–59.

19. According to Hunter, "the alteration from potency to form or actuality" in Aristotelian terms "is change or movement, which thus may exist in anything constituted of matter." Furthermore, in contrast with Plato, for whom "prime matter may exist in isolation from the realm of ideas," Aristotle maintains that "prime matter (or pure potency) has in fact never existed; it is not an existent substance, but only a logical distinction, for matter is always experienced in this world in some kind of actualization" (*JHI* 13:552–53).

20. Kroner 194.

21. Cf. Downame 152: "*Rerum igitur naturalium formae, quia internae sunt, et a sensibus remotae, latent plerumquenos, intelligentiamque in artificiosis rebus formae facilius occurrunt, quod earum scilicet formae externae sunt, ac sensibus ipsis expositae.*" See also Martinus, sig. E3v-r.

22. Thus Downame (154) suggests that while the external form pertains to the fashion and shape of things, internal form pertains to that which transcends outward appearance.

23. John Elof Boodin, "The Discovery of Form," *JHI* 4 (1943) 177.

24. St. Augustine, *The City of God*, trans. Gerald G. Walsh, S.J., et al. (Garden City,

New York: Doubleday and Co., 1958) 264–65. Latin interpolations are from *The City of God*, ed. T. E. Page (Cambridge: Harvard University Press, 1966).

25. In the *Patrologiae Cursus Completus* (Series Latina), ed. J.-P. Migne (Paris, 1861) 40:29–30.

26. Each of these attributes becomes important to Milton's depiction of divine form. In the case of discipline as a female with harmonious movements and gestures, we are reminded of "divinest Melancholy" in *II Penseroso*. With regard to the "quaterniond" formation of angelic order, we recall the shape of the angelic union in *Paradise Lost* (VI.62–63). The measuring of paradise, of course, recalls not only Milton's Heaven (*P.L.* II.1047–50) but Revelation 21:16–17.

27. Significantly, in *Christian Doctrine* the distinctions we are drawing between the ability to perceive form and the ability to act in accordance with it become the basis of Milton's methodology. Thus, Milton states that "Christian doctrine is comprehended under two divisions: *faith, or the knowledge [cognitio] of God; and Love, or the worship [cultus] of God*" (14:23). "These two divisions," Milton declares, "though they are distinct in their own nature, and put asunder for the convenience of teaching, cannot be separated in practice" (14:23).

28. "The essences of things and processes are therefore not merely logical genera or ontological existents. They are also 'ethical' entities" (Kroner 165).

29. In *Paradise Lost* those metaphysics give expression to the commonplace notion of the *scala naturae* or unilinear gradation by which "everything has an indwelling impulse towards the development of its own specific form, as is seen most clearly in the organic process of seed to plant or embryo to adult" (W. K. C. Guthrie, *A History of Greek Philosophy*, 2 vols. [Cambridge: Cambridge University Press, 1962] 1:12). According to Arthur O. Lovejoy, who treats the idea in depth, it was Aristotle who "chiefly suggested to naturalists and philosophers of later times the idea of arranging (at least) all animals in a single graded *scala naturae* according to their degree of perfection" (*The Great Chain of Being* [New York: Harper Brothers, 1960] 58).

30. Walter Clyde Curry, *Milton's Ontology, Cosmogony and Physics* (Lexington: University of Kentucky Press, 1957) 162.

31. See William B. Hunter, Jr., "Milton's Materialistic Life Principle," *Journal of English and German Philology* (hereinafter referred to as *JEGP*) 45 (1946) 68–76. The importance of that principle as an expression of Milton's monism, mortalism, traducianism, cosmology, and views of godhead has already been the subject of much illuminating analysis. Among other studies, see those mentioned by Hunter, as well as his article "Some Problems in John Milton's Theological Vocabulary," *Harvard Theological Review* 57 (1964) 353–65; Denis Saurat, *Milton, Man and Thinker* (London: J. M. Dent and Sons, 1944); George Williamson, "Milton and the Mortalist Heresey," *Studies in Philology* (hereinafter referred to as *SP*) 32 (1935) 553–79. The import of these studies should be seen within the context established by the present study.

NOTES TO CHAPTER THREE

1. Don A. Martindale, *The Nature and Types of Sociological Theory* (Cambridge: Harvard University Press, 1960), 78.

2. Martindale 79.

3. Edward Forsett, "To the Reader," *A Comparative Discourse*, reprinted in *Two Tracts* (Farnsborough, Hants.: Gregg International Publishers, 1969) 1; hereafter cited in the text as *Comparative Discourse*.

4. Michael Walzer, *The Revolution of the Saints: A Study in the Origins of Radical Politics* (Cambridge: Harvard University Press, 1965) 156.

5. Cited in Walzer 156–57.

6. Richard Hooker, *The Works*, ed. John Keble (New York: Appleton, 1845) 2:247; hereafter cited in the text by volume and page number.

7. See also Rom. 12:4–5; 1 Cor. 10:16–18, 11:3, 15:44; Eph. 1:22–23, 4:15–16, 5:23, 30, 32; Col. 1:18, 2:9, 10, 11, 19.

8. Ernst H. Kantorowicz, *The King's Two Bodies* (Princeton: Princeton University Press, 1957) 195–96.

9. Kantorowicz 199–200.

10. Malcolm Ross, *Poetry and Dogma: The Transfiguration of Eucharistic Symbols in Seventeenth Century English Poetry* (New Brunswick: Rutgers University Press, 1954) 189.

11. Darwell Stone, *A History of the Doctrine of the Holy Eucharist* (London: Longmans, Green, 1909) 1:94.

12. *The Rationale of Ceremonial*, ed. Cyril S. Cobb, Alcuin Club Collections 23 (London: Longmans, Green, 1910) 41–42.

13. Donald J. McGinn, *The Admonition Controversy* (New Brunswick: Rutgers University Press, 1949) 9.

14. McGinn 15–16.

15. John Wyclif, *The English Works*, ed. F. D. Matthew, Early English Text Society 74 (London: Trübner and Co., 1880) 471.

16. Cited by Hooker, *Laws*, *Works* 1:351.

17. In *English Puritanism from John Hooper to John Milton*, ed. Everett Emerson (Durham: Duke University Press, 1968) 265.

18. Cited by McGinn 256.

19. See Ernest Sirluck, introduction, *Complete Prose Works of John Milton* 2:69.

20. See Milton's Ramistic formulations in *The Art of Logic* 11:55–63, as well as a discussion of this idea in the previous chapter.

21. In Milton's *Complete Prose Works* 1:992.

22. Don M. Wolfe, ed., introduction, *Complete Prose Works* 1:129.

23. Lawrence Stone, *Sculpture in Britain* (Baltimore: The Johns Hopkins University Press, 1955) 2.

24. John Donne, *Sermons*, ed., George Potter and Evelyn Simpson (Berkeley: University of California Press, 1953–62) 10:221–22; hereafter cited in the text by volume and page number.

25. *Jonathan Swift: Selected Prose and Poetry*, ed. Edward Rosenheim, Jr. (New York: Holt, Rinehart, and Winston, 1959) 99.

26. Otto Friedrich von Gierke, *Natural Law and the Theory of Society*, trans. Ernest Barker (Cambridge: Cambridge University Press, 1934) 51–52.

27. Kantorowicz 208.

28. Kantorowicz 216, 223.

29. Cf. Walzer 171–72.

30. Quoted by Charles and Katherine George, *The Protestant Mind of the English Reformation, 1570–1640* (Princeton: Princeton University Press, 1961) 194.

31. For the Anglican point of view, see John Taylor's satiric tract *The Causes of the Diseases and Distempers of this Kingdom; found by feeling of her Pulse, Viewing her Urine, and Casting her Water* (1645).

32. "The Life of Martius Coriolanus," *Shakespeare's Plutarch*, ed. T. J. B. Spencer (Baltimore: The Johns Hopkins University Press, 1964) 303.

33. E. K. Chambers, Appendix B, *The Tragedy of Coriolanus* (Boston: D. C. Health, 1910) 195. According to Chambers, the fable is over three thousand years old.

34. In his edition of *Areopagitica*, in *The Prose of John Milton*, ed. J. Max Patrick (Garden City, New York: Doubleday and Co., 1967) 317 n. 326.

NOTES TO CHAPTER FOUR

1. William B. Hunter, Tr., "Milton on the Incarnation: Some More Heresies," JHI 21 (1969) 367. See, however, Hunter's more recent article, "Milton on the Exaltation of the Son: The War in Heaven in *Paradise Lost*," *English Literary History* (hereinafter referred to as *ELH*) 36 (1969) 219–29. This important article demonstrates the necessity of understanding the prefigurative nature of the Son's role, a point I shall stress later.

2. Vincent Taylor, *The Person of Christ in New Testament Teaching* (London: Macmillan, 1963) 279, 276.

3. Friedrich Loofs, "Kenosis," *Encyclopaedia of Religion and Ethics*, ed. James Hastings (New York: Charles Scribner's Sons, 1914) 7:680–87. For a discussion of the later Christologies, see *Cyclopaedia of Biblical, Theological, and Ecclesiastical Knowledge*, ed. J. M. M'Clintock and James Strong (New York: Harper, 1951) 5:46.

4. Clarence Augustine Beckwith, *"Kenosis," The New Schaff-Herzoq Encyclopedia of Religious Literature*, ed. Samuel M. Jackson (New York and London: Funk Wagnalls, 1919) 6:315.

5. J. M. Creed, "Recent Tendencies in English Christology," *Mysterium Christi*, ed. G. K. A. Belland and D. Adolf Deissruann (London: Longmans, Green, 1939) 133. I am indebted to Ralph P. Martin, "Kenosis," *The New Bible Dictionary*, ed. J. D. Douglas (Grand Rapids: Eerdmans, 1962) 689, for this reference.

6. Barbara Lewalski, *Milton's Brief Epic: The Genre, Meaning, and Art of Paradise Regained* (Providence: Brown University Press, 1966) 156–58. For additional discussion of kenosis in Milton, see, among other sources, the entry under that heading in *A Milton Encyclopedia*, gen. ed. William B. Hunter, 9 vols. (Lewisburg: Bucknell University Press, 1978–83) 4:181–82.

7. Lewalski 156–58.

8. In this regard, see also Maurice Kelley, *This Great Argument: A Study of Milton's De Doctrina Christiana as a Gloss upon Paradise Lost* (Princeton: Princeton University Press, 1941) 156, 159.

9. Lewalski 393 n. 69.

10. Hunter, "Milton on the Incarnation," 367.

11. Walter Lock, *"Kenosis," A Dictionary of the Bible*, ed. James Hastings (New York: Charles Scribner's Sons, 1899–1904) 2:835.

12. Mother Mary Christopher Pecheux, "'O Foul Descent!': Satan and the Serpent Form," *Studies in Philology* (hereinafter referred to as *SP*) 62 (1965) 193. According to Mother Mary Christopher 193 n. 9), "Milton may have been using a Latin text or making his own translations from the Greek. . . ."

13. Cited by Beckwith, 315.

14. Beckwith 315. See also Lewalski 159.

15. Alfred E. Garvie, *"Kenosis," Dictionary of Christ and the Gospels*, ed. James Hastings (New York: Charles Scribner's Sons, 1908) 927.

16. See, for example, Lock, 835; *The Interpreter's Dictionary of the Bible*, gen. ed. George Arthur Buttrick (New York: Abingdon Press, 1962) 3:7; *The New Scofield Reference Bible*, ed. C. I. Scofield (New York: Oxford University Press, 1967) glosses Phil. 2:7: "Lit. 'emptied himself,' i.e. divested himself of his visible glory."

17. Gregory of Nazianzen, *Oration* XXXVII.3, *A Select Library of Nicene and Post-Nicene Fathers of the Christian Church*, 2nd ser. ed. Philip Schaff and Henry Wace (New York: Christian Literature Co., 1894) 7:338–39. The association of "strips" and "exinanition" is so common that according to Charlton T. Lewis and Charles Short (*A Latin Dictionary* [Oxford: Oxford University Press, 1897]), the Vulgate uses *exinanivit* in the tropological sense of "laid aside his glory" (Phil. 2:7).

18. Hilary of Poitiers, *Homily on Psalm LIII*, *A Select Library*, 2nd ser. 9:245.

19. Cited by E. H. Gifford in *The Incarnation* (London: Longmans, Green, 1911) 78–79.

20. J. B. Lightfoot, *Saint Paul's Epistle to the Philippians* (London: Macmillan, 1894) 127–31.

21. *A Select Library*, 2nd ser., 9:159. See the *Patrologia Latina*, ed. J.-P. Migne (Paris, 1845) 10. Hilary makes similar statements in Book IX, chapter 38.

22. In his introduction to Hilary's works, William Sanday (lxxii) notes that Hilary's constant approach is one of describing the evacuation as a "change of apparel."

23. Cited by Donald G. Dawe in *The Form of a Servant* (Philadelphia: Westminster Press, 1963) 55, 59.

24. Dawe 30.

25. Dawe 21–22. See also Charles Gore, *Dissertations on Subjects Connected with the Incarnation* (New York: Charles Scribnes's Sons, 1895) 174–75.

26. Gore 175. "In an extreme form," says Gore, "this idea came to be known as Nihilianism."

27. Gore 176.

28. John Calvin, *Institutes*, ed. John T. McNeill (Philadelphia: Westminster Press, 1960) 20:474, 476.

29. Cited by Gifford 60.

30. *The New Bible Dictionary*, 689. See Martin's *An Early Christian Confession* (London: Tyndale Press, 1960) for further etymological distinctions.

31. Lightfoot 127–31.

32. Lightfoot 127–31. The supposed liturgical form of Phil. 2:6–11 does not negate its philosophical overtones.

33. Gifford 18.

34. In *The Poet's Life of Christ*, ed. Norman Ault (Oxford: Oxford University Press, 1927).

35. C. A. Patrides, *Milton and the Christian Tradition*, (Oxford: Oxford University Press, 1966) 133–34. According to Patrides, Augustine, Gregory the Great, and others held similar views.

36. Pecheux, "'O Foul Descent!" 188–96.

37. Cited in Pecheux, "'O, Foul Descent!'" 192.

38. John T. Shawcross "The Balanced Structure of *Paradise Lost*," *SP* 57 (1965) 698–99. This essay has been revised and incorporated into Shawcross's *With Mortal Voice: The Creation of Paradise Lost* (Lexington: The University of Kentucky Press, 1982).

39. Christ's stooping to enter the tabernacle is parodied by the debased soul's stooping to "migrate to the beasts" (compare Luke 8:27–33). Indeed, the parody becomes even more ironic if we consider Milton's treatment of the pagan deities in the *Nativity* ode. There "brutish gods" (211) such as Isis, Horus, Anubis, Osiris, and Typhon incarnate themselves in bestial forms that are also tabernacles. (Osiris, for example, is not only enshrined but incarnated in the bull Apis.) According to Hunter ("*Milton on the Incarnation*" 354–55), these and the other deities, enshrined in their "Temples dim" (198), stand in direct contrast to the incarnate Christ, enshrined in "a darksom House of mortal Clay" (14; compare *P.R.* IV:598–99; 1 Cor. 3:16, 17; 16:19; John 1:14). (Hunter suggests [355, 357] that the importance of the contrast resides in the action: the divinities forsake their temples as the result of Christ's having entered his.)

40. For a full treatment of this idea, see my book, *The Dialectics of Creation: Patterns of Birth and Regeneration in Paradise Lost* (Amherst: University of Massachusetts Press, 1970).

41. Albert S. Cook, "Notes on Milton's *Ode on the Morning of Christ's Nativity*," *Transactions of the Connecticut Academy of Arts and Sciences* (New Haven: Yale University Press, 1909) 15:320

42. William Riley Parker, *Milton: A Biography* (Oxford: Oxford University Press, 1968) 1:67. Parker suggests that "perhaps a psychological disturbance has inhibited [Milton's] art."

43. Milton associates Phil. 2 and John 13 also in *The Reason of Church-Government* 3:244.

44. For a full discussion of the iconographical and theological bearing of this concept, see Albert C. Labriola, "The Aesthetics of Self-Diminution: Christian Iconography and *Paradise Lost*," *"Eyes Fast Fixt": Current Perspective in Milton Methodology*, ed. Albert C. Labriola and Michael Lieb (Pittsburgh: University of Pittsburgh Press, 1975) 267–311 (vol. 8 in the *Milton Studies* series.) See also Labriola's important study "'Thy Humiliation Shall Exalt': The Christology of *Paradise Lost*," *Milton Studies*, vol. 15 ed. James D. Simmonds (Pittsburgh: University of Pittsburgh Press, 1981) 29–42.

NOTES TO CHAPTER FIVE

1. James Holly Hanford, "The Pastoral Elegy and Milton's *Lycidas*," *Publications of the Modern Language Association of America* (hereinafter referred to as *PMLA*) 25 (1910) 403–47. Hanford's essay has been often reprinted. It reappeared as part of his volume *John Milton: Poet and Humanist* (Cleveland: Western Reserve, 1966) 126–60. My references are to the version in *Milton's "Lycidas": The Tradition and the Poem*, ed. C. A. Patrides (New York: Holt, Rinehart, and Winston, 1961). This volume has since appeared in a revised edition (Columbia: University of Missouri Press, 1983).

2. *Variorum Commentary on the Poems of John Milton*, gen. ed. Merritt Y. Hughes, 4 vols. to date (New York: Columbia University Press, 1970–).

3. *The Poetical Works of John Milton, with Notes of Various Authors*, ed. H. J. Todd, 6 vols., 3rd ed. (London: R. Gilbert, 1826) 5:13–14. The edition was first published in six vomumes by J. Johnson, London, 1801.

4. The commentary editors of *Lycidas* in the *Variorum*, vol. 2, past 2 (1972) 639, are A. S. P. Woodhouse and Douglas Bush.

5. See poem no. 248, "On the death of the late county [sic] of Pembroke," in *Tottel's Miscellany* (1557–87), ed. Hyder E. Rollins, 2 vols. (Cambridge: Harvard University Press, 1928) 1:192. According to Rollins (2:302), the Lady is Anne Parr, sister of one of Henry VIII's wives. "The opening lines of this elegy," says Rollins, "remind one of the words with which Milton begins his lament for Lycidas."

6. *Variorum* 2:639.

7. Samuel Taylor Coleridge, in *The Romantics on Milton*, ed. Joseph Anthony Wittreich, Jr. (Cleveland and London: Case Western reserve, 1970) 256.

8. Wittreich 256.

9. The quote is from the opening of the proem to the first book of *The Faerie Queene*.

10. *Variorum* 2:639.

11. *Variorum* 2:639.

12. This and the following elegies are conveniently anthologized in *The Pastoral Elegy*, ed. Thomas Perrin Hamilton, Jr., and trans. Harry Joshua Leon (Austin: The University of Texas, 1939) 25–29, 37–40.

13. Watson Kirkconnell, *Awake the Courteous Echo: The Themes and Prosody of Comus, Lycidas, and Paradise Regained in World Literature* (Toronto and Buffalo: University of Toronto Press, 1973) 170 n. 105.

14. *The Pastoral Elegy*, 121–27, 134–45.

15. *The Pastoral Elegy* 34–36, 127–33, 174–80.

16. *The Pastoral Elegy* 233–49.

17. For a discussion of the structure of the epicedium, see Julius Caesar Scaliger, *The Poetics*, in *Milton's "Lycidas," Edited to Serve as an Introduction to Criticism*, by Scott Elledge (New York and London: Harper and Row, 1966) 109–10. See also George Norlin, "The Conventions of the Pastoral Elegy," *American Journal of Philology* (hereinafter referred to as *AJP*) 32 (1911) 294–312, and Thomas Rosenmeyer, *The Green Cabinet: Theocritus and the European Pastoral Lyric* (Berkeley and Los Angeles: University of California Press, 1969) 94–95, 118–19.

18. David S. Berkeley, *Inwrought with Figures Dim: A Reading of Milton's "Lyci-*

das" (The Hague: Mouton, 1974) 33–34. For Wittreich, see his "'A Poet Amongst Poets': Milton and the Tradition of Prophecy," *Milton and the Line of Vision*, ed. Joseph A. Wittreich, Jr. (Madison: University of Wisconsin Press, 1975), 117–23; and his *Visionary Poetics: Milton's Tradition and His Legacy* (San Marino, Cal.: Henry E. Huntington Library, 1979), esp. 138–41. More recently, see also the important work of Edward Tayler, *Milton's Poetry: Its Development in Time* (Pittsburgh: Duquesne University Press, 1980) 45–59. In its gloss of "Yet once more," the *Variorum* does little with the biblical dimensions of the phrase (2:639).

19. Berkeley 25–26. The expression "smite no more" has no specific scriptural antecedent. It represents a collocation of several passages (1 Sam. 26:8; Matt. 26:31; Mark 14:27; and Rev. 19:15).

20. Basically concerned with the Old Testament, "formula" critics derive many of their insights from the work of Parry, Lord, Bowra, and Magoun, among others. For the most important formula critics, see Stanley Gevirtz, *Patterns in the Early Poetry of Israel* (Chicago: University of Chicago Press, 1963); William Whallon, *Formula, Character, and Context: Studies in Homeric, Old English, and Old Testament Poetry* (Washington, D.C.: The Center for Hellenistic Studies, 1969); Robert C. Culley, *Oral Formulaic Language in the Biblical Psalms* (Toronto: University of Toronto Press, 1967); and William Watters, *Formula Criticism and the Poetry of the Old Testament* (Berlin and New York: Walter de Gruyter, 1967).

21. These works may be had in translation. See the *Theological Dictionary of the Old Testament*, ed. G. Johannes Botterweck and Helmer Ringgren, trans. John T. Willis, 5 vols. to date (Grand Rapids, Mich.: William B. Eerdmans, 1974), and the *Theological Dictionary of the New Testament*, ed. Gerhard Kittel and trans. Geoffrey W. Bromiley, 10 vols. (Grand Rapids, Mich.: William B. Eerdmans, 1964).

22. The statement is taken from Wilson's subtitle to A *Christian Dictionary*, 3d ed. (London, 1622). This is Thomas Wilson the exegete, not Thomas Wilson the rhetorician. For his discussion of "once more" and "no more," see sigs. Ooo5v, Fff44, Kkkg', and L116v.

23. For Salomon Glass (1593–1656), I am using the 1705 edition of *Philologia sacra, qua totius SS. Veteris et Novi Testamenti scripturae* (Leipzig, 1705); for Jacques Gousset or Jacobo Gussetio (1635–1704), I am using the 1702 edition of *Commentarii Linguae Ebraicae* (Amsterdam, 1702). In Glass's *Philologia sacra*, see, in particular, the discourse on *"non amplius"* and *"semel"* as repeated formulas, 966–72. Glass ties in all the motifs associated with "once more" and "no more" that I am dealing with here. In Gousset's *Commentarii*, see the discourses on *"yasaf," "a'od,"* and *"m'at,"* 331–32, 475–77, and 588–89. For comparable thesauri, see the *Christiani Noldii Concordantiae Particvlarum Ebraeo-Chaldaicarum* (Jena, 1734), sigs. Yyy4^r, B4v–B6r, Ttt3r, of Christian Nold (1626–1683); John Buxtorf, *Lexicon Hebraicum et Chaldaicum* (London, 1646) 301–2, 501–3, 506; [Alexander Rowley], *Sodalis Discipulis* (London, 1648) 48, 136; William Robertson, *Thesaurus Linguae Sanctae* (London, 1680) 323–24; and John Udall, *The Key of the Holy Tongue* (Leyden, 1593) 66, 99.

24. Culley 12.

25. See, in particular, Watters, *Formula Criticism*, which reviews and calls into question some of the basic assumptions of formula criticism. His discussion of the allied disciplines (Homeric, Old English, and so on) is also interesting.

26. Watters 74.

27. Whallon, 204–10. Whallon examines this phenomenon with particular reference to the language of Jesus.

28. For examples of the *"a'od m'at"* formula, see, among other texts, Job 24:24; Ps. 37:10; Isa. 10:25, 26:20, 29;17; Jer. 51:33; and Hos. 1:4. The formula is particularly characteristic of prophetic utterance. Comparative scriptural citation for the AV, the Hebrew, and the Greek are drawn from the *Biblia Polyglotta*, 6 vols. (London, 1657).

29. According to *A Greek-English Lexicon of the New Testament and Other Early Christian Literature*, trans. and ed. W. F. Arndt and F. W. Gingrich, 4th ed. (Chicago:

University of Chicago Press, 1957), s.v., *"deloi,"* from *"delow,"* suggests not only the idea of "signifying," "notifying," and "setting forth," but the concept of "revealing" (as of a revealing of secrets).

30. In the case of Heb. 12:26–27 versus Hag. 2:6–7, what the author of Hebrews considers impermanent about Haggai's "yet once more" is its focus upon the restored Temple as that which is made. In contrast, the author of Hebrews' "Yet once more" focuses upon the "kingdom which cannot be moved" (Heb. 12:28), the antitype prefigured in the restored Temple of Haggai. Typology, of course, is a fundamental constituent of the outlook that the author of Hebrews embodies.

31. See Moses Stuart, *A Commentary on the Epistle to the Hebrews*, 2 vols. (London: John Miller, 1828) 2:338; and Franz Delitzsch, *Commentary on the Epistle to the Hebrews*, trans. Thomas L. Kingsbury, 2 vols., 3rd ed. (Edinburgh: T. and T. Clark, 1926) 2:359–64.

32. David Dickson, *A Short Explanation of the Epistle of Paul to the Hebrews* (Aberdene, 1635) 306.

33. John Diodati, *Pious Annotations Upon the Holy Bible*, 3rd ed. (London, 1651), sig. Ooo 4ᵛ.

34. Frank Kermode, *The Sense of an Ending: Studies in the Theory of Fiction* (New York: Oxford University Press, 1967) 35, passim. According to Kermode, "Virgil and Genesis belong to our end-determined fictions" (6).

35. The term is Donald M. Friedman's, in *"Lycidas:* The Swain's *Paideia", Milton Studies*, vol. 3, ed. James Simmonds (Pittsburgh: University of Pittsburgh Press, 1971) 3–34.

36. Culley 15. For the most recent treatment of this dimension, see Heather Asals's "Echo, Narcissus, and Ambiguity in *Lycidas*," delivered before the Modern Language Association meeting in San Francisco, 1979. Although Asals is concerned primarily with epanalepsis (the act of ending a line with its opening word or words), other reverberative devices (such as anadiplosis, anaphora, atanaclasis, ploce, epiphora) are also important. See Edward S. LeComte, *Yet Once More: Verbal and Psychological Pattern in Milton* (New York: Liberal Arts Press, 1953) 25. Convenient explanations of individual devices may be found in the *Encyclopedia of Poetry and Poetics*, ed. Alex Preminger et al. (Princeton: Princeton University Press, 1965).

37. Claus Westermann, *Basic Forms of Prophetic Speech*, trans. Hugh Clayton White (Philadelphia: The Westminster Press, 1967) 93–95, 116, and passim. Westermann's discussion is also of importance for anyone interested in the significance of "woe" as a formula (190–94). In this context I am thinking, of course, of "woe" and its phonetic variations in Milton's Sonnet 18. For a review of Westermann's approach, as well as of "form criticism" (of which formula criticism is a kind) applied to the scriptural prophets in general, see W. Eugene March, "Prophecy," in *Old Testament Form Criticism*, ed. John H. Hayes (San Antonio: Trinity University Press, 1974) 159–77.

38. Italics for "no more" and "any more" are my own.

39. Westermann, pp. 95, 169–98.

40. James Hope Moulton, *A Grammar of New Testament Greek*, 2 vols. (Edinburgh: T & T Clark, 1906) 1:187–92. See further William Francis Gallaway, *On the Use of "me" with the Participle in Classical Greek*, 2d ed. (Cambridge: Cambridge University Press, 1959) 156; and William Watson Godwin, *Syntax of the Moods and Tenses of the Greek Verb* (Boston: Ginn and Co., 1900) 388–96.

41. Italics for "no more" and "any more" are my own. See also Isa. 10:20, 23:12. For accounts of the Hebrew negative, see A. B. Davidson, *Hebrew Syntax* (Edinburgh: T. & T. Clark 1901) 118; and Dean A. Walker, *The Semitic Negative* (Chicago: The University of Chicago Press, 1896). For the uses of *"yasaf,"* see *A Hebrew and English Lexicon of the Old Testament*, trans. Edward Robinson and ed. Francis Brown (Oxford: Oxford University Press, 1907).

42. *A Hymne to God the Father*, lines 5–6, 11–12, 17–18, *The Complete Poetry of John Donne*, ed. John T. Shawcross (Garden City, New York: Doubleday and Co., 1967).

43. William Haller, *The Rise of Puritanism* (New York: Harper and Row, 1957) 323.

44. John A. Via, "Milton's Antiprelatical Tracts: The Poet Speaks in Prose," *Milton Studies*, vol. 5, ed. James Simmonds (Pittsburgh: University of Pittsburg Press, 1973) 87–127.

45. *Works of John Owen*, ed. Rev. William H. Goold, 16 vols. (London and Edinburgh: Johnstone and Hunter, 1853) 8:269.

46. *Works of John Owen* 8:260.

47. For an overview, see *Variorum*, 2:ii, 565–636. Most recently, see Clay Hunt, *Lycidas and the Italian Critics* (New Haven: Yale University Press, 1979).

48. *Variorum* 2:ii, 639–49. See *The Poems of Milton*, ed. John Carey and Alastair Fowler (London: Longman, 1968) 239–40 n.

49. Julius Caesar Scaliger, *Select Translations from Scaliger's Poetics*, trans. Frederick M. Padelford (New York: H. Holt and Co., 1905) 21–24. Interpolations are from Scaliger's *Poetices libri septem* (Heidelberg, 1594) 15–16.

50. Theocritus, *Idyll XI* (19), in *The Idylls of Theocritus and the Eclogues of Virgil*, trans. C. S. Calverley (London: G. Bell and Sons, 1926). Further references to Theocritus, cited parenthetically in my text, are to this edition.

51. Hanford 27–55.

52. Hanford 30.

53. *Variorum* 2:ii, 653. For an account of the nuptials, see Theocritus, *Idyll VIII* (90). According to Hanford, Daphnis is "subdued by a new love, after his marriage to the fairest of the nymphs" (30). But the explanation of the *Variorum* editors seems to be closer to the truth. In any case, the nuptial dimension of the first *Idyll* is implicitly, rather than explicitly, delineated.

54. Bion, *Lament for Adonis* (59, 88–91), in Hanford 35–36.

55. Vergil, *Eclogue X* (29–31), in Hanford 108.

56. Sannazaro, *Piscatory Eclogue I* (54–59), in Hanford 108.

57. According to the *Variorum* editors (2: ii, 645), "there is perhaps the suggestion of the poet as wooer, the Muses as wooed." But there is certainly more than just a "suggestion" of this sort of thing: "coy" and "denial" are part of the very language of *carpe diem* rhetoric.

58. See *Variorum* 2:i, 128: "Todd and later editors compare: 'Sweet rose, fair flower, untimely pluck'd soon vaded, / Pluck'd in the bud, and vaded in the spring!' (Shakespeare, *Pass. Pil.* 1)."

59. *Variorum* 2:i, 706. Compare *Arcades*, which speaks "Of that renowned flood . . . / Divine *Alpheus*, who by secret sluse, / Stole under Seas to meet his *Arethuse* (29–31). See Ovid, *Metamorphoses* (V.512–641), trans. Frank J. Miller, 2 vols. (London: W. Heinemann, 1916). Parenthetical references are to this edition.

60. Moschus, *Lament for Bion* (6 and 7), in *Hanford* 37.

61. For a summary of sources, see *Variorum* 2:ii, 672. The story of Hyacinth's death is told in Ovid, *Metamorphoses* (X.174–219). Milton's interest in the Apollo-Hyacinth story can be seen in the *Fair Infant* elegy (22–28).

62. For a discussion of homoeroticism in Milton, particularly as this tendency is reflected in *Epitaphium Damonis*, see John T. Shawcross, "Milton and Diodati: An Essay in Psychodynamic Meaning," in *"Eyes Fast Fixt": Current Perspectives in Milton Methodology*. For a discussion of the erotic in Milton, see Edward Le Comte, *Milton and Sex* (New York: Columbia University Press, 1978).

63. *Variorum* 2:ii, 652. Compare the Lady's song to Echo in *A Mask* (229–42).

64. Ovid, *Metamorphoses* (III.400–01).

65. Bion, *Lament for Adonis* (38) and Ronsard, *Adonis* (251), in *Hanford* 34–35, 168. See also Moschus's *Lament for Bion* (30), in *Hanford* 37.

66. See *Variorum* 2:ii, 653, for a discussion of this and additional sources.

67. *Variorum* 2:ii, 655.

68. *Variorum* 2:ii, 657. See Ovid, *Metamorphoses* (X.3–85; XI.1–42).

69. Calliope's inability to save her son is documented in the *Variorum* 2:ii, 657.

70. In *Milton's Poetical Works (Facsimile Edition)*, ed. Harris Francis Fletcher, 4 vols. (Urbana: University of Illinois Press, 1943–48) 1:434, 435.

71. Bion, *Lament for Adonis* (69–77), in *Hanford* 35.

72. According to Ruby Nemser ("A Reinterpretation of 'The Unexpressive Nuptial Song,'" *Milton Newsletter* 2 [1968] 1–2), the word "unexpressive" in *Lycidas* means "expressionless" (in the sense of being inaudible) rather than "inexpressible" (in the sense of being incapable of expression). I feel, however, that "unexpressive" carries both meanings. Interestingly, Revelation 14:3, from which the idea is partially drawn, gives rise to a similar ambiguity. Whereas the AV renders the Greek *mathein* ("learn") as "no man could learn that song," some editions of the Vulgate translate *dicere* ("say") rather than *discere* ("learn"). The Rheims version (1582) has "and no man could say the song." See *Biblia Hexaglotta*, ed. Edward Riches de Levante, 6 vols. (New York: Funk and Wagnalls, 1901) 6:870–71; *The New Testament Octapla*, ed. Luther A. Weigle (New York: T. Nelson, 1962), s.v.; and *Biblia Sacra Vulgatae Editionis* (Rome, 1592) 1125. Seventeenth century exegetes were certainly aware of the problem. See William Cowper, *Pathmos: or, A Commentary on the Revelation of Saint John* (1623), in *The Workes of Mr. William Cowper* (London, 1623) 1063: "The Latine Translation hath, No man could say this Song: *nemo potuit dicere.*" But the Greek has "learn."

73. It is interesting to note in the *Obsequies to the memories of Mr. Edward King* (Cambridge, 1638), in which *Lycidas* first appeared, an elegy by Isaac Olivier, who depicts King as "a lustie bridegroom" who should have "leapt to land" in order to escape the amorous embraces of the waves (30). In *Justa Edovardo King*, reproduced from the original edition, 1638 (New York: Facsimile Text Society, 1939) 16.

NOTES TO CHAPTER SIX

1. John Clarke, *An Essay Upon Study* (1731), in *Milton: The Critical Heritage*, ed. John T. Shawcross, 2 vols. (London: Routledge and Kegan Paul, 1970–72) 1:263–64.

2. Alexander Pope, "The First Epistle to the Second Book of Horace" (102), *Poems of Alexander Pope*, ed. John Butt, 11 vols., 2nd ed. (New Haven: Yale University Press, 1953) 4:203.

3. William Empson, *Milton's God* (1961; rev. ed. Cambridge: Cambridge University Press, 1981) 146. For a counterstatement to the premises underlying the Empsonian conception, see Denis Danielson, *Milton's Good God: A Study in Literary Theodicy* (Cambridge: Cambridge University Press, 1982).

4. See, among other works, J. B. Broadbent's *Some Graver Subject: An Essay on Paradise Lost* (New York: St. Martin's Press, 1967) 144–57.

5. Irene Samuel, "The Dialogue in Heaven: A Reconsideration of *Paradise Lost*, III, 1–417," *Milton: Modern Essays in Criticism*, ed. Arthur E. Barker (New York: Oxford University Press, 1965) 233–45. (Reprinted from *PMLA* 72 [1957] 601–11.) See also Merritt Y. Hughes, "The Filiations of Milton's Celestial Dialogue (*Paradise Lost*, III.80–343)," *Ten Perspectives on Milton* (New Haven: Yale University Press, 1965) 104–35; and Kathleen M. Swaim, "The Mimesis of Accommodation in Book 3 of *Paradise Lost*," *Philological Quarterly* 63 (1984) 461–75. More recently, Albert C. Labriola has explored the deliberative and iconographical contexts of the dialogue in Heaven in an excellent study entitled "'God Speaks': Milton's Dialogue in Heaven and the Tradition of Divine Deliberation," *Cithara* 25 (1986) 5–30. Labriola's views are very much in accord with my own.

6. Jackson Cope, *The Metaphoric Structure of Paradise Lost* (Baltimore: The Johns Hopkins Press, 1962) 170–73.

7. Broadbent 146–48.

8. Samuel 234–35. Compare Hughes 105.

9. Stanley Fish, *Surprised by Sin: The Reader in Paradise Lost* (New York: St. Martin's Press, 1967) 86.

10. Fish 62. See Walter J. Ong's *Ramus, Method, and the Decay of Dialogue: From the Art of Discourse to the Art of Reason* (Cambridge: Harvard University Press, 1958) 287–88.

11. Ong 287.

12. Ong 287–88.

13. Fish 62. In this regard, see Francis C. Blessington, "Autotheodicy: The Father as Orator in *Paradise Lost*," *Cithara* 14 (1975) 49–60; and Blessington's *Paradise Lost and the Classical Epic* (London: Routledge and Kegan Paul, 1979) 39–49. See also Anthony Low, "Milton's God: Authority in *Paradise Lost*, *Milton Studies*, vol. 4, ed. James Simmonds (Pittsburgh: University of Pittsburgh Press, 1972) 19–38.

14. *The Dialogic Imagination: Four Essays by M. M. Bakhtin*, ed. Michael Holquist and trans. Caryl Emerson and Michael Holquist (Austin: University of Texas Press, 1981) 279. According to Bakhtin, "every word is directed toward an answer and cannot escape the profound influence of the answering word that it anticipates" (280). Barbara Lewalski has recently commented that *Paradise Lost* "manifests many of the characteristics . . . that Bakhtin finds in the emerging Renaissance novel" (*Paradise Lost and the Rhetoric of Literary Forms* [Princeton: Princeton Uniwersity Press, 1985] 17). For additional study of dialogue in Milton, see Joseph Stuart Moag, "Traditional Patterns of Dialogue and Debate in Milton's Poetry," diss., Northwestern University, 1964.

15. In short, I actually find myself closer to A. J. A. Waldock, who responds to God's first speech by saying that Milton has taken "the supreme risk . . . of permitting a theoretically perfect character to dilate on his own impeccability" (*Paradise Lost and Its Critics* [1947], paperback edition [Cambridge: Cambridge University Press, 1966] 102–04). Waldock is right for all the wrong reasons, as I shall attempt to show.

16. I prefer the Sumner translation of this passage in the Columbia *Works of John Milton* to the Carey translation in the Yale *Complete Prose Works of John Milton* 6:213: "all that play-acting of the persons of the godhead."

17. Milton's own prose summary of the dialogue in the "Argument" to Book III suggests something of the five act structure into which the dialogue might be divided:

Act I (80–134)

God sitting on his Throne sees Satan flying towards this world, then newly created; shews him to the Son who sat at his right hand; foretells the success of Satan in perverting mankind; clears his own Justice and Wisdom from all imputation, having created Man free and able enough to have withstood his Tempter; yet declares his purpose of grace towards him, in regard he fell not of his own malice, as did Satan, but by him seduc't.

Act II (144–66)

The Son of God renders praises to his Father for the manifestation of his gracious purpose towards Man.

Act III (167–217)

God again declares, that Grace cannot be extended toward Man without the satisfaction of divine Justice; Man hath offended the majesty of God by aspiring to Godhead, and therefore with all his Progeny devoted to death must dye, unless some one can be found sufficient to answer for his offence, and undergo his Punishment.

Act IV (227–65)

The Son of God freely offers himself a Ransom for Man.

Act V (274–343)

The Father accepts him, ordains his incarnation, pronounces his exaltation above all Names in Heaven and Earth; commands all the Angels to adore him.

18. In this regard, see Arthur O. Lovejoy's classic essay, "Milton and the Paradox of tie Fortunate Fall," *ELH* 4 (1937) 161–79.

19. The terms *anagnorisis* and *peripeteia*, of course, are derived from Aristotle's *Poetics* (XI.1–5). See further, Martin Mueller, *Children of Oedipus and Other Essays on the Imitation of Greek Tragedy 1500–1800* (Toronto: University of Toronto Press, 1980), esp. 217: "The central action of *Paradise Lost* is in Aristotle's words a *mythos dramatikos*." Although "the term dramatic, as Aristotle uses it, does not primarily refer to drama" but to "composition of the action," *Paradise Lost*, as Mueller observes, embodies both this strict Aristotelian definition and a "more conventional sense" of drama as heightened action as well.

20. To this end, he viewed himself as having assumed the prophetic role. In that role, Milton prayed "to that eternal Spirit who can enrich with all utterance and knowledge, and sends out his Seraphim with the hallow'd fire of his Altar to touch and purify the lips of whom he pleases" (3:241; Isa. 6:1–8). As a result of this inspiration, Milton saw himself not only as re-creating the drama of Scripture but as veritably participating in that drama. At this solemn music, Milton became an actor, a participant along with the angelic hosts that surround the throne. His song became their song: he became one of them. This was his way of fulfilling the commission of one who appeared before the divine throne as prophet. Such a commission is that to which Milton as celebrant of this high drama dedicated his poetic career.

21. John Demaray, *Milton's Theatrical Epic: The Invention and Design of Paradise Lost* (Cambridge: Harvard University Press, 1980).

22. This is Psalm 84 in the Vulgate. As Milton's *Cambridge Manuscript* plans attest, the debate among the Daughters of God in one form or another was to assume an important part in his projected drama on the Fall. Scholars such as Robert L. Ramsay have already documented Milton's interest in and indebtedness to the allegory not only in such poems as the *Fair Infant* elegy and the *Nativity* ode but in the poems *On Time* and *Upon the Circumcision*, not to mention Milton's own translation of Psalm 85, which elaborates upon the allegory ("Morality Themes in Milton's Poetry," *SP* 15, [1918] 123–59, esp. 133–53). In Milton's translation of Psalm 85, there is no sense of either conflict or debate among the Daughters. On the contrary, Milton celebrates the union of the Daughters: "Mercy and Truth *that long were miss'd*, Now *joyfully* are met; / *Sweet* Peace and Righteousness have kiss'd *And hand in hand are set*" (10; the italics represent Milton's own interpolations). This quality of reconciliation underlies Milton's references to the allegory in the earlier poetry as well, perhaps because the occasion (the Incarnation as a means of harmony) warrants it. In other words, Christ has already offered himself as a sacrifice: there is no longer any need for contentiousness. In *Paradise Lost*, the occasion is prelapsarian and moves toward reconciliation. Most recently, John T. Shawcross has shown how significantly the allegory underscores Milton's concept of covenant ("Milton and the Covenant: The Christian View of Old Testament Theology," *Milton and Scriptural Tradition: The Bible into Poetry*, ed. James H. Sims and Leland Ryken [Columbia: University of Missouri Press, 1984] 160–91, esp. 181–83). What has not been sufficiently emphasized, however, is the degree to which the sense of heightened drama implicit in the conflict among the Daughters pervades the celestial parliament in Book III of *Paradise Lost*.

23. See Hope Traver's *The Four Daughters of God: A Study of the Versions of this*

Allegory with Especial Reference to those in Latin, French, and English (Philadelphia: The John C. Winston Co., 1907), and Samue Chew, *The Virtues Reconciled: An Iconographic Study* (Toronto: The University of Toronto Press, 1947).

24. Traver 12–15.

25. *The Corpus Christi Play of the English Middle Ages*, ed. R. T. Davis (Totowa: Rowman and Littlefield, 1972) 123–29. For the most extensive morality rendering of the scene, see *The Castle of Perseverance* (ca. 1425).

26. The full titles are *Christ's Victory and Triumph in Heaven and Earth over and after Death*, (1610) and *The History of the Perfect-Cursed-Blessed Man: Setting forth Man's Excellency, Misery, Felicity by his Generation, Degeneration, Regeneration* (1628).

27. Lewalski, *Paradise Lost and the Rhetoric of Literary Forms* 119. Lewalski quite correctly sees other literary forms underlying the dialogue as well. She traces the scene, for example, to the tradition of the *Concilia Deorum*, made evident in the *Odyssey* I.31–98, as well as to such interchanges as that between Apollo and Phaethon in Ovid's *Metamorphoses* II.1–152 (114–17). God's first speech she sees as a mode of forensic or judicial oratory in which God argues a case publicly before an angelic court (120–21).

28. In this regard, see Joseph A. Wittreich, Jr., "'All Angelic Natures Joined in One': Epic Convention and Prophetic Interiority in the Council Scenes of *Paradise Lost*," *Composite Orders: The Genres of Milton's Last Poems*, ed. Richard S. Ide and Joseph A. Wittreich, Jr. (Pittsburgh: University of Pittsburgh Press, 1983) 43–74, esp.48: The council scenes in *Paradise Lost* are "objectifications of inner turmoil and emblems of mental divisions." For a telling biblical analogue that brings into focus the idea of a divine psychodrama, see Isaiah 54:5–10, esp. 6–8: "For the Lord hath called thee as a woman forsaken and grieved in spirit. . . . In a little wrath I hid my face from thee for a moment; but with everlasting kindness will I have mercy on thee, saith the Lord thy Redeemer."

29. Milton's statement here raises the vexed question of *anthropopatheia*, the attribution of human emotions to God. Although Milton is opposed to this notion, his commentary draws upon the language of those who endorse the idea. See the full and helpful annotations in the Yale *Complete Prose Works* 6:134–37.

30. In this respect, the divine anger of God (what Milton in *Upon the Circumcision* had earlier called "the full wrath" of "vengefull Justice" [11.22–31]) offers fit contrast to the diabolic anger of Satan, that is, what God Himself in *Paradise Lost* refers to as the "rage" that "transports our adversarie" (III.80–81). Whereas the first is justified and finally resolved in the assertion of mercy (III.134), the second is unjustified and self-defeating (III.85–86). *Paradise Lost* is an epic that implicitly contrasts the *ira Dei* with the *ira diaboli*. For the appropriate background, see Lactantius, *On the Anger of God, The Works of Lactantius*, trans. William Fletcher, 2 vols. (Edinburgh: T. and T. Clark, 1871 1:32 and passim.

31. The distinction is implicit in the interchange between God and Adam in Book VIII of *Paradise Lost*. God refers to Himself as one who is "alone / From all Eternitie" (405–06). In that state, God, as Adam comments, is "accompanied" with Himself, that is, the "self" with whom He converses. When does converse with others, He raises His creatures to what "highth" He wishes "Of Union or Communion, deifi'd" (427–31).

32. Broadbent, 148.

33. John Peter, *A Critique of Paradise Lost* (1960; rpt. n.p.: Archon Books, 1970) 12.

34. Allan Gilbert, "Form and Matter in *Paradise Lost*, Book III," *Milton Studies in Honor of Harris Francis Fletcher* (Urbana: University of Illinois Press, 1961) 52.

35. The phrase "creature late so lov'd" (III.151) contains its own criticism: it implies that he who was loved of late is perhaps not loved now. The word "late" might also modify "creature" and thereby suggest the idea of one who has died. (According to the *OED*, such usage was commonplace in the seventeenth century. Compare Milton's own usage in "late espoused saint" [Sonnet 23, 1].)

36. Milton provides a full discussion of "blasphemy" in *Christian Doctrine* (17:154–61).

37. For a detailed analysis of this biblical motif, see Sylvia Scholnick's important study

"Lawsuit Drama in the Book of Job," Brandeis University, 1976. The technical term for such a lawsuit in Job is *riv*, but there are also a number of other such terms that suggest the idea of litigation, among them, *yachach*. In this regard, see also William Holladay, "Jeremiah's Lawsuit with God," *Interpretation* 17 (1963) 280–87; Herbert Huffmon, "The Covenant Lawsuit in the Prophets," *Journal of Biblical Literature* 78 (1959) 285–95; James Limburg, "The Lawsuit of God in the Eight-Century Prophets," Th.D. thesis, Union Theological Seminary (Virginia) 1969, among others.

38. Hughes 116.

39. In this regard, see H. Wheeler Robinson, "The Council of Yahweh," *Journal of Theological Studies* 45 (1944) 151–57; G. Ernest Wright, *The Old Testament Against Its Background* (Chicago: Henry Regnery Co., 1950) 30–41; and Frank M. Cross, Jr., "The Council of Jahweh in Second Isaiah," *Journal of Near Eastern Studies*, 12 (1953) 274–77. For these references, I am indebted to Mother Mary, Christopher Pecheux's excellent article, "The Council Scenes in *Paradise Lost*," in *Milton and Scriptural Tradition* 82–103.

40. For a discussion of the concept of the holy mountain, see my *Poetics of the Holy* 140–70.

41. See John E. Parish, "Milton and an Anthropomorphic God," *SP* 56 (1959) 619–25; and Hughes 114–18. See also Kitty Cohen, *The Throne and the Chariot* (The Hague: Mouton, 1975) 103–16. Returning us unequivocally to the Abrahamic-Mosaic milieu that characterizes the dialogue in Heaven, Adam's rationalization provides the occasion for reconsidering the dialogue within a new perspective.

42. The impact that the Abrahamic and Mosaic passages had upon Milton, in this respect, is particularly discernible in *The Reason of Church-Government*, which ends with an ironic reversal of Abraham's appeal to God to spare the Sodomites for the sake of ten worthy people. Adopting the role of Abraham, Milton appeals to the Lords to spare the prelates if there can be found "but only one good thing in prelaty." The implication here, of course, is that *nothing* good can be found, and that "prelaty" should, as a result, be shown no mercy (3: 278–79).

43. Marvell's poem can be found, among other places, in the Columbia edition of Milton's *Works* (2: 3–5).

NOTES TO CHAPTER SEVEN

1. In *Samson Agonistes*, the word "strength" is used forty-one times; in *Paradise Lost*, it is used thirty-four times; in *Paradise Regain'd*, six times. In *Paradise Lost*, it appears most often in Books I and II, where it is associated primarily with Satan, and in Book VI, where it suggests the nature of the confrontation between Satan and God. In *Paradise Regain'd*, it is applied to both Satan and Jesus. In the distinction between strength and weakness, both epics, however, invoke the idea in a special sense that forms the basis of the discussion that follows.

2. As opposed to "weak," "weakness," etc., such terms as "strong," "strongest," and "power," among others, are at issue here.

3. See, in this regard, the *Theological Dictionary of the Old Testament*, 2:367–82 (hereinafter referred to as *TDOT*). In addition to the *TDOT*, see the *Theological Dictionary of the New Testament*, 2:284–317 (hereinafter referred to a *TDNT*); and William Wilson, *Old Testament Word Studies* (Grand Rapids: Kregel Publications, 1978) 321.

4. According to the *TDOT*, the root *gbr* extends to such forms as *gabhar*, *gebhurah*, *gebhir*, *gibbor*, and *gebher*, all of which associate strength and power (367–82). Related to these terms are others, such as *koach*, which will be discussed fully in connection with Samson.

5. Cyril H. Powell, *The Biblical Concept of Power* (London: The Epworth Press, 1963) 7.

6. *TDNT* 2:291–92.

7. "It should be no surprise, therefore, that in the Rabbinic age, when the name Yahweh was no longer uttered, the word *gebhurah* [might] was used along with other words as a substitute for the proper name of God" (*TDOT* 2:370).

8. *TDOT* 2:372.

9. *TDNT* 2:293.

10. *TDNT* 2:301.

11. Rudolf Otto, *The Idea of the Holy: An Inquiry into the non-rational factor in the idea of the divine and its relation to the rational* (1923), trans. John W. Harvey (New York: Oxford University Press, 1958). See, in this regard, Otto's discussion of "Over-poweringness" or *majestas* (19–23). For a full treatment of the concept in Milton, see my *Poetics of the Holy*.

12. Although Milton is at pains here to distinguish between God as the source of power and the Spirit as a "symbol and minister of divine power," the thrust of the argument remains appropriate for our purposes nonetheless.

13. As Milton indicated in his translations, the italicized words are his own. From this perspective, his emphasis upon God's strength is telling.

14. From the perspective of Milton's prose works, this epic image of power is fully anticipated, of course, in *An Apology for Smectymnuus*. There

> Zeale, whose substance is ethereal, arming in compleat diamond ascends his fiery Chariot drawn with two blazing Meteors figur'd like beasts, but of a higher breed then any the Zodiack yeilds, resembling two of those four which *Ezechiel* and S. *John* saw, the one visag'd like a Lion to expresse power, high autority and indignation, the other of count'nance like a man to cast derision and scorne upon perverse and fraudulent seducers; with these the invincible warriour Zeale shaking loosely the slack reins drives over the heads of Scarlet Prelats, and such as are insolent to maintaine traditions, brusing their stiffe necks under his flaming wheels.

In this manner, observes Milton, the true prophets of old combated the false and Christ, that "fountaine of meeknesse," galled and vexed the prelatical pharisees. This Milton refers to as "a sanctifi'd bitternesse against the enemies of truth" (3:313–14). For corresponding discussions of this idea, see my two articles "Milton's 'Chariot of Paternal Deitie' as a Reformation Conceit," *Journal of Religion* 65 (1985) 359–77; and "'Hate in Heav'n': Milton and the *Odium Dei*," *ELH* 53 (1986), 519–36. In the same vein, compare Milton's discussion of Justice in *Eikonoklastes*: "We may conclude therfore that justice, above all other things, is and ought to be the strongest: Shee is the strength, the Kingdom, the power and majestie of all Ages." Free men, says Milton, have been delivered from the captivity of kings by "the strength and supreme Sword of Justice." Celebrating the power of Justice, Milton likewise extols the strength of Truth as a corresponding virtue (5: 292–94).

15. Significantly, the Son's act is associated with Jesus' exercise of his *dynamis* in driving out the diabolic spirits from the demoniac (VI.856–57; cf. Matt. 8:28–34).

16. *TDOT* 2:372, 376–77.

17. The phrases *b'chayyil* and *b'koach* both signify strength, power, might. The term *b'ruchiy* is from *ruach*, which signifies spirit. As indicated, *koach* will be discussed later, with respect to the Samson narrative.

18. The phrase *he-gar dynamis mou en astheneia teleioutai* literally means "for the power of me in weakness is perfected."

19. Milton inscribed the biblical text in Greek, and in the Arnold Album continued the inscription in Latin: "*To the most learned man, and my most cultured champion, Mr. Christopher Arnold, I have given this in memory of his virtue and my zeal towards him*" (as translated in the Columbia edition).

20. For the biblical basis of the foregoing, see n. 17 above.

21. The aspersions cast upon Milton in *The Cry of the Royal Blood* (attributed by Milton to Alexander More but in fact by Peter du Moulin) depict him at once as a Cyclops ("A monster horrible, deformed, huge, and sightless") and as a disgusting little animal than whom "nothing is more weak, more bloodless, more shrivelled" (in the Yale *Complete Prose Works* 4: 1045; cf. 1050–51). In a chapter devoted exclusively to "That Foul Rascal John Milton," the insults are doubly compounded: "Scourge his whole body to make it one big welt," the author cries. "Shall you ever stop? Beat him until he has evilly poured forth his fearful bile and diseased blood through his tears." Milton is described as a disgusting thing of the gallows, an unclean being one can scarcely bear to touch. Seen as fit for nothing more than to "turn a hand-mill in the condition of an ass," he is nevertheless challenged to physical combat: "Come hither, you impious tormentor, I want a few words with you" (Yale *Complete Prose Works* 4: 1078–80). The situation is strikingly like that depicted in Samson's confrontation with Harapha in Milton's drama. In fact, in his response to the *Cry* in the *Second Defence*, Milton treats the assaults very much in the form of a drama reminiscent of a Samson-like figure encountering his enemies as they approach him: "But hark! again some strange and cackling cry! I suppose a flight of geese is on the wing, coming from some quarter or other! Oh, I now perceive what it is. I remember that it is the clamour of a tragedy. The chorus makes its appearance," etc. (The Columbia *Works*, 7: 77).

22. Given the extent to which this point of view permeates such works as *The Reason of Church-Government* and the *Second Defence*, it should come as no surprise that it underscores *A Treatise of Civil Power in Ecclesiastical Causes*. Applying the Pauline distinction between strength and weakness to matters of polity, Milton argues that physical power is not only inappropriate but totally ineffectual in compelling matters of religion. Citing such texts as 1 Corinthians 1:27 and 2 Corinthians 10:3–6, Milton observes that God has not chosen the force of this world to subdue conscience and conscientious men, "who in this world are counted weakest"; rather, He has chosen conscience, as being weakest, "to subdue and regulate force." In comparison with spiritual power, outward force, says Milton, is "uneffectual and weak" (6: 22–23). Such ideas are repeated and elaborated upon throughout. In the same vein (but, of course, in response to a different set of political circumstances), see Milton's earlier poetic rendering *On the New Forcers of Conscience*.

23. For the biblical contexts, see n. 4 above, especially 1 Cor. 3:18–19 and 4:10.

24. The phrase alludes, of course, to Milton's plans for a drama on the subject in the Cambridge Manuscript (18: 240). Compare Isaiah 49:7.

25. According to the *Theological Wordbook of the Old Testament*, ed. R. Laird Harris et al, 2 vols. (Chicago: Moody Press, 1980), *koach* appears one hundred and twenty-six times in the Old Testament (1:436–37; hereinafter referred to as *TWOT*). "It is relatively evenly distributed in its occurrences, the most in any book being twenty in Job. It also occurs twelve times in Isa. and Dan., and eleven times in Ps. The only cognate language in which this root appears is Arabic where it has the verbal idea 'to batter down.'"

26. *TWOT* 1:436–37.

27. *TDOT* 2:367.

28. The term used in Judges 3:5 is *l'hosiah* (cf. *mosiah*: "deliverer"), which implies the ideas of freedom, renewal, and redemption.

29. As the various commentaries on the composition of the Book of Judges indicate, the Nazaritical dimension initiated in chapter 13 is a later addition. According to C. F. Burney, chapters 14 through 16 are *sui generis*, "full of the rough vigour and broad humour of the rustic story-teller," whereas "the religious motive which colours the narrative of *ch.* 13 is altogether absent from *chs.* 14–16. The birth narrative prepares us for a Gide'on or a Samuel, keenly alive to the fact that he holds a divine commission, and upheld in his performance of it by consciousness of the divine support. Samson, however, proves to have no commission at all, and recognizes no higher guide than his own wayward passions." Chapters 14 through 16, moreover, contain "a mythological

element which must be very primitive." They are the product of an "ancient cycle ot folk-tales" current at the time the Samson narrative was composed (*The Book of Judges* [London; Rivingtons, 1918] 337–42). See also Cuthbert Aikman Simpson, *Composition of the Book of Judges* (Oxford: Basil Blackwell, 1957) 53–55.

30. For a full account of the Nazaritical code, see Numbers 6:1–21. For discussions of the code itself, see the entry "Nazirite" in the *Encyclopaedia Judaica*, ed. Cecil Roth, 16 vols. (Jerusalem: Keter Publishing House, 1971) 12:907–910; and the entry "Nazirites" in the *Encyclopaedia of Religion and Ethics*, ed. James Hastings, 12 vols. (New York: Charles Scribner's Sons, 1917) 9:258–60. According to the earliest conception of the Nazarite, such a figure was a holy man and a warrior whose power was manifested in psychic and physical, rather than in ethical, forms. There are, accordingly, "many affinities between the Nazirite and the warrior. Samson, who is called a Nazirite, was a holy warrior much like Saul." Brought like Saul to holy fury by the Spirit of God (cf. 1 Sam. 10:9–13; 11:5–11), the Nazarite experienced special physical power. He was a charismatic figure with long hair. As delineated in Numbers 6, the Nazaritical code "indicates that the charismatic aspects were subsiding in favor of a standardized communal control." It is doubtful, in fact, that the older Nazarites observed all the laws that later became the hallmarks of the Nazaritical code (*The Interpreter's Dictionary of the Bible*, ed. George Arthur Buttrick, 4 vols. [New York: Abingdon Press, 1962] 526–27).

31. It certainly does not appear in the Numbers account, or anywhere else in the Bible, for that matter. For the specific regulations regarding the cutting of the hair according to the Nazaritical code, see especially Numbers 6:5, and 18. For the uniqueness of the connection between divine strength and the Nazaritical injunctions against cutting the hair in Judges 16:17, see J. Alberto Soggin, *Judges: A Commentary*, trans. John Bowden (Philadelphia: The Westminster Press, 1981) 257–58: In the texts about the Nazaritical injunctions, it is never mentioned that such ideas as "the length of hair produces a particular strength." According to James L. Crenshaw, "the secret that Samson had guarded zealously until Delilah's successful onslaught of his patience comes as something of a surprise to the most attentive listener or reader. It returns to an element of the saga that has been ignored since the opening episode. Samson attributed his great strength to a Nazirite vow. Apart from the birth narrative, nothing in the saga reinforces this interpretation of his special power." "Furthermore," observes Crenshaw, "nothing in Samson's conduct suggests that he took a Nazirite vow very seriously. Instead, he played an active part in wedding festivities where wine would have flowed freely, and he ate honey which he would have gathered from a lion's carcass" (*Samson: A Secret Betrayed, a Vow Ignored* [Atlanta: John Knox Press, 1978] 95–96).

32. According to A. Smythe Palmer, "it would hardly be too much to say that the *motif* which actuates the entire narrative is his [Samson's] extraordinary endowment in the matter of hair. It is the distinctive characteristic which marks off Samson from every other personage in the Biblical history and, indeed, in literature. There are many mighty men of valour celebrated for their doughty achievements in saga, romance, or story; but none who owes his peculiar gift of strength to the abundant and unchecked growth of his hair. On this the interest of the narrative turns and the *denouement* of his career depends." (*The Samson Saga and Its Place in Comparative Religion* [London: Sir Isaac Pitman, 1913] 33–34). Nonetheless, the association of the length of one's hair and physical prowess and strength is, according to a number of scholars, very much in keeping with ancient beliefs and customs. For a full account of those beliefs and customs, see Theodor H. Gaster, *Myth, Legend, and Custom in the Old Testament*, 2 vols. (Gloucester, Mass.: Peter Smith, 1981) 2:436–43; Ignaz Goldziher, *Mythology Among the Hebrews and Its Historical Development*, trans. Russell Martineau (London: Longmans, Green, 1877), 407–14; and Sir James George Frazer, *Folk-Lore in the Old Testament: Studies in Comparative Religion, Legend, and Law* (New York: Tudor, 1923) 272–73.

33. *The Jewish Antiquities*, trans. H. St. J. Thackeray and Ralph Marcus, 9 vols. (Cambridge: Harvard University Press, 1958) 5:125, 129.

34. *Jewish Antiquities* 5:128–29. As the editors point out, the name Samson is, in fact, most probably derived from the Hebrew *shemesh*, "sun." By deriving the etymology of "Samson" from the word "strong," Josephus, the editors suggest, no doubt had in mind the commonplace notion that the sun symbolized strength (129). This aspect will be discussed in more detail. According to William Riley Parker, there is a traditional etymology that associates "Samson" with *shamam*, "to waste," an etymology from which is apparently derived the meaning of "the strong." Parker does not elaborate upon this association (*Milton's Debt to Greek Tragedy in Samson Agonistes* [Baltimore: Johns Hopkins, 1937] 13 n. 35.) According to the pseudo-Philo, the etymology of the name Samson is "holy unto the Lord" or "anointed to the Lord," an allusion to the Hebrew *semen*, "oil" (Louis Ginzberg, *The Legends of the Jews*, 6 vols. [Philadelphia: Jewish Publication Society of America, 1959] 6:205–6).

35. *Jewish Antiquities* 5:139. Approximating that of the Septuagint (*Daleida*), Josephus' spelling, of course, anticipates Milton's own rendering "Dalila."

36. *Jewish Antiquities* 5:143. Josephus' judgment of Samson's error is not as harsh as one might otherwise expect: "That he let himself be ensnared by a woman," Josephus comments, "must be imputed to human nature which succumbs to sins; but testimony is due him for his surpassing excellence in all the rest."

37. Ginzberg 4:47–49. Ginzberg's sources are *Sotah* 9b, *Midrash Bereshit Rabba* 4.4, and *Midrash Yikrah Rabba* 8.2. According to the *Midrash Rabbah*, there were three occasions when the Holy Spirit began to affect Samson: when he went down to Timnah (Judg. 14:5), when he went down to Ashkelon (Judg. 14:19), and when he came to Lechi (Judg. 15:14) (ed. Rabbi H. Freedman and Maurice Simon, 10 vols. [London: Soncino Press, 1951] 4:102).

38. *The Babylonian Talmud*, trans. R. I. Epstein, 35 vols. (London: Soncino Press, 1936) 16:45. Much has been made of the Samson narrative as a reformulation of a solar myth. Gaster formulates the assumptions of this theory as follows:

> (i) The name Samson derives from the Hebrew word *shemesh*, meaning "sun," and much of the action takes place near Beth-Shemesh . . ., presumably an ancient shrine of the sun-god, where solar myths would very probably have been current. (ii) The story of how Samson burned up the standing grain and olive crop of the Philistines by sending into their fields foxes with fire-brands tied to their tails (15:4–6) might well represent the action of the scorching sun. (iii) The shearing of Samson's locks at the instigation of Delilah (16:16–19) might, in the same way, reflect the curtailment of the sun's rays by the shades of night. (434)

Although Gaster is at pains to discount this theory, it was a commonplace one with ancient origins. See also Soggin 257, Goldziher 407–10, and Palmer 34–37, among others. Approaching the idea from the Miltonic perspective, see Don Parry Norford, "The Sacred Head: Milton's Solar Mysticism," *Milton Studies*, vol. 9, ed. James Simmonds (Pittsburgh: University of Pittsburgh Press, 1976) 37–75; and Anthony Low, "The Phoenix and the Sun in *Samson Agonistes*," *Milton Studies*, vol. 14, ed. James Simmonds (Pittsburgh: University of Pittsburgh Press, 1980) 219–31, among others.

39. *Talmud* 16:46.

40. According to *Sotah* 9b, Delilah is so called because "she weakened [*Dildelah*] his [Samson's] strength, she weakened his heart, she weakened his action" (*Talmud*, 16:43; cf. *Midrash Rabbah* 5:286). By succumbing to the weakness represented in the figure of Delilah, Samson became unclean. From both a Talmudic and a Midrashic point of view, this uncleanness is graphically characterized in sexual terms. Discoursing upon Samson's humiliation at being made to "grind" in the prison house (Judg. 16:21), the *Talmud* says of the term "grind": "It teaches that everyone brought his wife to him [Samson] to the prison that she might bear a child by him [who would be as strong as he was]" (*Sotah* 10a, *Talmud* 16:45; cf. *Midrash Rabbah* 5:286). Even in its disparagement of Samson, Talmudic and Midrashic commentary places the concept of strength at the center of its focus. Here the ironic assumption is that it can be infused from one person to the next.

41. From the Miltonic point of view, see Samuel S. Stollman, "Milton's Samson and the Jewish Tradition," *Milton Studies*, vol. 3, ed. James Simmonds (Pittsburgh: Univer-

sity of Pittsburgh Press, 1971) 185–200, which is an interesting exploration of the Talmudic and Midrashic backgrounds.

42. Although ascribed to Paul from the time of the early church onward, "Hebrews has no claim to having been written either by Paul or one of his disciples (Norman Perrin, *The New Testament: An Introduction* [New York: Harcourt, Brace, Jovanovich, 1974] 137).

43. As Perrin notes (140), "the idea of listing the heroes of the faith is Jewish." See Sirach 44:1–50:21.

44. The phrase *enedynamothesan apo astheneias* literally means "acquired strength out of weakness," whereas the phrase *egenethesan iskyroi en polemow* literally means "became mighty in war." Both suggest the idea of becoming strong.

45. The particular Old Testament elder to whom the author alludes here is Moses, but the statements apply to the others as well.

46. See in this regard Franz Delitzsch, *Commentary on the Epistle to the Hebrews*, trans. Thomas L. Kingsburg, 2 vols. (Grand Rapids: Eerdmans, 1952) 2:274–80.

47. Cited by F. Michael Krouse, *Milton's Samson and the Christian Tradition* (1949; New York: Farrar, Straus and Giroux, 1974) 41. Throughout the entire body of exegetical literature on Samson, "strength," observes Krouse, "was always the key-note" of the focus concerning the significance of the biblical account (100).

48. Krouse 44–45.

49. See, among other writers, Ambrose, *De Spiritu Sancto*; Diodorus of Tarsus, *In Librum Judicum*; and Cyril of Alexandria, *De Sancta et Consubstantiali Trinitate Dialogus VI*, all cited by Krouse. For such writers (who transformed Samson into a saint), this hero was "impelled and strengthened throughout his career by the Holy Spirit." In the later Middle Ages, see Petrus Comestor, *Liber Judicum*, Haymo Halberstatensis, *In Divini Pauli Epistolas Expositio*, Aton of Vercelli, *Expositio in Epistolas S. Pauli*; Theophylactus of Bulgaria, *Expositio in Epistolam ad Hebraeos*, and Harvey of Burgundy, *Commentarii in epistolas Pauli* (cited in Krouse 36, 46–49).

50. Krouse 71–72. In his *In Librum Judicum Commentarius*, Sebastian Schmidt made it clear that Samson's strength did not reside in the hair per se and that the cutting of the hair in itself did not make Samson weak. Rather, the hair was "a symbol of his [Samson's] falling away from virtue—he had sinned, and he lost his strength for that reason, not merely because his hair was cut" (Krouse 72, 75–76).

51. William Gouge, *A Learned and Very Useful Commentary on the Whole Epistle to the Hebrewes* (London, 1655).

52. Interestingly, Gouge refers to the Samson-Hercules association, not to endorse it but to suggest its shortcomings: "The Heathen report much of *Hercules*. Certainly the ground of that strength which they divulge about their *Hercules*, arose from some fragments that they had heard concerning this *Samson*. Many of their reports concerning *Hercules*, are fabulous: but if all were true, yet are they not comparable to that which is recorded in the Word of Truth of *Samson*" (174).

53. Gouge 174–75.

54. Gouge 175–76.

55. Gouge 176.

56. Gouge 178–79.

57. For corresponding treatments in the seventeenth century, see Henry Ainsworth, *Annotations upon the Five Bookes of Moses* (London, 1639) 34–44; John Diodati, *Pious Annotations on the Holy Bible*, 3rd ed. (London, 1651), sig. Bb4v; and Matthew Poole, *Annotations upon the Holy Bible*, 2 vols. (London, 1683) 1: sig. Iii4v-r. According to Diodati, the Nazaritical dimension of the Samson narrative is of great importance in determining the nature of strength. It was to be understood not only as a sign of God's singular favor toward Samson but as a symbol of Christ's own "perfect holiness" and "infinite strength and power."

58. In *Eikonoklastes*, Milton employs the same allegory not to support kingship but, as might be expected, to call it into question: "*The words of a King*, as they are *full of power*, in the autority and strength of Law, so like *Sampson*, without the strength of that

Nazarites lock, they have no more power in them then the words of another man"
(5:257).

59. Compare Milton's later statement in the *First Defence*:

> Samson, that renowned champion, though his countrymen blamed him (Judg. 15,
> 'Knowest thou not that the Philistines are rules over us?'), yet made war
> singlehanded against his rulers; and whether instigated by God or by his own
> valor only, slew not one, but many at once of his country's tyrants. And as he had
> first duly prayed to God to be his help, it follows that he counted it no
> wickedness, but a duty, to kill his masters, his country's tyrants, even though the
> greater part of his countrymen refused not slavery. (7: 218–19)

The emphasis upon Samson's singlehanded strength in executing God's vengeance is
pervasive in Milton's thought.

60. See, for example, the entry *"Nazar"* in John Buxtorf, *Lexicon Hebraicum et
Chaldaicum* (London, 1646) 433–35. See also Ainsworth 34–44. More recently, Palmer
invokes the same association (31).

61. Compare the reference to Samson in *Paradise Lost*. After Adam and Eve have
fallen, they copulate in lust until they are enveloped by "dewie sleep." After their
awakening, Adam's plight, in particular, is delineated in terms of Samson's own: "So
rose the *Danite* strong / *Herculean Samson* from the Harlot-lap / Of *Philistean Delilah*,
and wak'd / Shorn of his strength" (IX.1059–62). Like Samson, Adam, in his own way,
regains his strength. It is in fact this regaining of strength that is the focus of the final two
books of *Paradise Lost*.

62. "Muing" or "mewing" is, of course, literally a shedding or molting (cf. *mutare*,
"to change"), and as such recalls the earlier reference to "casting off the old and
wrincl'd skin of corruption." Implicit in the term is the sense of renewal that earlier
critics have ascribed to it. See Yale *Prose* 2:558 n. 254.

63. According to J. Max Patrick (*The Prose of John Milton* 324 n. 366), Milton has in
mind here the account of the conversion of Saul (Acts 9:3–22). After his conversion, he
was three days without sight. With the eventual return of vision, "immediately there fell
from his eyes as it had been scales." Also, "Saul increased the more in strength." Such
an increase in strength, of course, recalls Samson as well.

64. Krouse 108–18. For additional discussion of the term *agon* in general, see *TDNT*
1:134–40. With regard to Milton, see also Paul M. Sellin's learned and illuminating study
"Milton's Epithet *Agonistes*," *Studies in English Literature* 4 (1964) 137–62. As Sellin
demonstrates, the term *agonistes* implies not only *certator* ("champion"), *pugil*
("fighter"), or *athleta* ("athlete") but *ludio, actor scenicus*, and even *hypocrites*.

65. For this dimension of the drama, see my analysis of *Samson Agonistes* in *Poetics of
the Holy*, esp. 73–80.

66. For Milton's own discussion of renovation as theological process, see *Christian
Doctrine*, Bk. 1, ch. 17 (15: 342–65). This chapter should be read in the context of those
concerning redemption (1.16) and regeneration (1.18). With specific reference to
Samson Agonistes, see John M. Steadman, "'Faithful Champion': The Theological
Basis of Milton's Hero of Faith," *Anglia* 77 (1959) 13–28; William O. Harris, "Despair
and 'Patience as the Truest Fortitude' in *Samson Agonistes*," *ELH* 30 (1963), reprinted
in *Critical Essays on Milton from ELH* (Baltimore: Johns Hopkins University Press,
1969) 277–90. Corresponding studies that move in the same general direction are those
of Arnold Stein, *Heroic Knowledge* (Minneapolis: University of Minnesota Press, 1957)
and Anthony Low, *The Blaze of Noon: A Reading of Samson Agonistes* (New York:
Columbia University Press, 1974), among many others. Of immense importance to the
idea of spiritual development, as well as to the action of *Samson* as a whole, is Mary Ann
Radzinowicz, *Toward Samson Agonistes* (Princeton: Princeton University Press, 1978)
passim. In a major reassessment of prevailing attitudes, Joseph A. Wittreich has more
recently questioned traditional ways of approaching *Samson* as renovative drama. See
Wittreich's seminal study *Interpreting Samson Agonistes* (Princeton: Princeton University Press, 1986) passim.

67. Although Samson maintains that his "riddling days are past" (1064), the whole

drama fosters a sense of the enigmatic and of a character's ability to decipher hidden meanings.

68. In this regard, see especially the excellent discussion of Harapha in *A Milton Encyclopedia* 3:150–54, as well as the glosses in *The Poems of John Milton*, ed. John Carey and Alastair Fowler (London: Longman, 1968) 380; and *John Milton: Complete Poems and Major Prose*, ed. Merritt Y. Hughes (New York: Odyssey Press, 1957) 577. The Hebraic underpinnings are discussed by Jack Goldman, "The Name and Function of Harapha in Milton's *Samson Agonistes*," *English Language Notes* 12 (1974) 84–91. For biblical antecedents, see 2 Sam. 21:16 and 1 Chron. 20:4, among others. For the various etymologies explored in the present discussion, see the entries on *raphah*, *ha-rapha*, and *rephaim* in *A Hebrew and English Lexicon of the Old Testament*, ed. Francis Brown (Oxford: Clarendon Press, 1907) 950–52, hereinafter abbreviated as *HELOT*; and *TWOT* 2:857–59.

69. Harapha speaks of "*Og* or *Anak* and the *Emins* old / That *Kiriathaim* held" (1078–80), and Samson refers to the "Giant-brood" of Harapha, who might be reputed by Fame to be "Father of five Sons / All of Gigantic size, *Goliah* chief" (1248–49). For a discussion of these figures, see Goldman, and John M. Steadman, *Milton's Epic Characters: Image and Idol* (Chapel Hill: University of North Carolina Press, 1968) esp. 185–93.

70. See the references in *HELOT* 950–52 and *TWOT* 2:857–59 and such biblical texts as 2 Sam. 4:1; Job 12:21; Isa. 13:7; and Jer. 6:24, 38:4, and 50:43, among others. See also Carey and Fowler 380 n.

71. As a symbol of pride, Harapha represents the third in a series of temptations that constitute what is commonly referred to as "the triple equation." See Krouse 128–32. Compare the references to Satan as a tower in *Paradise Lost* I.591.

72. Having done so, Harapha comments, "thou knowst me now / If thou at all art known" (1080–81), lines that recall Satan's own challenge to Ithuriel and Zephon in *Paradise Lost*: "Not to know mee argues your selves unknown" (IV.830).

73. For a full treatment of this subject, see my discussion of holy war in *Poetics of the Holy* 246–312.

74. See, in this regard, the entries on *rapha'* (with terminal *aleph*) and *raphah* (with terminal *he*) in *HELOT* 950–52. Under *raphah*, *HELOT* has "Vid. also *rapha'* heal" (952), a cross reference that suggests their correspondence. *Rapha'* appears repeatedly in the Old Testament (e.g., Gen. 20:17 and 50:2, Isa. 19:22, Jer. 33:6). To indicate the meaning "giant," *raphah* and *rapha'* are also used interchangeably in the Old Testament (*raphah* in 1 Chron. 20:4, 6, 8; and *rapha'* in 2 Sam. 21:16, 18, 20, 22). See in this connection the entry on "Giants" in *The International Standard Bible Encyclopaedia*, gen. ed. James Orr, 5 vols. (Chicago: The Howard-Severance Co., 1915) 2:1224. The *TWOT* provides a full and detailed account of both forms (2:857–59), but does not relate them. The first person to call attention to what might be termed the "healing" dimension of the name Harapha was Milton's own nephew Edward Phillips in the 1671 edition of *The New World of Words*, 3rd edition (London, 1671): "*Haraphah*, (Hebr.) a Medicine, a Philistim [*sic*] whose sons being gyants were slain, by *David* and his servants" (sig. X2^r). This definition was recorded in a fascinating note by William Riley Parker in the correspondence section of the *Times Literary Supplement* (hereinafter referred to as *TLS*) 2 Jan. 1937: 12. In the note, Parker establishes that Phillips, in his entries on both Harapha and Samson, was engaging in effect in the first interpretation of *Samson Agonistes*. For Phillips, Samson or *Shimshon* means "*There the second time*," a rendering that finds no etymological justification in the Old Testament itself but much justification in *Samson Agonistes*, for, as Parker maintains, "the etymology helps to explain the theme of that poem—regeneration" (12). For its earliest critic, Milton's drama clearly embodied the regenerative or restorative meaning, a meaning consistent with the etymology of Harapha that Edwards cites as well. Parker's note provoked a rejoinder by a Jacob Leveen, whose criticism is generally narrow and unenlightening (except for an attempt to find an etymology for *Shimshon* in the Hebrew *sham* ["there"]

and *sheni* ["second"]) and a comment by an H. Loewe, who emphasizes that dimension of *Harapha* which suggests "weakness" (*TLS* 23 Jan. 1937: 60). Incidentally, it should also be noted that *rephaim* likewise carries the meaning of "shades" or "ghosts" in connection with its suggestion of "*powerless ones*" (see *HELOT* 952). It might be suggested here that Harapha, in his connection with the idea of healing, becomes a kind of unwitting Raphael (*rapha-el*). Philip Gallagher has seen fit to write an essay entitled "The Role of Raphael in *Samson Agonistes*," *Milton Studies*, vol. 18, ed. James Simmonds (Pittsburgh: University of Pittsburgh Press, 1983) 255–94, but not with the above ideas in mind.

75. As has been recognized before, the homeopathic principle of like curing like has manifold implications for Milton's drama. See Milton's discussion of catharsis in the Preface to *Samson*. For interpretations of that discussion and its bearing upon the drama, see, among others, William Riley Parker, *Milton's Debt to Greek Tragedy in Samson Agonistes* 67–71. The Renaissance contexts of catharsis are established by John M. Steadman, "'Passions Well Imitated': Rhetoric and Poetics in the Preface to *Samson Agonistes*," *Calm of Mind: Tercentenary Essays on Paradise Regained and Samson Agooistes*, ed. Joseph A. Wittreich, Jr. (Cleveland: Case Western Reserve, 1971) 175–207. See also Martin Mueller, "Pathos and Katharsis in *Samson Agonistes*," *ELH* 31 (1964) 156–74.

76. Tragedy is said by Aristotle to "purge the mind" of passions like pity and fear or terror and "reduce them to just measure." "For so in Physic things of melancholic hue and quality are us'd against melancholy, sowr against sowr, salt to remove salt humours" (Preface 573). The concept of "lustration" is drawn from the Latin rendering ("*lustrationem*") of the Aristotelian concept that is cited on the title page of Milton's drama (1:[330]).

77. This constitutes the fourth (and penultimate) choral stasimon (Parker 48).

78. For this dimension, see Sellin, cited above. See also the language of the prose Argument to *Samson*: Samson is called "to play or shew his strength" in the presence of the lords and people.

79. As Albert C. Labriola convincingly argues in "Divine Urgency as a Motive for Conduct in *Samson Agonistes*," *PQ* 50 (1971) 99–107, Samson's "rouzing motions" here must be distinguished from the "intimate impulse" (1223) alluded to earlier.

80. For a discussion of *Samson Agonistes* as a form of apocalypse, see Barbara K. Lewalski, "*Samson Agonistes* and the 'Tragedy of the Apocalypse,'" *PMLA* 85 (1970) 1050–62.

81. See the language of the prose Argument to *Samson*.

82. In this regard, Samson is fulfilling that dimension of the role of *agonistes*, which implies not only *ludio* and *actor scenicus* but *hypocrites*. See Sellin, cited above.

83. For a discussion of this aspect, see Albert R. Cirillo, "Time, Light, and the Phoenix: The Design of *Samson Agonistes*," in *Calm of Mind* 209–33.

84. Among discussions of this passage, see Cirillo, Lee Sheridan Cox, "The 'Ev'ning Dragon' in *Samson Agonistes*: A Reappraisal," *Modern Language Notes* 76 (1961) 577–84, and Anthony Low, "The Phoenix and the Sun in *Samson Agonistes*, *Milton Studies*, vol. 14, ed. James Simmonds (Pittsburgh: University of Pittsburgh Press, 1980) 219–31.

85. See, however, John T. Shawcross's important essay, "Irony as Tragic Effect: *Samson Agonistes* and the Tragedy of Hope," *Calm of Mind* 259–306.

Index

Absolute Being, 88
Accommodated Being, 88
Accommodation, 17
Actor scenicus, 136
Adam and Eve, 48–51
Adiaphorism, 28–29
Agon, 136, 138
Agonistes, 120, 124, 128, 129, 132–133, 134, 136
Alammani, 55
Alexander the Great, 7
Alpheus, Milton's allusions to, 71
Anonymous Biographer, 2
Aquinas, Saint Thomas, 10
Arethuse, Milton's allusions to, 71
Aristotle, 5, 10, 13
Arnold, Christopher, 103
Ascham, Roger, 5
Athletes, 120
Augustine, Saint, 14–15, 18, 113

Bacon, Francis, 10, 42
Bakhtin, Mikhail, 79
Barak, 112
Bastwick, John, 66
Bentley, Richard, 47
Berkeley, David S., 56
Bernard, Richard, 21
Bible: Acts, 79; II Chronicles, 100, 108; I Corinthians, 22, 36, 102, 103, 106; II Corinthians, 129; Ephesians, 47, 120, 129; Exodus, 94, 95, 99, 108; Ezekiel, 64; Genesis, 42, 92, 94, 108; Habakkuk, 46; Haggai, 58, 59; Hebrews, 46, 56, 58, 59, 63–64, 111–112, 119; 133; Isaiah, 57, 65, 92, 108; Jeremiah, 93, 101, 102, 108; Job, 93, 99, 108, 121; John, 51; Joshua, 99; Judges, 99, 109, 113, 119; Luke, 61, 100; Numbers, 94–95; I Peter, 51; Philippians, 39, 40, 41, 51, 103; Psalms, 65, 82, 93, 94, 100, 108; Revelation, 50, 57, 63, 64–65, 73, 74, 135; I Samuel, 130; I Timothy, 100; Zechariah, 50, 101–102
Bion, 68–69, 71, 72, 73
Body, Milton's use of, as metaphor, ix, 21–37

Boodin, John Elof, 14
Botterweck, Johannes, 57
Brailsford, Dennis, 2
Brinsley, John, 5
Broadbent, J. B., 88
Burton, Henry, 66

Calvin, John, 29, 41
Cartwright, Thomas, 22, 27
Castiglione, Baldassare, 5
Cecil, Sir William, 27
Celestial dialogue, conventions of, x, 76–97
Certator, 120, 132, 136
Chambers, E. K., 36
Charles I, 66
Chorus of Danites, 122, 123, 132, 133, 138
Christus patiens, 105–106, 107
Cicero, 6, 7
Clarke, John, 76, 80
Clement of Alexandria, 39
Closet drama, Milton's analysis of, x
Coleridge, Samuel Taylor, 54
Comenius, John Amos, 4
Comus, 46
Concisio corporis, 31–32
Controversia, 6–7
Convention, as generic imperative, ix
Cook, Albert S., 49
Cope, Jackson, 77
Cornelius a Lapide, 114
Corpus mysticum, concept of, 22–26
Corpus reipublicae mysticum, 32
Creed, J. M., 38, 40
Cromwell, Oliver, 2
Culley, Robert, 62
Currey, Walter Clyde, 19
Cyril of Alexandria, 41, 44

Dagon, 124
Dalila, 125–127
Dante, 91
David, 112
Dawe, Donald G., 41
Delilah, 107–108, 110, 125, 127
Demaray, John, 81
Dickson, David, 59

Milton, John: *Ad Patrem*, 71, 73; *Animadversions*, 9, 30, 74; *Apology, An*, 73; *Areopagitica*, 7, 8, 36, 37, 66, 88, 119, 122, 140; *Art of Logic*, 9, 10, 12, 14, 16, 17, 18–19, 42; *At a Solemn Musick*, 73–74; Cambridge Manuscript, 72–73, 80, 81; *Christian Doctrine*, 12, 17, 19, 22, 23, 24, 26, 39, 40, 42, 45, 59, 74, 79, 91, 95, 96, 100, 101; *Considerations touching the likeliest means to remove hirelings out of the Church*, 33; *Doctrine and Discipline of Divorce, The*, 95; *Of Education*, 1, 2, 3, 4, 7, 8, 15, 17, 140–141; *Epitaphium Damonis*, 68, 74; *Epitaph on the Marchioness of Winchester*, 54; *Fair Infant* elegy, 45, 54, 59, 70; *Il Penseroso*, 43; *Lycidas*, 53, 54, 55, 56, 57, 60–61, 62, 65, 66, 67, 68, 69, 70, 71, 72–73, 74, 75; *On the Morning of Christs Nativity*, 8, 44, 45, 46, 49, 60, 73; *Mask, A*, 8, 17, 24, 45, 47, 48; *Paradise Lost*, 8, 12, 15, 19, 45–46, 105, 106, 128, 133–134; *Paradise Regain'd*, 8, 45, 46, 105, 106, 107, 128; *Passion, The*, 8, 46, 60; Prolusions, 6–7, 9, 47–48; *Reason of Church-Government, The*, 16, 23, 30, 31, 33–34, 43–44, 80, 81, 103, 107, 117, 118, 119, 133, 139, 140; *Of Reformation*, 24, 25, 30, 34, 35, 44; *Samson Agonistes*, 8, 46, 80, 98, 107, 120, 128, 131, 135, 137; *Second Defence*, 1, 2, 15, 104, 133; Sonnets, 3, 60; Tetrachordon, 13–14; *Upon the Circumcision*, 40, 45
Moschus, 55, 71
Moulton, James Hope, 64
Mulcaster, Richard, 6
Muse, 61
Music, in education, 2

Nazaritical code, 108–109
Nazir, 117

Oedipus, 106–107
Old Dispensation, 23–24
Ong, Walter J., 78
Organicism, 21–37
Origen, 39, 44
Orpheus, 4
Otto, Rudolf, 100, 136
Ovid, 71
Owen, John, 66

Parish, John E., 94
Parker, William Riley, 49
Pastoral, Milton's handling of, x, 53–75
Patrick, J. Max, 37
Patrides, C. A., 46
Pauline transvaluation, 103, 105, 106, 111
Pecheux, Mother Mary Christopher, 47
Peripeteia, 135
Peter, John, 88
Philastrius, 113
Pindar, 8
Plato, 4–5, 10, 12, 13, 14, 17–18, 32
Platonism, 19–20
Prynne, William, 27, 35, 66

Ramism, influence of, on Milton, 78
Rapha, 131
Raphael, 15
Rationale of Ceremonial, The, 26
Rephaim, 128
Ronsard, Pierre de, 55
Ross, Malcolm, 24

Saint Paul, 102
Saint John the Divine, 63, 64
Samson, 8, 93–138
Samuel, Irene, 77, 78, 112
Sannazaro, Jacopo, 54, 69
Scaliger, Julius Caesar, 67
Scholastic philosophy, Milton's attacks on, 9
Self-divestiture, 49–50; relating of, to self-emptying, 40
Self-investiture, 45
Shawcross, John T., 47
Shemesh, 117, 137
Simon Peter, 51
Socrates, 13
Sophocles, 81, 96
Spenser, Edmund, 55
Strength, Milton's delineation of, x, 98–138

Talmud, 110–111
Taylor, Vincent, 38
Tertullian, 39
Theocritus, 54, 55, 67, 68, 69, 72
Todd, H. J., 54
Tomkis, Thomas, 22
Traver, Hope, 82
Trismegistus, Hermes, 21
Truth, 3, 7–8; Milton's vision of, 36–37
Tuckney, Anthony, 33

INDEX